DONATION

D0908966

THE
BATTLE
FOR
EUROPE

ASSAULT FROM THE WEST 1943–45

THE BATTLE FOR EUROPE

ASSAULT FROM THE WEST 1943–45

ROY CONYERS NESBIT

Sutton Publishing

First published in the United Kingdom in 2004 by
Sutton Publishing Limited · Phoenix Mill
Thrupp · Stroud · Gloucestershire · GL5 2BU

British Library Cataloguing in Publication Data
A catalogue record for this book is available from the British Library.

ISBN 0-7509-3316-X

Typeset in 10/14pt Sabon.
Typesetting and origination by
Sutton Publishing Limited.
Printed and bound in England by
J.H. Haynes & Co. Ltd, Sparkford.

CONTENTS

ACKNOWLEDGEMENTS

I am extremely grateful to staff members at the National Archives for initiating this book and providing a considerable amount of help in researching the content as well as supplying many of their official photographs. They are Anne Kilminster, Sheila Knight, Paul Johnson, Hugh Alexander and Brian Carter.

My thanks are also due to staff members of Sutton Publishing Ltd who liaised with the staff at the National Archives and brought the book to fruition. They are Jonathan Falconer and Nick Reynolds.

Further cooperation was provided in the USA by Jo King of King Visual Technology, who supplied official photographs from the National Archives and Records Administration in her country.

I am also grateful to the artists Mark Postlethwaite GAvA and Charles J. Thompson GAvA, ASAA, GMA, EAA, who provided some of their excellent paintings for the book.

Finally, this book could not have been written without the advice and contributions made by my friends Georges Van Acker and Dudley Cowderoy.

SOURCES OF PHOTOGRAPHS

This book was initiated by staff of the Image Library at the National Archives, who provided many of the photographs contained within the narrative. All these photographs, together with costs of prints and reproduction fees, are available from the National Archives Image Library, Kew, Surrey TW9 4DU, Tel: 020 8392 5225, fax: 020 8392 5266, email: Image-library@pro.gov.uk

Other photographs originated from the National Archives and Records Administration, Still Picture Branch, NWCS, Room 5360, 8501 Adelphi Road, College Park, MD 20740 6001, USA, tel: (001) 301 713 6625, x234, fax: (001) 301 713 7436. However, such photographs can be obtained only via 'Participating Vendors for the Reproduction Sales of Still Photographs, Aerial Film, Maps and Drawings'. A list of these vendors, who also provide costs of prints inclusive of reproduction fees, is available from the above authority. The photographs for this book were obtained from King Visual Technology, PO Box 441374, Port Washington, MD 20749, tel: (001) 301 583 3533, fax: (001) 301 583 3535, email: archives@kvt.com

The remaining photographs in this book are part of the author's private collection, built up over many years and not for sale to the general public. The majority of these were originally official wartime photographs. Her Majesty's Stationery Office at St Clements Lane, 2–16 Colegate, Norwich NR3 1BQ, provided information as follows: 'Crown copyright in photographs taken prior to 1 June 1957 have a copyright life of fifty years from the end of calendar year in which the photographs were taken. Schedule 7, paragraph 30 of the Copyright Act 1956 refers.'

CHAPTER ONE

PREPARATION FOR INVASION

The War Cabinet never gave up hope of re-entering the Continent of Europe after the evacuation of the British Expeditionary Force from France in the summer of 1940. The success of the RAF in the Battle of Britain in the latter part of the year removed the possibility of a German invasion but it was obvious that the country did not possess the means to defeat her enemy on her own, even with the support of her Commonwealth. The Wehrmacht controlled France, the Low Countries, Denmark and Norway, and had been joined by Italy, which possessed strong forces in the Mediterranean and East Africa.

The British pinned their hopes on the entry of powerful allies in the war, and this expectation was justified when Germany attacked the Soviet Union on 22 June 1941 and declared war on the USA after the Japanese attacked Pearl Harbour on 7 December 1941. Nevertheless, it would be four long years from 1940 before the plans for a counter-invasion could be fully formulated and put into effect. For two of those years the tide of war seemed to move irresistibly in favour of the Axis and its partner in the Far East. The Wehrmacht crushed Russian armies and swept over the plains of their country to the outskirts of Moscow and Leningrad. Axis forces soon occupied the Balkans, Greece and the Aegean Islands. They drove the British forces back from Libya to Egypt, threatening the Suez Canal. The Japanese moved with astonishing speed through Southeast Asia and islands of the Pacific, defeating the ill-prepared forces of America, Britain and the Netherlands and creating the myth that they were military supermen. Most dangerous of all for Britain, U-boats of the Kriegsmarine and a handful of submarines of the Regia Marina sank millions of tons of Allied shipping in the Atlantic, severely restricting the flow of military and other supplies to the country and even endangering her ability to feed her population.

It was not until the middle of 1942 that the tide of war began to turn, at first almost imperceptibly and then with increasing momentum. It began with the victory of an American fleet over Japanese aircraft carriers at Midway in June 1942. Then the British Eighth Army defeated the Afrika Korps at the Battle of El Alamein in October 1942, sending the remainder in full retreat across North Africa towards the Anglo-American forces which landed in Algeria and French Morocco to await their arrival. The Axis forces were reinforced and fought desperately until they finally surrendered in May 1943.

Even worse for the Wehrmacht was the Battle of Stalingrad, when the whole of its Sixth Army was first cut off and then wiped out by the end of January 1943. This was followed by the immense Battle of Kursk in July 1943, which ended in a decisive victory for the Russians, who sent the Panzer armies back in a fighting retreat across the eastern plains to their home country. In the same period, the Western Allies finally achieved superiority over the menace of the U-boats in the Atlantic, by a combination of decrypts of their signals, stronger naval escorts including aircraft carriers, long-range aircraft and improved radar technology. U-boat losses became so severe that their commander, Grossadmiral Karl Dönitz, had no option but to order the survivors to withdraw temporarily from the North Atlantic. They were never able to return with their previous effectiveness. Supplies of war materials and personnel streamed across the Atlantic from America, with a degree of safety hitherto unknown.

Sicily was invaded by Anglo-American forces in July 1943, followed by the Italian mainland on 3 September. Italy had had enough of the war and surrendered four days later, leaving German forces and a few diehard Fascist units to defend the peninsula after reinforcement. By this time, it was clear that the Wehrmacht was becoming so overstretched and beleaguered that the Western Allies could attempt an invasion of France.

The decision for this invasion rested with the Combined Chiefs of Staff, consisting of Franklin D. Roosevelt and Winston S. Churchill with their top commanders. At the end of April 1943, these had appointed Lieutenant-General Frederick E. Morgan as 'Chief of Staff to the Supreme Allied Commander (designate)' with instructions to prepare plans for the invasion. Morgan was given a list of the forces available for the operation, which included five infantry divisions and two airborne divisions for the initial assault, two more infantry divisions as follow-up, and twenty more when a lodgement had been secured. The number of naval vessels and aircraft were also listed.

Morgan and his staff, abbreviated to COSSAC, were able to draw on provisional but detailed plans formulated over the previous years by other teams. By the end of the following July, they were able to produce an outline plan, which was submitted to the Combined Chiefs of Staff. This proposed that the initial landings should be made by three infantry divisions on the beaches of Normandy to the west of Ouistreham on the mouth of the river Orne, near the inland city of Caen. Although this involved a passage of about 100 miles across the Channel, the beaches were less heavily defended than the nearer Pas de Calais and had fewer high cliffs. The outline plan also listed in detail the parts to be played by the airborne forces, the air forces and the naval forces.

This plan was recommended by the Combined Chiefs of Staff and considered by Roosevelt and Churchill at their 'Quadrant' meeting in Quebec in August 1943. It was approved in general, although Churchill urged an increase in the forces by at least 25 per cent. It was also considered that the invasion should be synchronised with another on the south coast of France (later known as operation 'Anvil') and that pressure should be maintained on the German forces defending the Italian peninsula.

Subsequently, there was disagreement among the Combined Chiefs of Staff as to the resources to be devoted to the invasion of France at the expense of operations elsewhere in the world, particularly in the Pacific. The Americans put forward the view that these could not be resolved until a Supreme Allied Commander for the invasion was appointed. It had already been agreed by Roosevelt and Churchill that he should be an American, thus representing the larger part that his country would play in the enterprise, in terms of military resources.

The man chosen by Roosevelt was General Dwight D. Eisenhower, who had led the Anglo-American invasion of north-west Africa with skill and distinction. Eisenhower was known as a talented administrator rather than an experienced battlefield commander. He was an excellent organiser who had become highly respected by the various nationalities under his command, and such qualities were precisely correct for the forthcoming operation. His appointment was announced on 6 December 1943. Churchill chose Air Chief Marshal Sir Arthur W. Tedder as his British deputy, representing the crucial role that air power would play in the success of the invasion and the later thrusts towards Germany. Tedder was also an excellent organiser and had worked in harmony with Eisenhower in the Mediterranean theatre.

Admiral Sir Bertram H. Ramsay was appointed as Commander-in-Chief of the naval forces for the invasion of France and the subsequent reinforcement and supply. He possessed special qualifications for his position, for he had organised the evacuation of the British Expeditionary Force from France in 1940 and played a major part in the Allied landings in north-west Africa in 1942. He had also commanded the British naval task force for the landings on Sicily. Thus he was also accustomed to working successfully with both Eisenhower and Tedder.

A meeting of high commanders of the Allied Expeditionary Force took place on 1 February 1944. Left to right, seated: Air Chief Marshal Sir Arthur Tedder (Deputy Supreme Commander); General Dwight D. Eisenhower (Supreme Commander); General Sir Bernard Montgomery (Commander of British and Canadian 21st Army Group). Left to right, standing: Lieutenant-General Omar Bradley (Commander of US 1st Army Group); Admiral Sir Bertram Ramsay (Commander of Allied Naval Expeditionary Force); Air Chief Marshal Sir Trafford Leigh-Mallory (Commander of Allied Expeditionary Air Force); Lieutenant-General W. Bedell Smith (Chief of Staff for operation 'Overlord'). *British Official*

The most famous American bomber in the Second World War was the Boeing B-17, which formed part of the vast armada of the US Eighth Air Force in Britain. The B-17F variant was powered by four Wright R-1820-07 Cyclone engines, carried a crew of up to ten, was normally armed with twelve 0.50in machine-guns and had a maximum bomb load of 9,600lb. This photograph was taken on 22 June 1943 when 235 Fortresses were sent against the synthetic rubber factory at Hüls. No long-distance fighters were available for escort and sixteen bombers failed to return. *Author's Collection*

The man chosen to command the Army, at least in its initial assault phase, was General Sir Bernard L. Montgomery. He had served on the Western Front in the First World War and in the early stage had been severely wounded. His first major opportunity for high command came when Churchill appointed him to take over the Eighth Army in Egypt. His victory over Feldmarschall Erwin Rommel at El Alamein had earned him the status of a national hero in Britain. He was also extremely popular with his troops, for not only did he inspire them with personal appearances on front lines but was successful in keeping their casualties to the barest minimum. But he could be arrogant and acerbic with his superiors and was to try Eisenhower's patience to the limit.

The Air Commander-in-Chief was Air Chief Marshal Sir Trafford L. Leigh-Mallory. He had commanded No. 12 Group of Fighter Command during the Battle of Britain and then taken over Fighter Command from 28 November 1942. In fact, his new command already existed, having been formed on 1 June 1943 for this purpose. It was named the Allied Expeditionary Air Force and consisted of two major components, the RAF's Second Tactical Air Force and the US Ninth Air Force. The squadrons involved were already actively involved in tactical operations over Western Europe.

These five men, one American and four British, held the success of the liberation of Europe in their hands. Before taking over his new position, Eisenhower studied the COSSAC outline plan and decided that the initial assault should be made on a broader front, extending further west as far as the Cotentin peninsula. This would enable some of the forces to swing northwards and capture the port of Cherbourg. Before leaving for a short visit to Washington, he asked Montgomery to study the plan with the other commanders-in-chief and report on his return.

Montgomery concurred with this opinion and was ready with his comments when Eisenhower returned on 15 January 1944. The invasion area should be extended from the original 25 to about 50 miles and five infantry divisions should carry out the initial landings, backed by two airborne divisions and overwhelming air cover. This would also involve a considerable increase in naval strength, to sweep the area clear of mines, carry the troops and bombard enemy positions.

The partner of the B-17 Fortress in the US Eighth Air Force was the Consolidated B-24 Liberator. There were many variants of this heavy bomber, of which the first to be mass-produced was the B-24D. This was powered by four Pratt & Whitney R-1830-43 engines of 1,200hp, had up to ten crew members, was armed with ten 0.50in machine-guns and carried 8,800lb of bombs. This photograph was taken on 1 August 1943, after three Bombardment Groups of the Eighth Air Force had flown out to the Benghazi area of Libya to join two Bombardment Groups of the Ninth Air Force in an attack on the Romanian oil installations at Ploesti and Campina. Long-range fighter escorts were not available and forty-five Liberators were shot down, mostly by enemy fighters. Eight others were so badly damaged that they were forced to land in Turkey. *Author's Collection*

Eisenhower's appointment was confirmed on 12 February 1944 by a simple but awe-inspiring directive issued by the Combined Chiefs of Staff. It began:

1. You are hereby designated as Supreme Allied Commander of the forces placed under your orders for operations for the liberation of Europe from the Germans. Your title will be Supreme Commander, Allied Expeditionary Force.
2. *Task*. You will enter the Continent of Europe and, in conjunction with the other United Nations, undertake operations aimed at the heart of Germany and the destruction of her armed forces. The date for entering the Continent is the month of May, 1944 . . .

The directive continued by setting out details of the command structure, logistics, coordination with other forces, relationships with United Nations forces in other areas and the re-establishment of civil governments in liberated territories. The operation was codenamed 'Overlord'.

Eisenhower set up his headquarters at Bushey Park, near Hampton Court on the western outskirts of London, this being named Supreme Headquarters, Allied Expeditionary Force (SHAEF). A period of intense planning began in this establishment. One of the initial problems concerned air power. It was of paramount importance that the railway system in north-east France and Belgium be crippled or even put completely out of action in advance of the Allied landings, to prevent the Wehrmacht rushing reinforcements to the areas of action. The Allied Expeditionary Air Force was already engaged on this task, which was named the 'Transportation Plan', but it was equipped only with fighter-bombers and light or medium bombers. It was felt that some of the railway yards and other centres should be plastered with heavy bombs, even if civilian casualties were caused.

All the Allied heavy bombers were on the strength of the US Eighth Air Force, under General Carl Spaatz, and the RAF's Bomber Command under Air Chief Marshal Sir Arthur T. Harris, and were thus not subject to the direction of SHAEF. Both these immensely strong strategic forces were engaged on bombing targets in the German heartland, under their previous directive. Spaatz and Harris objected strongly to any major diversion from their appointed tasks, although the latter had already begun making a few heavy raids on targets in France in anticipation of the invasion. Spaatz argued that his efforts were best employed on the destruction of German synthetic oil plants, which would have a more detrimental effect on Germany's capacity to continue to wage war. Their main objection seemed to be losing their independence by placing their forces under the direction of Air Chief Marshal Sir Trafford Leigh-Mallory of the AEAF.

The obduracy of these two senior officers drove Eisenhower close to despair, and the matter was not resolved until he called all interested parties together for a discussion on 25 March 1944. The result was a compromise. It was decided that the heavy bombers could be called upon by Eisenhower personally on occasions, but would be allowed for the most part to continue with their previous directive. Even then, Churchill objected to the policy, for he was disturbed at the prospect of heavy civilian casualties in the countries he intended to liberate. It took persuasion from Roosevelt before he withdrew his objections. Meanwhile, Spaatz began sending out small numbers of aircraft at night, dropping leaflets over the forthcoming targets and warning the citizens to vacate their homes.

Another problem, which proved less capable of resolution, was the shortage of landing craft for the increased number of assault forces. Britain's industries were far too overstretched to make good the shortfall and even the mighty industrial power of America could not provide sufficient craft by the following May. The outcome was a deferment of D-Day to 5 June, by which time enough landing craft could be supplied from America. Moreover, the anticipated invasion of southern France, operation Anvil, could not be synchronised with the landings in Normandy and would have to await further deliveries of landing craft.

The ground forces to be employed in the invasion of Normandy were the 21st Army Group commanded by General Sir Bernard L. Montgomery, and the United States 12th Army Group commanded by Lieutenant-General Omar N. Bradley. The former consisted of two Armies, the British Second Army and the First Canadian Army, while the latter consisted of the United States First Army and the United States Third Army. The initial assault forces were three division groups of the British Second Army commanded by Lieutenant-General Sir Miles C. Dempsey, and two division groups of the United States First Army commanded by Lieutenant-General Courtney H. Hodges. The British occupied the left flank of these forces, with the 3rd Division Group landing on 'Sword' beach to the west of the mouth of the river Orne, the 3rd Canadian Division Group on its right on 'Juno' beach, and the 50th Division Group further to the

The Republic P-47 Thunderbolt was built in greater numbers than any other single-seat American fighter in the Second World War. It was a large machine for its day, sometimes called the 'Jug', short for juggernaut. The first arrived in Britain in November 1942 and made their first operational flights with the US Eighth Air Force on 8 April 1943, on patrols over the French coast from Debden in Essex. These were P-47Cs, as shown here. The P-47D was the most numerous variant, powered by a Pratt and Whitney R-2800 engine of 2,535hp and armed with eight .50in machine guns. The Thunderbolt was employed as a long-range escort for bombers when fitted with drop-tanks, and its other role was as a fighter-bomber carrying up to 2,000lb of bombs. *Author's Collection*

The Ford and General Motors factories at Antwerp, manufacturing military vehicles for the Wehrmacht, were bombed by sixty-five B-17 Flying Fortresses of the US Eighth Air Force on 4 May 1943. Hits were scored on warehouses, docks and railway sidings. No aircraft were lost but fourteen were damaged. *Author's Collection*

right on 'Gold' beach, which ended at Port-en-Bessin. The Americans on the right flank of the British were to land their 1st Division Group on 'Omaha' beach to the west of Port-en-Bessin and their 4th Division Group on 'Utah' beach at the south-east corner of the Cotentin peninsula.

These seaborne landings were to be preceded in darkness by the British 6th Airborne Division, which would land behind the coastal defences on the left of the British sector, and the United States 82nd and 101st Airborne Divisions, which would land behind enemy defences on the right flank. The assault divisions were to be followed by successive landings of seaborne forces, and it was hoped that seventeen divisions would be ashore by D-Day plus four. More divisions would be landed on subsequent days, when the lodgement areas had been secured.

Responsibility for the carrying of the seaborne forces and their supplies rested with the Naval Commander-in-Chief, Admiral Sir Bertram H. Ramsay. The number of vessels under his control was enormous, numbering almost 7,000. These included 138 warships – battleships, cruisers, destroyers, sloops, frigates and patrol craft. There were also 287 minesweepers and 495 light coastal craft. The number of landing ships was over 4,000, of which about half could cross the Channel under their own steam while the remainder would be either towed or carried on larger ships. Apart from these, there were depot ships, salvage vessels, smoke-laying vessels and numerous other smaller craft.

To transport and cover the initial landings, two Task Forces were formed. The Eastern Naval Task Force, commanded by Rear-Admiral Sir Philip Vian, RN, supported the landings to be made by the British and Canadian divisions of the British Second Army on Gold, Juno and Sword beaches. The Western Naval Task Force, commanded by Rear-Admiral A.G. Kirk, USN, supported the landings to be made by the divisions of the United States First Army on Utah and Omaha beaches. In turn, these two Naval Task Forces were split into five forces to correspond with each of the five assault divisions. Within each, Bombardment Forces would open a colossal fire on the enemy's coastal defences in advance of the landings, from battleships, monitors, cruisers, gunboats and destroyers. As the troops approached the shores, this fire would be lifted to targets further inland. The part that the Navy would play in the invasion was codenamed operation 'Neptune'.

One of the main difficulties in supplying the armies from the sea was that there were only a few tiny ports in the lodgement areas. It was expected that the port of Cherbourg would be captured after about forty days, as well as ports in Brittany and on the Loire, but even then damage to the dock facilities would have to be made good and the harbours cleared. Thus a remarkable scheme was devised. The navies would take artificial harbours with them, one for the British sector and one for the American.

The idea was not new but this was the first time it was put into practice. The first stage would be to create breakwaters by sinking lines of blockships off Gold and Omaha beaches, five days after D-Day. Fifty-five merchant ships and four obsolete warships were selected for this purpose. They would be reinforced with ferro-concrete caissons towed over the Channel and sunk into lines, leaving two entrances in each harbour for supply ships. Floating piers for shallow-draught vessels would be anchored to the sea bottom within each harbour, connected to the shores by roadways to be made of articulated steel. Other piers for deep-draught vessels would be positioned to seaward of the harbours. The piers and roadways would be free to float up and down with the tides. Work on building the caissons, piers and roadways had begun during the previous August. These artificial harbours were codenamed 'Mulberries' and they would be heavily protected by anti-aircraft batteries.

While these preparations were under way, the Allied Expeditionary Air Force commanded by Air Chief Marshal Sir Trafford L. Leigh-Mallory was fully occupied with the Transportation Plan as well as attacks on enemy airfields within a radius of 150 miles of Caen in Normandy. Other potential targets were the enemy radar and wireless stations which stretched in a chain along the coastline.

The American component of the AEAF, the US Ninth Air Force under General Lewis H. Brereton, was equipped with Mustang, Thunderbolt, Lightning and Havoc fighters or fighter-bombers, with Marauder bombers and Dakota transports. It was slightly larger numerically than its RAF counterpart, the Second Tactical Air Force commanded by Air Marshal Sir Arthur Coningham, although the types of aircraft in the latter were more varied. They consisted of Spitfire, Typhoon, Beaufighter, Hurricane and Mustang fighters or fighter-bombers, with Boston, Mitchell and Mosquito bombers, together with Dakota transports and Albemarles, Stirlings and Halifaxes converted as transports.

On 15 April, Tedder issued a list of the Transportation targets to Harris and Spaatz. Although by this time both forces were already engaged on bombing some of these targets, they complied with their new orders. All three forces, RAF Bomber Command, the US Eighth Air Force and the Allied Expeditionary Air Force, made concentrated bombing attacks on locomotives, troop and freight trains, rail junctions, marshalling yards and enemy airfields. Their fighters swept over the area, seeking combat with enemy aircraft, and numerous combats took place. The most effective attacks proved to be those carried out by American and British fighter-bombers on the bridges leading to the Normandy battle area. These were hit with precision and destroyed for the expenditure of only a few medium-weight bombs. Unlike rail tracks, bridges could not be repaired or replaced quickly. These attacks brought the enemy's transport system in the region close to paralysis. Fortunately, civilian casualties in these operations, although serious, were far less than Churchill had feared.

Reconnaissance aircraft brought back a series of photographs showing the results of these efforts. Others swept at extreme low level over beaches and cliffs from the Netherlands to the coasts of Brittany, taking photographs of enemy defences and providing precise information for the commanders of each landing craft. Nearer D-Day, the fighter-bombers turned their attention to enemy radar stations along a wide coastline, knocking out most of these and drastically reducing their capacity to detect approaching vessels or aircraft. Other attacks were made on coastal positions which were believed to house some of Germany's new V-1 weapons, or flying bombs.

Although some 200 Allied aircraft were lost in 200,000 sorties in these preliminary operations, the enemy suffered far more. In addition to the destruction of the transport system, the strength of the Luftwaffe's Luftflotte 3 in the region, commanded by Feldmarschall Hugo Sperrle, was reduced to under 900 aircraft of all types. Only about 500 of these were serviceable at any one time. To oppose this small force, the Allies could muster about 5,000 heavy bombers, over 1,500 medium or heavy bombers, and over 2,800 fighters or fighter-bombers. To these could be added the squadrons of RAF Coastal Command and the Fleet Air Arm, which were ready and eager to provide support on D-Day and beyond.

A heavy raid against the shipyards at Kiel was mounted by the US Eighth Air Force on 14 May 1943, when 115 B-17 Flying Fortresses and 21 B-24 Liberators were despatched. Three Fortresses and five Liberators were lost and nine other Liberators damaged. These four Liberators were photographed on their bombing run. *Author's Collection*

In the afternoon of 13 May 1943, the US Eighth Air Force despatched ninety-seven B-17 Flying Fortresses to bomb the Henri Potez aircraft factory at Méaulte airfield, 19 miles north-east of Amiens in France. They dropped 863 general-purpose bombs of 500lb and 16 of 300lb, causing severe damage. Three aircraft failed to return. *Author's Collection*

The enemy forces on the other side of the Channel were known in considerable detail by the Allied commanders-in-chief, from decrypts of the 'Enigma' signals picked up by the 'Y' listening service and then decrypted at the Government Code and Cypher School at Bletchley Park in Buckinghamshire. Other intelligence came from air reconnaissance and reports by agents in the Resistance.

The Wehrmacht (German Armed Forces, including the various armies, Luftwaffe and Kriegsmarine) was under the direct control of Adolf Hitler and his Oberkommando der Wehrmacht (OKW). Within France and the Low Countries, the Commander-in-Chief West under the OKW was the veteran Feldmarschall Gerd Von Rundstedt, who had been brought out of retirement. His command included fifty-eight divisions, which included two Army Groups. To the north was Army Group B, commanded by Feldmarschall Erwin Rommel, who had come close to wresting control of North Africa from the British. This consisted of the Seventh Army commanded by General Friedrich Dollmann and the Fifteenth Army commanded by Generaloberst Hans von Salmuth. In the centre and the south of France was Army Group G, commanded by General Johannes Blaskowitz. This also consisted of two Army Groups, the First commanded by General Kurt von der Chevallerie and the Nineteenth commanded by General von Sodenstern. Apart from these two Army Groups, von Rundstedt had under his direct control the extremely powerful Panzer Group West.

The Naval Group West in France was commanded by Vizeadmiral Theodore Krancke, who was responsible to Hitler via Grossadmiral Karl Dönitz. Unlike the arrangement with the Allied command, the German Navy, Army and Air Force were not under a unified command in the west, but were responsible to Hitler and his OKW.

Hitler had taken a personal interest in the coastal defences of France and the Low Countries from as early as March 1942. Fortifications were built along them, designed to repel any attempt at invasion, while behind these more troops were positioned to drive the enemy back into the sea if he obtained a foothold. Hitler called this arrangement, inaccurately in terms of geography, the 'Atlantic Wall'. After Rommel was transferred from Italy to France in December 1943, he gradually came to the opinion that improvements in this largely static defence were desirable, in contrast to his experience and success in mobile warfare. He was also ordered to report direct to Hitler on this subject, bypassing von Rundstedt.

Along the front to be invaded by the Allies, from the port of Ouistreham to the Cotentin peninsula, fortifications had been built at all the small ports. Strongpoints had been constructed between these at intervals of about 1,000 yards. These consisted of pillboxes and systems of trenches protected by barbed wire, behind thousands of mines. They were heavily guarded, the troops being armed with machine-guns, mortars and field guns, giving direct and enfilading fire over all the beaches. However, the defence lacked depth, and the Allies were well aware of this weakness.

Over half the German divisions were positioned in such static defences along the whole 'Atlantic Wall'. Moreover, their quality varied considerably. Some were soldiers beyond the age of normal military service, others had been wounded on the Russian front and were in poor physical condition, while there were contingents recruited from conquered countries whose allegiance was questionable. However, there were undoubtedly many troops who could be expected to fight with great resolution, such as those in the parachute division which acted as infantry and in the Panzer divisions. Ominously for the Allies, there were about 1,500 German tanks in the West, and these were very dangerous opponents.

The Germans in France were also harried by the Resistance. When France fell in 1940, the population had been stunned by their defeat, and had little alternative but to accept an indefinite fate, albeit sullenly. There seemed little prospect that their ally, Britain, could hold out for long against the mighty Wehrmacht. As the years wore on, however, glimmers of hope arose in the more patriotic Frenchmen, and the tiny Resistance grew in strength. The BBC were instrumental in keeping these hopes alive, sending news of German defeats and coded messages to Resistance groups. The numbers of recruits increased when Germany began to send young Frenchmen out of their country as forced labourers. Many went into hiding, particularly in the southern region of France where they became 'Maquisards', named after the maquis evergreen bushes in their region.

Sabotage was their main activity, and here they were helped by the British Special Operations Executive (SOE). Operatives were parachuted by the RAF into France, or even landed in small clearings by Lysander high-wing monoplanes. Arms and explosives were provided by the British. These teams became Anglo-American as the war progressed, with members of the SOE combining with the American Office of Strategic Services (OSS). By April 1944, teams of these combined forces had been fully trained, being known as 'Jedburghs'. There were three men in each team, one British or American officer

in charge, one French national to act as a guide, and one wireless operator. They would be dropped after D-Day behind enemy lines, in areas where Resistance elements were known to exist. They would help by organising and equipping these for acts of sabotage, and providing leadership where necessary.

The Free French forces in Britain and elsewhere were nominally led by General Charles de Gaulle, but his relations with the Allied commanders-in-chief were less than cordial, primarily because of a refusal to accept his claim to be the head of a 'Provisional Government of the French Republic'. French warships in British waters formed part of operation Neptune under Admiral Ramsay, there were several French squadrons in the RAF, while four French divisions were fighting in Italy under the command of General the Hon Harold Alexander. None of these came under the direct command of de Gaulle, while French ground forces in Britain were commanded by General Pierre Koenig. Neither de Gaulle nor Koenig were admitted to detailed plans of operation Overlord until the former was asked to return from Algiers and given information on D-Day minus one. His reaction was extreme hostility to the Allied commanders-in-chief.

Hamburg photographed around midday on 26 July 1943, after the US Eighth Air Force despatched 121 B-17 Flying Fortresses to add to the damage caused by 791 aircraft of Bomber Command which raided the port on the two preceding nights. The Fortresses encountered much cloud and only 54 aircraft reached the target. Two aircraft failed to return. This raid was followed by Bomber Command's massive raid on 27/8 July when a violent firestorm was caused; about 40,000 people died and most of the survivors fled the city. *Author's Collection*

Absolute security was paramount for the forthcoming invasion, as well as deception regarding the location of the landings. These were arranged under the codename of operation 'Bodyguard'. Detailed knowledge of the plans was confined to only a few high-ranking officers, who were not allowed to travel abroad. In April 1944 a belt 10 miles deep, along the Firth of Forth and stretching from the Wash down the coasts of England to Land's End, was closed to all visitors without special permits. Diplomats were not allowed to enter or leave the country and, most unusually, mail in their 'diplomatic bags' was subject to censorship.

The main purpose of the deception planning was to convince Hitler and his OKW that the major airborne and seaborne assault would take place across the narrows of the Channel towards the Pas de Calais, under the codename of 'Fortitude South'. There would also be a diversionary attack against Norway, under 'Fortitude North'. These deceptions played on Hitler's known fears that landings would be made in these areas. Thus the most powerful German troops would be in the wrong positions to repel the invaders.

An imaginary 'British Fourth Army' was created in Scotland for the invasion of Norway, under the Commander-in-Chief Northern Command, Lieutenant-General Sir Andrew N. Thorne. A larger force was created in the south-east of England with the title 'First United States Army Group' (FUSAG). This fictitious Group was notionally commanded by the charismatic Lieutenant-General George S. Patton, who chafed against inaction but in fact was being held in readiness to command the genuine United States Third Army, which was destined to follow the United States First Army after the initial assault.

The fictitious FUSAG was represented as a million strong. To support the deception, dummy camps and depots were set up, with smoke rising from them. Dummy tanks were made of rubber, dummy airfields had landing lights and aircraft made of wood and fabric. Landing craft were also made of wood and fabric. All this was for the benefit of German reconnaissance aircraft, although Allied mastery of the skies usually prevented these from putting in an appearance. At the same time, a steady stream of signals were sent to code by the 'Y' wireless service in the south-east of England, simulating intense military activity.

But perhaps the most convincing for the Germans were the activities of British double agents. The development of the XX (or Double Cross) system by the Twenty Committee was one of the most successful accomplishments of British Intelligence during the Second World War. This Committee had been created by the Joint Intelligence Committee as early as January 1941, to supervise the use of double agents for 'the dissemination of false information'. By 1944 the whole of the intelligence system which the Germans believed was working on their behalf in Britain was in fact controlled by the Twenty Committee.

Several double agents were involved in operation Bodyguard, but three of these were probably the most effective. One of these, codenamed GARBO, was a Spaniard named Juan Pujol. He had attempted to join the British Secret Service soon after the outbreak of war but had been rejected. Thereupon he had approached the Abwehr (German Intelligence Service) via Madrid in February 1941, with the objective of convincing the British that he could become a successful double agent. He provided the Abwehr with several fabricated reports, supposedly from England, with the cover that he was employed by the Spanish section of the BBC. These reports were accepted by the Abwehr. When MI5 learnt of this success, he was taken to England in April 1942 and became active until the end of the war. GARBO was the main agent who transmitted messages to the Abwehr about the fictitious FUSAG formation. He was the only double agent to be awarded both the Iron Cross and the MBE.

Another double agent was codenamed BRUTUS. He was a Polish fighter pilot, Roman Garby-Czerniawski, who had escaped to France after the German invasion of his country. He had built up an intelligence network after the fall of France but was captured and interrogated by the Germans. These forced him to act as their agent in return for sparing the lives of his relatives. He was given the objectives of joining the Polish forces in Britain, where he would foment anti-Russian feelings and report on military formations. He was sent to Madrid, with orders to use the cover that he had escaped from prison, and ultimately reached Britain in October 1942, where he disclosed his true situation. In April 1944, he informed the Abwehr that he was posted to Scotland, and duly reported on the 'British Fourth Army' in position to invade Norway. He then informed them that he was posted to south-east England, where he provided false information about FUSAG.

The other double agent was Elvira Chaudoir, the socialite daughter of a Peruvian diplomat, who was codenamed BRONX. She lived in England and was in contact with the Secret Service when she visited her parents in Vichy in July 1942. While there, she made contact with the Abwehr and was recruited by them

In the morning of 29 July 1943, eighty-one B-17 Flying Fortresses of the 4th Bombardment Wing, US Eighth Air Force, were despatched to the Heinkel assembly plant engaged on Focke-Wulf Fw190 production on the Warnemünde peninsula, near Rostock. They scored direct hits and near misses on hangars, barracks and administration buildings. Four aircraft were lost. *Author's Collection*

in payment of a salary of £100 a month. She became highly trusted by them, communicating in plain language to her bank in Lisbon. In April 1944 she was asked to find out anything about the forthcoming invasion. Her response was to send on 15 May a telegram 'Envoyez vite cinquante livres. J'ai besoin pour mon dentiste.' This meant to the Abwehr 'I have definite news that a landing will be made in the Bay of Biscay in about one month.'

Although there were serious worries about the possibility that these deception measures would be detected by the enemy, it is evident that they were believed by the Abwehr, whose members appear to have been somewhat gullible. A German map dated 15 May 1944 which was later captured in Italy showed details of the Allied order of battle, complete with coloured maps and divisional signs, all of which were false. There is no evidence that there were any significant troop movements to oppose these fictitious forces, but the Wehrmacht did not reinforce the Normandy coast.

By late May 1944, the Allies had completed their immensely complex preparations for operation Overlord, which was still scheduled to take place on 5 June. The training had been marred by a disastrous episode in the early hours of 28 April, when the five naval assault forces were making practice approaches with their troops. In one of these exercises, off the Devon coast, the landing ships destined for Utah beach had been attacked by nine motor torpedo-boats (called Schnellboote by the Germans and E-boats by the British). These had left Cherbourg and were heading for the waters off Portland Bill. The escorting British destroyer had been damaged in a collision and already forced to withdraw, and the remaining corvette had been unable to stave off the attack. The Schnellboote had sunk two landing ships and damaged another, resulting in the deaths of 197 naval personnel and 441 military.

As the time for D-Day drew near, the weather took a turn for the worse. On Saturday 3 June, the wind began to increase and the seas became turbulent. Eisenhower, who by this time was in his Advanced Command Post at Southwick House on the outskirts of Portsmouth, called his senior commanders for a conference on the following day. Also present was Group Captain James M. Stagg, a 48-year-old Scot who served as Chief Meteorological Adviser to the Supreme Commander. Stagg depended primarily on reports from weather ships stationed in the Atlantic and meteorological aircraft of the RAF for constructing synoptic charts and making long-range weather forecasts. The high-pressure areas which had prevailed over the Azores during May had given way to a series of severe depressions. Air and airborne operations over Normandy had become impossible. D-Day was deferred by one more day, to 6 June.

But the weather did not improve, leaving this revised day in doubt. Eisenhower reassembled his team during the evening of the same day, 4 June. They were told by Stagg that there might be an improvement in the weather. Admiral Ramsay pointed out that vessels already at sea needed immediate orders or would have to return to port and await the next period of favourable tide. The Supreme Commander told Ramsay to assume that the invasion would be carried out as planned. He then asked his team to meet again at 04.00 hours on the following morning, 5 June.

The senior commanders gathered once more at this critical time. On this occasion, Stagg was able to be slightly more optimistic. He told them that there would probably be breaks in the weather, giving fair to fine periods during 6 and 7 June. All was silent for a few moments, until Eisenhower made the most momentous decision of his military career. 'OK, let's go,' he said. The gathering broke up immediately, leaving him alone.

A Messerschmitt Bf110 can be seen going down in flames in this photograph taken on 17 August 1943, when the US Eighth Air Force despatched 230 B-17 Fortresses to bomb the Vereinigte Kugellager Fabrik and the Kugelgfisher Fabric ball-bearing factories at Schweinfurt in Bavaria. The formations were attacked by swarms of Focke-Wulf Fw190s, Messerschmitt Bf109s and Bf110s on the return journey. Some 36 Fortresses did not return and 116 others were damaged. The censor has 'adapted' the river Main in this official photograph, in an attempt to conceal the exact location. *Author's Collection*

The Douglas A-20 Havoc was the main light bomber employed by the US Ninth Air Force. There were several variants, but the A-20G was powered by two Wright R-2600-23 Double Cyclone engines and armed with nine .50in machine-guns. It carried up to 3,000lb of bombs and there were usually three in the crew. In RAF service, this bomber was known as the Boston III. *US National Archives and Records Administration # 18-WP-21-100189*

In daylight on 26 August 1943, Bostons of No. 342 'Lorraine' Squadron, part of the Second Tactical Air Force, took off from Great Massingham in Norfolk to attack a transformer station near the Lac de Guerlédan in Brittany. This photograph shows a Boston over the target covered with explosions from bombs. *British Official*

Opposite page: In the early evening of 31 August 1943, 319 B-17 Flying Fortresses of the US Eighth Air Force were despatched to bomb the airfield at Amiens-Glisy and the Meulan aircraft factory, escorted by 160 P-47 Thunderbolts. Three Fortresses were lost, two in a collision, and forty-four damaged. Two Thunderbolts failed to return, having also collided. *Author's Collection*

Left: A daylight attack on 18 August 1943 by thirty-five Bostons of the Second Tactical Air Force was made against the steel and armament works of the Société de Constructions Mécaniques and the Société des Hauts Fourneaux Forges et Aciers de Denain, close together about 5 miles south-west of Valenciennes in France. Severe damage was done to the plants, as shown by this photograph of Bostons above the target. They were escorted by seven squadrons of Typhoons, but six aircraft failed to return. *British Official*

General-purpose bombs of 300lb falling on Lille-Vendeville airfield during a raid by thirty-six B-26 Marauders of the 387th Bombardment Group, US Eighth Air Force, in the early morning of 31 August 1943. One aircraft was lost in the operation and eleven others damaged. *Author's Collection*

The Arado Flugzeugwerke at Anklam, south-east of Greifswald, which manufactured component parts for the Focke-Wulf Fw190, was bombed during an attack on Marienburg when the US Eighth Air Force despatched 100 B-17 Flying Fortresses on 9 October 1943. Eighteen bombers were shot down and fifty-one damaged. *Author's Collection*

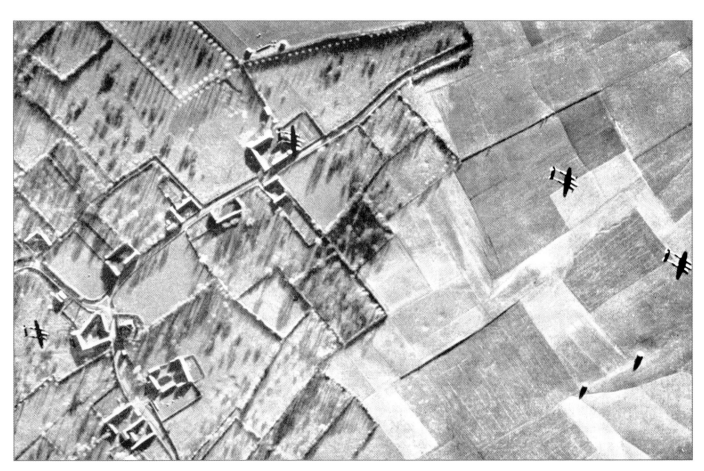

Four P-38 Lightnings of the USAAF photographed over France on 25 November 1943, with two of them more difficult to spot over broken country. *The National Archives: AIR 34/239*

Heinkel He177s and Heinkel He111s were identified by interpreters from this reconnaissance photograph of the airfield at Bourges in central France, taken on 20 December 1943. *The National Archives: AIR 34/239*

This reconnaissance photograph of the railway centre at Valenciennes, an industrial town in northern France, was taken from low level on 19 March 1944 after several attacks by the Second Tactical Air Force and the US Ninth Air Force. The double track bridge over the river Escaut (Schelde) is lying on the bed, preventing any canal traffic to Douai or Lille. There is also widespread damage in the locomotive sheds (top left) and the large factory on the other side of the river. *The National Archives: AIR 34/835*

Widespread devastation was caused during a daylight operation on 9 April 1944 when ninety-six B-17 Fortresses of the 1st Bombardment Division, US Eighth Air Force, raided the Focke-Wulf factory at Marienburg (now Malbork in Poland), where the famous Focke-Wulf Fw190 fighter was assembled. It was the second time they had attacked this factory and on this occasion all the main buildings were hit. Some were completely destroyed while the others were severely damaged. All the Fortresses returned but many were damaged. This photograph was taken five days later by a reconnaissance Mosquito of the RAF. *The National Archives: AIR 25/792*

A B-17 Flying Fortress of the 3rd Bombardment Division, US Eighth Air Force, attacking the aero-engine factory at Arnswalde (now Choszczno), 24 miles east-south-east of Stettin (now Szczecin), on 11 April 1944. The target is situated in a wood, blanketed by a heavy concentration of bomb bursts. *The National Archives: AIR 34/240*

A spectacular photograph of a B-17 Flying Fortress of the 3rd Bombardment Division, US Eighth Air Force, over Rostock during a daylight raid by 172 of these bombers on 11 April 1944. Other bomb clusters are visible above the aircraft as well as below on the left. *The National Archives: AIR 34/240*

The airfield at Tours-Parcay in France was attacked in daylight on 28 April 1944 by forty-five P-38 Lightnings of the 20th Fighter Group, US Eighth Air Force. Thirty-four of these were 'drop-snoot' Lightning P-38Js, fitted with a pexiglass nose and a cabin where a bombardier sat with a Norden bombsight. One Lightning was lost. The same Group attacked again two days later, also losing one aircraft. Then RAF Bomber Command attacked the target on the night of 7/8 May, with fifty-three Lancasters and four Mosquitos, losing two aircraft but causing great damage. The result of all these attacks was the almost complete destruction of all the main buildings, hangars and barracks. This photograph was taken on 8 May by a reconnaissance Spitfire of the RAF. *The National Archives: AIR 25/792*

Hirson viaduct, 38 miles south of St-Quentin in France, was partly destroyed by the US Ninth Air Force on 8 May 1944. *The National Archives: AIR 37/1231*

This close-up of a B-17 Flying Fortress in action was taken on 9 May 1944, when the US Eighth Air Force began its attacks on enemy installations in France as a prelude to the D-Day invasion. Bombs are exploding on the airfield at St-Dizier, south-east of Reims, during an attack by 75 Fortresses of the 1st Bombardment Division, escorted by fighters. They dropped 140 tons of bombs and returned safely. *The National Archives: AIR 34/240*

On 12 May 1944, a special cameraman in a B-17 Fortress opened the radio hatch and leant out to take this superb photograph of a Messerschmitt Me410A-1/UA breaking away after an attack, showing its 50mm BK5 cannon beneath the fuselage as well as the damaged wing of the Fortress. This was the day when the US Eighth Air Force made its first attack on German oil plants by despatching 621 Fortresses and 265 B-24 Liberators, escorted by 153 P-38 Lightnings, 201 P-47 Thunderbolts and 361 P-51 Mustangs. Some 46 bombers and 7 fighters failed to return. *The National Archives: AIR 34/240*

Bombs from an A-20 Havoc of the US Ninth Air Force falling through scattered clouds in May 1944 towards a road junction in northern France. *US National Archives and Records Administration # 342-FH-3A-18237-52896*

Opposite page: An A-20H Havoc of the US Ninth Air Force in early May 1944, attacking a rail junction at Busigny, about 15 miles south-east of Cambrai in northern France. *US National Archives and Records Administration # 342-FH-3A-18522-51357*

Right: The railway bridge at Conflan-Ste-Honorine, over the river Seine north-west of Paris, was rendered impassable on 29 May 1944 by a formation of B-26 Marauders and P-47 Thunderbolts of the US Ninth Air Force. In this instance it was the Thunderbolts which scored the direct hits. *The National Archives: AIR 37/1231*

The Douglas B-26 Marauder, such as this example serial 41/34680 'Gipsy Rose' photographed in March 1943, was medium bomber employed by the US Ninth Air Force from the autumn of 1943. There were several variants but the B-26B was powered by two Pratt & Whitney R-2800-43 engines of 1,920hp, carried a bomb load at 4,000lb, was armed with up to eight .50in machine-guns, and carried a crew of up to seven. *US National Archives and Records Administration # 18-WP-40-100249*

A B-26 Marauder of the US Ninth Air Force, part of a force attacking a German military objective in northern France on 9 May 1944, flying through a flak barrage while releasing eight 500lb bombs on the target 12,000ft below. *US National Archives and Records Administration # 342-FH-3A-18213-51513*

A-20 Havocs of the US Ninth Air Force attacking German defences at the Pointe du Hoc on the coast of northern France prior to D-Day. *US National Archives and Records Administration # 342-FH-3A-18295-57352*

The North American P-51 Mustang was arguably the finest long-distance fighter of the Second World War. The early version, such as the P-51-1A here, was fitted with an Allison V-1710 engine of 1,150hp but was considered underpowered. Later versions were fitted with a Packard Merlin V-1630-7 engine of 1,590hp, built in America under licence from Rolls-Royce. It served in both the USAAF and the RAF, armed with four .50in machine-guns and carrying drop-tanks. There was also provision for 1,000lb of bombs or eight rocket projectiles. *US National Archives and Records Administration # 18-WP-45-100145*

The Lockheed P-38 Lightning, shown here in pre-production form, first entered squadron service in August 1941 as a long-distance fighter. There were numerous variants but the most widely produced was the P-38L. This was fitted with two Allison V-1710-111/113 engines of 1,600hp and had a normal armament of one 20mm cannon and four .50in machine-guns, plus provision for up to fourteen underwing rockets. *US National Archives and Records Administration # 18-WP-37-100113*

The German coastal fortifications in north-west Europe, known as the *Atlantikwall*, stretched from the North Cape of Norway to the Franco-Spanish border. They were at their strongest between Den Helder in the Netherlands and Brest in France. Some of the propaganda showpieces were between Calais and Boulogne, such as this small bunker housing a KwK 43 L/71 gun of 8.8cm calibre. These bunkers provided protection for German long-range guns as well as defence posts. *The National Archives: CAB 106/1004*

Low-level air reconnaissance before D-Day revealed these beach defences in France. They were known as 'Belgian Gates' by the Germans, or 'Cointet structures' after the name of the inventor. The first were captured in 1940, and they were mounted on concrete rollers to make them movable. *The National Archives: AIR 37/1231*

The Lockheed F-5A photo-reconnaissance aircraft was an adaptation of the Lockheed P-38G. It was a single-seater powered by two Allison V-1710-51/55 engines

'Belgian Gate' beach defences in the Pas de Calais.
The National Archives: AIR 37/1231

Concrete obstacles erected by the Germans along
the beaches of France, photographed from extreme
low-level. *The National Archives: AIR 37/1231*

Some of the German coastal guns were mounted on railway carriages. The most formidable were those built in Krupp factories, the K5 of 28cm calibre and the K12 of 21cm calibre. These were positioned between Dunkirk and Boulogne, but not near the beaches where the Allied landings took place. They could be mounted on rail turntables, giving them a field of fire of 360°, or otherwise were concealed in bomb-proof shelters of about 250ft in length. This K5, which could fire a shell of 561lb for 38 miles, was completely destroyed by air bombing, leaving part of the turntable visible. *The National Archives: CAB 106/1004*

Below: Father (Major) Edward J. Waters, a Catholic Chaplain from Oswego in New York, conducted Divine Service on Weymouth pier for American troops before they embarked as part of the first wave to land on the Normandy beaches on D-Day. *US National Archives and Records Administration: War & Conflict # 1039*

This photograph was taken on the eve of D-Day, showing preparations for the Allied invasion which left Littlehampton in Sussex. The landing craft, each with a balloon as protection against low-flying enemy aircraft, joined the greatest Armada in history. *The National Archives: DEFE 2/502*

The Supreme Commander, General Dwight D. Eisenhower, giving the order of the day – 'Full victory – nothing else!' – to paratroopers of the US 101st Airborne Division before they boarded their transport aircraft for the invasion of Normandy. *US National Archives and Records Administration: War & Conflict # 1040*

CHAPTER TWO

A DAY TO REMEMBER

All high commanders have to enter into contingency planning and General Dwight Eisenhower was no exception. Having given final authority for the launch of operation Overlord, he wrote a communiqué announcing its failure and accepting blame for a wrong decision. This missive was never released. His next move, after turning in for overdue sleep on 5 June, was to travel by staff car to Greenham Common airfield in Berkshire, where pathfinder units of the US 101st Airborne Division were preparing to take off. He addressed the aircrews as well as the paratroopers with their blackened faces. Some of those present remembered that his words included: 'The eyes of the world are on you tonight.'

American and British airborne troops preceded the seaborne forces. The American contribution was twice the size of the British and consisted of the 82nd as well as the 101st Airborne Division. The paratroopers were carried by over 800 Douglas C-47 and C-53 transports, followed by about 100 transports towing WACO CG-4A gliders carrying heavier weapons and infantry. All these aircraft were part of the IX Troop Carrier Command of the US Ninth Air Force, based at twenty-two airfields in the eastern, southern and western counties of England. As with all other aircraft on operation Overlord, they sported broad black and white recognition stripes over their wings and fuselage, to distinguish them from enemy aircraft.

The first US pathfinders took off at 22.48 hours on 5 June, followed by the main stream of transports. Escorted by Mosquitos of the RAF's Second Tactical Air Force, they flew over the Channel to the west of the Cotentin peninsula before turning east towards their targets. Meanwhile, Stirlings of the RAF's Bomber Command carried out a feint further south to simulate another operation, dropping 'Window' aluminium foil to confuse enemy radar screens.

The task of the pathfinder paratroopers was to employ specially designed 'Eureka' beacons to guide the other transports and the gliders to their appointed dropping zones. The target area for the 101st Division was to the west of Utah beach, in order to secure the far right flank for the American seaborne forces. The 82nd Division was to land further inland, near the town of Ste-Mère-Eglise, where it would assist the American seaborne forces in their objective of cutting off the Cotentin peninsula and eventually capturing the port of Cherbourg.

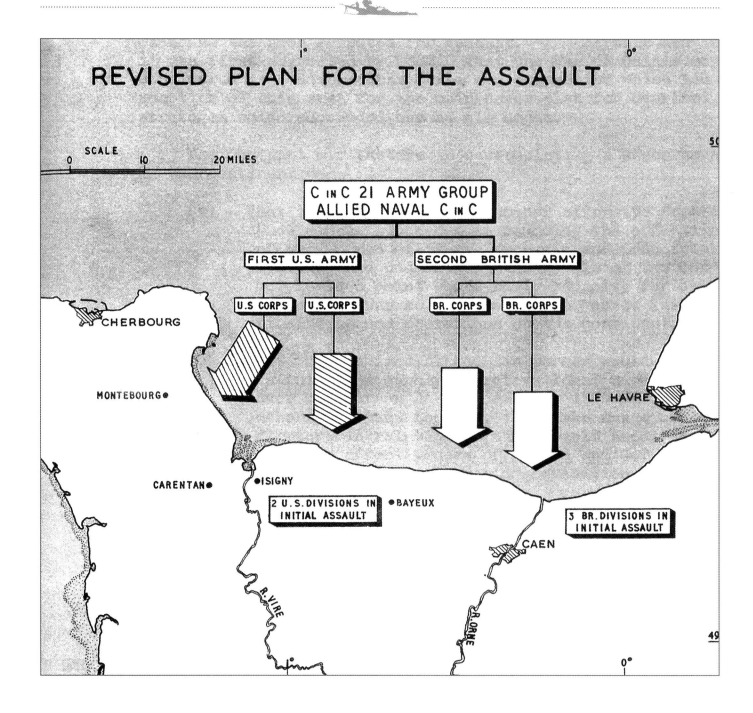

Revised plan for the assault. *The National Archives: AIR 41/66*

The various sections of the American air armada kept their formations until the final leg to the east. Then the aircraft encountered thick cloud and heavy flak. They began to break up, and those which descended below the cloud to identify positions on the dark ground were greeted with intense light flak. The last arrived at 04.04 hours on 6 June but the aircraft losses were reasonably light. Twenty-one troop carriers and one glider were shot down, while two glider tugs failed to return. But the paratroopers became scattered far more widely than intended and had great difficulty forming up. It is estimated that only about 1,100 of the 6,000 men despatched from the 101st Division landed on or near their intended zones.

The situation with an equivalent number of men from the 82nd Division was even worse, especially since many landed on ground occupied by the German 91st Infantry Division, which happened to be on manoeuvres in the area, and fierce gun battles ensued. Nevertheless, small groups of these airborne soldiers managed to form into larger units and, after bitter fighting at close quarters, eventually succeeded in securing the western flank of Utah beach in time for the arrival of the seaborne troops.

The British 6th Airborne Division on the far left flank of the invasion forces also experienced adverse weather conditions. The paratroopers and other airborne troops were either carried in Dakotas or towed in gliders by Dakotas, Stirlings, Halifaxes and Albemarles of the RAF's Nos 38 and 46 Groups. A total of 264 aircraft carried 4,310 men, while 98 others towed gliders with 493 troops and heavier equipment.

These airborne forces consisted of the 3rd Parachute Brigade, the 5th Parachute Brigade and the 6th Airlanding Brigade. Each of these included three battalions, and their main objectives were threefold. They had to capture intact two bridges over the river Orne and the Caen canal and then defend them, in order to facilitate the advance of the British seaborne troops. Next, two bridges over the river Dives to the east had to be destroyed, to hinder the German Fifteenth Army if it attempted to attack the left flank of the seaborne troops. Lastly, they had to destroy a powerful gun battery at Merville, on the coast overlooking Sword beach.

The first objective was achieved by a spectacular *coup de main*. Among the first aircraft were six Halifaxes which took off from Tarrant Rushton in Dorset at about 23.00 hours, towing six Horsa gliders flown by Army pilots of C Squadron, Glider Pilot Regiment. These Horsas carried 138 soldiers of the 6th Airlanding Brigade's 2nd Battalion, Oxfordshire & Buckinghamshire Light Infantry. There were also sappers, medics and a liaison officer from the 7th Parachute Battalion. The tows were released on crossing the French coast and five of these gliders landed in precisely the correct positions. The troops attacked the surprised German defenders and captured the bridges intact, which they held until reinforced by paratroopers of the 5th Parachute Brigade.

Elsewhere, not all the parachute drops and glider landings went so well. The low cloud and dark night which beset the Americans to the west produced a similar effect on the British operations. Many of the pathfinders with their 'Eureka' beacons were dropped incorrectly. Thus the paratroopers of the 3rd and 5th Parachute Brigades landed across widely dispersed areas instead of within their appointed dropping zones, and the men had great difficulty in forming up. There was confused fighting with elements of the enemy, although the latter were less numerous than those encountered by the Americans. Some landing strips for the gliders which followed the paratroopers were not prepared in time, although most gliders landed safely. Nevertheless, men of the 8th Battalion, 3rd Parachute Brigade, covered sappers while they blew up the bridges over the river Dives at Troarn and Bures.

The fiercest fighting took place against the defences of the Merville battery. It had been intended that these would be stormed by 600 paratroopers of the 9th Battalion, 3rd Parachute Brigade, but in the event only about 150 men were dropped close enough for the assault. But this reduced force carried out the task, wiping out the defenders and putting the four 75mm guns of the battery out of action. The paratroopers suffered 70 casualties, including wounded.

Seven aircraft and twenty-seven gliders were lost in these British operations. The airborne airlift was classed as very successful, despite the difficulties caused by the unfavourable weather. But these were only part of the RAF's activities on this momentous night. Bomber Command despatched over 1,000 aircraft to bomb enemy batteries along the coast where the seaborne forces were destined to land. Most of these attacks had to be made solely by radar marking, since cloud covered all but two of the targets, with a resulting loss of accuracy. Over 5,000 tons were dropped, with an average of 100 aircraft and 500 tons for each battery, for the loss of three bombers. This was the largest tonnage dropped during a single night up to this date. The last of the night bombers turned back towards England as the sky began to lighten.

Meanwhile, during the night, thirty-six RAF bombers dropped dummy paratroopers and explosive devices in the areas of Marigny in the American sector and Caen in the British sector, as well as at Yvetot, inland between Dieppe and Le Havre. These helped to deceive the enemy as to the true locations of the airborne landings. Twenty-two other bombers carried out a very complex duty, circling over a fleet of small ships carrying balloons, while dropping specially cut Window aluminium foil. This operation was designed to simulate a large convoy of ships heading for the beaches between Boulogne and Le Havre. Twenty-four more bombers patrolled the skies, fitted with special apparatus to jam the enemy's R/T directions to his night-fighters while substituting false directions from German-speaking aircrew in the bombers. Twenty-seven other bombers took bearings on enemy radar, while thirty-four more dropped Window to blot out their screens. Twenty-five light bombers made 'Intruder' attacks against enemy airfields. Five aircraft were lost in these special operations.

While these events were taking place, the great armada of about 2,700 ships was ploughing through five sea lanes cleared of mines, heading towards the landing beaches. Years of planning and preparation had preceded this enormous undertaking but, in spite of the efforts of the air forces and the airborne troops, there could be no certainty about its outcome. The seas were heavy and the skies were overcast. The pitching and rolling of the ships created misery among the troops, especially those in the smaller vessels. Many were seasick and cold, adding to the grinding tension they must have felt before the forthcoming battle. Large numbers had never been under fire before and did not know how they would react when the shooting began, although they hoped they would acquit themselves well. They must have longed for the end of the waiting, in spite of the danger ahead.

Soon after 05.00 hours on 6 June, two midget submarines of the Royal Navy rose to the surface off Sword and Juno beaches. These were *X23* and *X20*, each manned by a crew of five, which had left Portsmouth over three days before and spent most of that time underwater. Each flashed a green light to guide the bombarding squadrons of the great armada to their positions. These followed minesweepers down the approach channels to their chosen anchorages.

At about 05.30 hours, the great warships opened a thunderous barrage on enemy defences along the 50-mile strip of coast where the seaborne troops were destined to land. Heavy shells from six British and American battleships, two monitors, twenty-three cruisers and two gunboats poured down on these fortifications, continuously and stupefyingly. Overhead, four Seafire squadrons of the Fleet Air Arm, together with five squadrons of Spitfires and Mustangs of the

Admiral Sir Bertram H. Ramsay RN, Allied Naval Commander-in-Chief Expeditionary Force. *Author's Collection*

Rear-Admiral Sir Philip Vian RN, commander of the Eastern Naval Task Force. *Author's Collection*

RAF's Air Defence of Great Britain, plus fifteen squadrons of Spitfires flown by pilots of the USNAF, spotted the falls of these shells. Each pilot relayed the information by R/T to his allotted warship. Some of the shore batteries were eventually silenced.

In the early morning of 6 June, Vizeadmiral Theodor Krancke, the German commander of Naval Group West, was woken up and advised that something was happening in this part of the English Channel. He immediately ordered the 8th Destroyer Flotilla to move north from the Gironde estuary to the port of Brest, but for the present these warships could not reach the invasion armada. For immediate action, he ordered twelve *Schnellboote* (fast motor torpedo boats) of the 5th and 9th Flotillas to leave Cherbourg and attack the western flank of this force. At the same time, four warships of the 5th Torpedo Boat Flotilla (the size of small destroyers) were to leave Le Havre and attack the eastern flank.

The 9th Flotilla of *Schnellboote* left their concrete bunkers at 05.30 hours and the crews witnessed the awe-inspiring spectacle of the great invasion fleet. There was nothing they could do but fire their torpedoes ineffectually from extreme range and flee back to their shelters. The 5th Flotilla, which left Cherbourg after them, was raked by Allied fighter-bombers and had to return immediately or face certain destruction. The larger torpedo boats had better luck. Their approach to the eastern flank was concealed by an Allied smokescreen and they managed to fire fifteen torpedoes at the eastern bombarding force. Many of these passed close to Allied warships but one struck the Norwegian destroyer *Stremmer* amidships, breaking her back and causing her to sink immediately. Most of her crew were picked up, while the four German warships zigzagged wildly and raced back to harbour.

By this time the ships and craft carrying the troops had reached their lowering positions. Fifty-four of the landing craft had been lost during the overnight passage. They were so overloaded with heavy equipment such as tanks that they proved unseaworthy in the weather conditions. But huge numbers of assault vessels with their troops and equipment began to form up for the final run to the coast. Those destined for the British sector began this part of the operation at 05.30 hours. In the vans of each formation were landing craft carrying DD (Duplex Drive) tanks. These were Sherman tanks fitted with canvas floats and propellers, so that they were amphibious and could steer through shallow water ahead of the troops. Behind these were craft carrying 'Flail' tanks, Shermans fitted with rotary chains for exploding mines. Other craft carried 'Crocodile' tanks, Churchills fitted with flame-throwers instead of the machine-gun. Then there were swarms of landing craft with assault companies of infantry, sappers, armoured vehicles, self-propelled artillery and other equipment.

Not all these landing craft left at the same time, for the configuration of the enemy coast determined the sequence. On the far right flank, the American Utah beach formed a right angle, so that the craft could be fired on from two sides. For this reason, the Americans decided that their lowering positions should be

11 miles offshore, as against 7 miles in the British sector. They also decided that their first troops should assault the Utah and Omaha beaches at approximately 06.30 hours (known as H-hour), whereas the average time in the British and Canadian sector was 07.30 hours.

As the streams of landing craft began their journeys to the beaches, seventy-five destroyers of the bombarding squadrons closed the shore and opened fire by direct observation with their 4.7in and 4in guns. The whole of the enemy front was blanketed with their fire, providing reassurance to the troops in the assault craft.

Ahead of these craft, the US Ninth Air Force went into action. Its IX Bomber Command despatched 269 Marauders to attack coastal batteries on seven localities along both the British and American sector, accompanied by twelve groups of Lightnings for fighter cover and ground attack. A group in the USAAF was the equivalent of the RAF wing. Four more groups of Lightnings from the US Eighth Air Force also escorted these bombers, which flew at low level to keep under the cloud base so far as possible. The timing of these attacks varied in accordance with the H-hours in both sectors. Not all the results of this bombardment could be observed, but it is known that they were particularly effective in the westerly Utah sector.

These attacks were followed by streams of heavy bombers from the US Eighth Air Force, along the entire front. Over 1,600 Fortresses and Liberators continued in daylight the work carried out during darkness by the RAF's Bomber Command. The aircraft bombed from high level and had varied success, owing to the extent of the cloud beneath them. Conditions over Utah were favourable and the bombs fell accurately, but those over Omaha were dropped with the aid of pathfinder aircraft relying on instruments and most fell up to 3 miles inland. The results over the British sectors were similarly mixed. The American air attacks ended only ten minutes before the troops left their landing craft.

General Sir Miles C. Dempsey, commander of the British Second Army. *Author's Collection*

The US Eighth Air Force also despatched over 1,700 fighters during the day. These were Lightnings, Thunderbolts and Mustangs, hunting for any Luftwaffe aircraft which dared to put in an appearance. Further inland, about 400 fighter-bombers tackled with bombs and rockets ground targets such as enemy fighting vehicles and transport. The fighters on D-Day, both USAAF and RAF, were controlled by three Fighter Direction Ships, one in the American sector and two in the British. This close air-to-sea collaboration was a notable feature of the invasion, and similar air-to-ground collaboration began when the troops gained a foothold.

The German defenders on the coast were subjected to further bombardment. Five minutes before the assault troops landed, a murderous stream of projectiles was fired from LCT(R)s – Landing Craft Tanks carrying rockets. Each of these specialised craft could fire salvoes of rockets at the rate of about 650 per minute. Over 38,000 of these screaming and terrifying weapons were fired along the entire front. The assault troops began to land a few minutes after the rockets soared over their heads and the warheads exploded on their targets. The range of the barrages from the destroyers and the landing craft was then increased slightly, to fall further inland.

The entire front was 50 miles wide but the invading forces did not intend to land everywhere along its length. Instead, they hoped to punch holes in the enemy defences, each of about a mile in width. There were five landing beaches in the American sector, on Utah and Omaha, and five in the British and Canadian sector, on Gold, Juno and Sword. These ten landing beaches were given individual code-names. Footholds on them would enable reinforcements to land rapidly and in reasonable security. Then the troops would begin to penetrate inland, wipe out the remainder of the enemy along this stretch of his 'Atlantic Wall' and eventually form a continuous and powerful bridgehead, constantly supplied and reinforced. As so often occurs in warfare, events did not take place exactly as planned.

On the far right flank of the American Utah sector, two assault battalions of the 8th Regimental Combat Team (RCT), part of VII Corps, landed on 'Tare' and 'Uncle' beaches at the south-east corner of the Cotentin peninsula, accompanied by DD tanks and bulldozers with their naval and engineer teams. These landings began at 06.30 hours, about an hour earlier than in the British sector. The bombardment which preceded the troops had been extremely heavy but had lasted for only about forty minutes. The landing craft had had a long run-in of about three hours from their parent ships 11 miles from the shore, and some of the men must have felt seasick. Nevertheless, they entered sheltered water during the last part of their passage and met beaches with sand dunes which were only a few feet above sea level. Two battalions landed first, supported by DD tanks, closely followed by a third battalion.

Opposition was only light and quickly overcome, although inevitably there were casualties. The men managed to breach the sea wall behind the shore and began moving inland, towards the paratroopers of the 82nd Airborne Division who had been dropped during the night. Their main hindrance was fields which had been flooded, but contact was soon made.

More progress was made on this far right flank. The 12th and 22nd Regimental Combat Teams followed the 8th, so that about 23,250 men landed, together with numerous vehicles and huge quantities of stores. These new arrivals were almost unimpeded but the American destroyer *Carry* hit a mine and was sunk. The 12th and 22nd pushed north while the 8th headed inland to link up with the 82nd Airborne Division at Ste-Mère-Eglise, but the latter was opposed by troops of the German 91st Division. Attempts were made to reinforce the 82nd with airborne troops in gliders, but some landed in the wrong positions and suffered heavy casualties. Other gliders landed inland to reinforce the 101st Airborne Division, but these had fierce encounters with the German 6th Parachute Regiment which fought as infantry and was ordered to counter-attack.

The successful occupation of the Utah beaches was in sharp contrast with the grim experiences of the Americans on the beaches at Omaha, codenamed 'Dog', 'Easy' and 'Fox'. A combination of adverse circumstances resulted in near-disaster. There were cliffs

Rear-Admiral A.G. Kirk USN, commander of the Western Naval Task Force. *Author's Collection*

of up to 150ft high behind the beaches and the flat trajectory of naval fire had failed to silence many of the emplacements behind them, while the air bombardment had missed these targets entirely. The German troops, from the 352nd Infantry Division, were of a higher calibre than those at Utah. Their division was highly trained and mobile, and had recently arrived to strengthen the defences in the area. Even more unfortunate, the assault troops became dispersed, lost much of their heavy equipment, and some landed on the wrong beaches.

The assault troops landing on the three beaches consisted of the 116th and 16th Regimental Combat Teams, part of V Corps. They had set off in darkness and cohesion was lost at the outset. Thirty-two DD tanks were launched too far from the coast and twenty-seven of these sank. Fifty-one others were launched nearer the shore but many of these were sunk by gunfire. Most of the amphibious DUKWS* carrying artillery foundered in the seas. The landing craft became scattered and some landed too far to the east. When the infantrymen began wading through the surf to the shore, a murderous fire was opened from German artillery pieces, mortars and machine-guns. Many were mown down and the wounded were hit

General Omar N. Bradley, commander of the United States 12th Army Group. *Author's Collection*

again, while medics who tried to attend to them were also hit. The Americans had relied on bulldozers to clear obstructions on the beaches but many of those which landed were knocked out. Those infantrymen who remained unwounded from the first waves were pinned down behind banks of shingle or whatever shelter they could find, such as wrecked vehicles. Succeeding waves, from battalions of the Ranger Group and the 18th Regimental Combat Team, jammed up behind them while the incoming tide covered beach defences which had not been cleared by the engineers. The men could not advance, move sideways or even retreat. It seemed to the German defenders on this stretch of coast that the Allied invasion had failed.

Nevertheless, small parties of these Americans cut their way through barbed wire and began working their way through the mined beaches. Some began to scale the cliffs with ladders and ropes, under intense fire. Relief came from eight American and three British destroyers which closed the shore and opened accurate fire on the German batteries and other positions. By 10.00 hours, after one of the worse episodes in American military history, the situation began to change. The British on the left flank, who had not experienced such extreme difficulties, began to move behind the German defenders on Omaha and threaten to surround them. Leaving huge numbers of casualties behind them, the surviving American troops gradually fought their way into these German positions and gained the upper hand.

These assault troops did not began to reach the high ground behind the beach until 13.00 hours. In their rear, the beach was littered with tanks, armoured

* D being the year of origin, U meaning Utility, K meaning front-wheel drive and W meaning six-wheeled.

Lieutenant-General Courtney H. Hodges, commander of the United States First Army. *Author's Collection*

vehicles, bulldozers and tractors, many of which had been knocked out by enemy fire. The dead were everywhere but the wounded were being tended. One by one, enemy garrisons in strongpoints on the cliff tops surrendered when they were surrounded and under intense fire. Engineers cleared the mines laid in a track which led to these positions and ways inland were opened. But progress along these ways was slow against two regiments of the 352nd Division, which was familiar with the territory and could fire on the Americans from concealed positions. There was hard fighting in the approaches to the small towns of Vierville-sur-Mer, St Laurent and Colleville-sur-Mer, for the Americans were still short of tanks, field artillery and ammunition. Limited progress had been made by nightfall but over 34,000 men had landed on the beaches.

On the left flank of Omaha was the British Gold sector, where the 1st Hampshire and 1st Dorset landed on 'Jig' beach while to their left the 6th Green Howards and 5th East Yorkshire landed on 'King' beach. These regiments formed part of the 50th Division Group under XXX Corps. Here the coast and sand dunes were low-lying and there were no cliffs behind them, but the defences consisted of fortified buildings, pillboxes, trenches, barbed wire, mines and an anti-tank ditch. The German troops were well armed with mortars, anti-tank guns, field guns and machine-guns, and many of their emplacements had escaped the sea and air bombardments.

Events did not go well at the outset for the assault troops on Jig beach. The strong tides and currents which had beset the Americans at Omaha swept the leading landing ships of the 1st Hampshire too far to the east, while the DD tanks which should have preceded them were delayed by heavy seas. The first to land came under strong crossfire yet they managed to storm one of the enemy's strongpoints and then turned to attack another, still under withering fire. They were supported by other companies of the 1st Hampshire which landed twenty minutes later and began to make further headway.

The 1st Dorset on their left flank of Jig beach had fewer problems. The flail tanks landed punctually and cleared paths for the infantrymen, who established a firm foothold and then began to push inland. At 08.30 hours the troops on this beach were reinforced by the 2nd Devon Regiment, who joined in the fight, gradually storming the enemy positions westward to Omaha beach. More forces landed punctually and in good order. These were the 47th Royal Marine Commandos with the 90th and 147th Field Regiments of the Royal Artillery.

Towards the east, the assault troops landed in good order on King beach, the 6th Green Howards on the left and the 5th East Yorkshire on the right, with clearance units and Assault Vehicles Royal Engineers (AVREs) ahead of them. They overcame strongpoints, using 'petard' explosive devices to knock out pillboxes and breaching a sea wall with the tanks. Some of the enemy's guns had already been put out of action by the naval bombardment. Of course, there were casualties but prisoners were taken and the village of la Rivière was occupied after accurate gunfire from destroyers. The 7th Green Howards landed in support, as well as the 86th Field Artillery Regiment, and more enemy batteries were subdued.

The whole of the 50th Division Group had landed on the Gold beaches by midday. One brigade attacked westwards along the coast to occupy the little seaport of Arromanches against determined opposition. From there, Royal Marine Commandos were the first to link up with the Americans on Omaha. Other brigades struck southwards, crossing the meandering river Seulles and advancing towards the important town of Bayeux. The advance parties reached the Bayeux–Caen road, about 7 miles south of the coast, after stiff fighting during which they were assisted by naval gunfire and rocket attacks from the RAF's Typhoons. By nightfall, almost 25,000 had been landed in this sector.

Further on the left flank, the beaches on the Juno sector were stormed by assault troops of the 3rd Canadian Division Group, part of the British I Corps. From west to east, the Royal Winnipeg Regiment landed on 'Mike' beach, while the Regina Rifles, the Queen's Own Rifles of Canada and the North Shore Regiment landed on 'Nan' beach. This was the shortest of the five sectors, with the low-lying coast only about 6 miles in length and protected by an offshore reef of rocks which were submerged at high tides. There was, however, a gap of about a mile wide where the river Seulles ran into the sea by the small port of Courseulles, which was one of the objectives of the Canadians on Mike beach. As with the Gold sector, the entire stretch of coast was defended by fortified houses, pillboxes, minefields, barbed wire, and machine-gun and mortar positions.

The assault was delayed by rough seas and the difficulty in forming up the landing craft. The rising tide prevented the clearance groups from demolishing underwater obstructions and it was estimated that about 90 of the 300 landing craft were sunk or damaged on their approaches or return passages. Not all the DD tanks landed in advance of the assault troops on the beaches, having been delayed by swimming through the wrong swept channel. They were followed by two Canadian Armed Regiments, two batteries of Royal Marines, and two squadrons of sappers.

Mike beach was attacked on both sides of Courseulles. This was strongly defended and continued to rake the beach, the port not being cleared completely until the late afternoon, after difficult street fighting. Meanwhile, attempts to punch an exit from the beach were hindered by thickly sown mines, barbed wire, flooding, tank traps and mortar fire. It was not until about 09.15 hours when the first DD tank got across.

The assault troops on Nan beach were supported by thirty-four DD tanks which landed soon after them. One of their worst obstacles was a sea wall of up to 12ft in height, where a strongpoint had survived the air and sea bombardment. This strongpoint fell after the Canadians managed to attack it from the flank.

Other regiments from the 7th and 8th Canadian Brigade Groups followed a few hours later, finding the beaches jammed with damaged vehicles and troops. But by this time several exits from both beaches had

Feldmarschall Gerd von Rundstedt, Commander-in-Chief of Army Group West. *Author's Collection*

been achieved and a movement inland began, making good progress in spite of sniper fire. The Royal Winnipeg Regiment, the Canadian Scottish and the Regina Rifles penetrated up to 5 miles inland, taking many prisoners and sending three companies of the German 726th Regiment into retreat. These Canadians occupied three villages over the river Seulles. Meanwhile, other forces advanced eastward along the coast, overcoming strongpoints in small ports and then also breaking through the defences up to 5 miles inland. However, by nightfall, these Canadians came up against tanks of the German 21st Panzer Division, which separated them by about 2 miles from the British in the Sword sector. They took up defensive positions and awaited daybreak for their next moves. By this time, some 21,400 Canadians had landed in their Juno sector.

The fifth and last sector was Sword on the far left flank. where the beach was codenamed 'Queen'. The 1st South Lincolnshire Regiment with the 2nd East Yorkshire Regiment formed the initial assault troops. These regiments were part of the 3rd Division Group of the British I Corps. Their landing area was a single narrow stretch of beach between the little seaside resort of Lion-sur-Mer and the larger port of Ouistreham at the mouth of the river Orne. The British 6th Airborne Division had landed inland from the latter port during the night and subdued the battery at Merville, overlooking Queen beach. The airborne forces were still holding the bridges over the river Orne and the Caen canal.

The German defences consisted of the fortified ports of Lion-sur-Mer and Ouistreham, with the usual mixture of strongpoints, guns, mortars and machine-guns between them. There were also trenches, barbed wire and minefields, while behind the coast road was a continuous belt of houses occupied by the enemy. The assault troops were protected effectively during their run-in by the barrage from destroyers and rockets from landing craft. Thirty-eight DD tanks of the 13th/18th Hussars landed soon afterwards although some were knocked out on the beaches. These were followed by armoured vehicles and breaching teams of the Royal Marines and the Royal Engineers. Of course, the troops came under continuous enemy fire and there were heavy casualties, but they managed to overcome an enemy strongpoint.

Reinforcements poured ashore, headed by the 1st Suffolk, with Royal Marine Commandos and field regiments of the Royal Artillery. The Commandos began to storm the port of Ouistreham. So many vehicles arrived that they became jammed in front of a beach exit. By the early afternoon, the beach-head was secure but still under fire from defences inland.

When the commander of the German LXXXIV Corps, part of the Seventh Army, became aware that British tanks had landed to the west of the river Orne, he ordered the 21st Panzer Division of 16,000 men to tackle the intruders. This formidable force was stationed south-east of Caen and consisted of 127 Mark IV tanks, 40 assault guns and 24 88mm anti-tank guns. However, the regiments were dispersed and could not go into action immediately.

Meanwhile, the British forces made good progress from Queen beach. By this time, almost 29,000 men had landed. Many enemy defences had been cleared but the strongpoint of Lion-sur-Mer held out against determined attacks. Other forces pushed inland, capturing small towns and villages in the direction of their main objective, the important town of Caen. There was a memorable scene when the 1st Special Service Brigade, led by Brigadier the Lord Lovat, crossed the canal bridge near the river Orne, with Piper Bill Millin ranting *The Black Bear*.

In this period, the vigilant RAF had spotted enemy armoured vehicles moving towards Caen from the south and south-west. This force consisted of ninety tanks of the 21st Panzer Division together with two battalions of infantry. Lieutenant-General Sir Miles Dempsey, who commanded the British Second Army, requested assistance from the air. Typhoons of the RAF's Second Tactical Air Force, armed with rockets and bombs, duly delivered a continuous series of deadly attacks. At about 16.00 hours the remaining tanks came up against the British at Biéville-sur-Orne, about 4 miles north of Caen, and were met with well-directed fire from anti-tank and field guns. At least thirteen were knocked out and the enemy's counter-attack was stalled. A German report states that fifty-four tanks of the 21st Panzer Division were lost during the day. The infantry accompanying them were probably deterred by the sight of numerous gliders landing behind the British lines. These carried a reinforcement of two battalions of the 6th Airborne Division.

Thus all these landings on D-Day were successful, in spite of some errors in execution. The Atlantic Wall, built with so much effort and expenditure of material, had proved ineffectual against a determined and well-planned attack. One of the most remarkable aspects of the day was the failure of the Luftwaffe to appear over the enormous targets provided by the thousands of

Feldmarschall Erwin Rommel, commander of German Army Group B. *Author's Collection*

Allied troops and their equipment on the beach-heads, at a time when they were at their most vulnerable to air attack. In fact, its response was barely perceptible. Less than 100 sorties were flowing during daylight, the majority by single-engined aircraft, but these German aircraft were simply overwhelmed by the great swarms of Allied fighters eager to intercept them. In contrast, the Allied air forces flew over 14,500 sorties during the previous night and the daylight hours of D-Day, keeping the skies almost clear throughout the operation. They had lost only 113 aircraft, mostly from flak. The landings would not have been possible but for this complete air superiority.

The British reached positions about 3 miles north of Caen on this day. It had been hoped to capture this strategic town but the objective was not achieved. Nevertheless, the whole day had gone as well as could be reasonably expected. Over 75,000 British and Canadian troops had landed on the beaches, with 57,500 Americans. In addition to these, almost 8,000 British and about 15,500 American airborne troops had landed. The casualties had been heavy but not merely so serious as had been feared.

A Waco CG-4A glider brought down on D-Day near Ste-Mère-Eglise, about 21 miles south-east of Cherbourg. The wings are pitted with holes and much of the fabric has gone from the fuselage, exposing the welded steel frame. *The National Archives: CAB 106/1004*

The Short Stirling was the first four-engined monoplane bomber to serve in the RAF. In August 1940, No. 7 Squadron was the first to receive the Mark I as shown here. Powered by four Hercules XI engines of 1,595hp, it was armed with two Browning .303in machine-guns in nose and dorsal turrets, with four more in the tail turret. The maximum bomb load was 14,000lb. The role of the Stirling as a bomber ended in the latter part of 1943 but variants were produced for glider towing, transport of troops, dropping supplies to Resistance workers in occupied Europe, and other specialised tasks. *British Official*

Keeping a vigilant watch from the sea, at night in the Sword area, where the British invasion troops had landed. *The National Archives: ADM 199/1662*

The cruiser HMS *Mauritius* engaging German coastal batteries and firing at infantry positions, soon after dawn on D-Day. *The National Archives: ADM 199/1662*

A British LCT (Landing Craft Tank) hit by enemy shellfire, burning on D-Day. There were several versions of this craft, such as the LCT(R) which was armed with two 20mm anti-aircraft guns and could fire 1,080 5in rockets to support the troops on the beaches. *The National Archives: ADM 199/1662*

Enemy medium batteries firing high-explosive shells at British warships at dawn on D-Day, with one explosion visible in the water. *The National Archives: ADM 199/1662*

British LCT 789 leading a convoy of landing craft through choppy seas to the beaches of Normandy. *The National Archives: DEFE 2/502*

A B-26 Marauder of the US Ninth Air Force over the Normandy invasion beaches on D-Day, one of many giving support to the troops below. *US National Archives and Records Administration # 342-FH-3A-17154-51988*

An air view of the American landing operations on the coast of Normandy. Three LSTs (Landing Ships Tank) can be seen in shallow water about 200yd offshore while tanks and other vehicles are ploughing through the surf. Soldiers are spread over the beaches while others are wading or swimming ashore. *US National Archives and Records Administration # 342-FH-3A-17156-52286*

American assault vehicles and troops on the Normandy beaches, some pushing inland while other waves of the invading forces approach through the surf in support. *US National Archives and Records Administration # 342-FH-3A-17140-51580*

An oblique photograph taken from 2,000ft on D-Day over Gold Beach in the British sector, showing great activity among shipping and landing craft at Asnelles, east of Arromanches. The pilot was Captain Frank Cassady of the US Ninth Air Force, flying a Lightning F-5. *The National Archives: AIR 25/792*

American troops of the 1st Infantry Division struggling through the surf under intense enemy fire to Omaha Beach, after leaving the ramp of their Coast Guard landing craft. In the distance, a solitary armoured vehicle is trying to clear a path through obstacles on the beach. *US National Archives and Records Administration: War & Conflict # 1041*

Juno Beach near Graye-sur-Mer, where the Canadian units of the British Second Army landed in the early morning of D-Day. This photograph was taken at low tide on the same day, showing landing craft and heavy traffic building up ready to move inland. *The National Archives: AIR 37/1231*

British DD (Duplex Drive) swimming tanks among the landing craft going ashore on the right flank of Gold Beach on D-Day. The troops met less resistance than feared in this part of the invasion beaches. The DD was a Sherman tank made watertight and fitted with two ship's screws driven by its engine. It was kept afloat by a waterproof bag containing thirty-six rubber tubes, inflated by two compressed air bottles on the afterdeck. This bag was discarded when the beach was reached. The engine was then switched to the caterpillar drive wheels and the tank was ready for action. *The National Archives: DEFE 2/502*

Crossed rifles in the sand marked the body of an American soldier who died on D-Day near one of the wooden obstacles that littered the invasion beaches. By 10.30 hours, the US 1st Division had suffered 3,000 dead or wounded. *US National Archives and Records Administration: War & Conflict # 1044*

Below: American assault troops of the 16th Infantry Regiment, wounded while storming Omaha Beach, wait by the chalk cliffs of Colleville-sur-Mer, 8 miles north-west of Bayeux in Normandy, for evacuation to a field hospital. *US National Archives and Records Administration: War & Conflict # 1043*

Soldiers of an American landing party helping others whose landing craft was sunk by enemy fire on D-Day. These survivors reached Utah Beach near Quineville by means of a life raft. *US National Archives and Records Administration: War & Conflict # 1042*

After the beach-heads had been secured, a combat photographer of the US Coast Guard came across this German MG 34 heavy machine-gun stuck in the ground with a helmet on it, somewhere in shell-blasted shores of Normandy. In the foreground is a box containing cartridge belts and a German hand-grenade. *US National Archives and Records Administration: War & Conflict # 1045*

The wreckage of a P-47 Thunderbolt which crash-landed on one of the battle-scarred beaches of Normandy, photographed on 22 June 1944. *US National Archives and Records Administration # 342-FH-3A-17188-72625*

An LCT (Landing Craft Tank) preparing to discharge its cargo on Omaha Beach after the area had been cleared of the defending German troops. *The National Archives: CAB 106/1004*

Amphibious DUKWs landing with equipment and supplies on the British invasion beaches, before returning empty to beached coasters for further supplies. A large white X has been painted for guidance on the wall of the building flying the Royal Navy's White Ensign. *The National Archives: DEFE 2/502*

British LCT406 unloading its cargo on one of the Normandy beaches. The tank appears to be a version of the Cromwell fitted with a double-barrelled weapon. *The National Archives: DEFE 2/502*

British launches on D-Day tied up off the Normandy beaches, seen in the distance. The crews are awaiting the order to go ashore and unload their cargoes. *The National Archives: DEFE 2/502*

British Commandos landing on one of the Normandy beaches on D-Day. Some are carrying bicycles as they wade through the surf to the shore. *The National Archives: DEFE 2/502*

A German gun battery silenced by Allied bombing on
the coast of Hitler's 'West Wall', photographed by a
US Coast Guard. The walls were found to be 13ft
thick and the emplacement housed four heavy guns.
US National Archives and Records Administration: War &
Conflict # 1046

The White Ensign of a Royal Navy beach party flying on a Normandy beach as troops move inland from their landing craft. *The National Archives: DEFE 2/502*

Coasters ran aground on the invasion beaches at low tide and unloaded their cargoes into amphibious DUKWs. Then they waited for high tide, refloated and set off for more supplies from an English port. *The National Archives: DEFE 2/502*

The Supermarine Spitfire XIV, fitted with a Rolls-Royce Griffon 65 engine of 2,050hp driving a five-bladed propeller and rated to give a maximum speed of 448mph at 26,000ft, first entered RAF service in January 1944. It had elliptical wings and was armed with two 20mm cannons as well as four .303in machine-guns. From June 1944, the squadrons equipped with this fighter claimed the destruction of over 300 V-1 flying bombs. Spitfires XIVs served in home defence and with the Second Tactical Air Force. *British Official*

Two Royal Norwegian squadrons in the RAF, Nos 331 and 332, gave fighter cover and close support to the Allies' navies and armies during the D-Day landings. They were equipped with Spitfire XIs and based at Bognor Regis in Sussex as part of No. 132 Wing, No. 84 Group, Second Tactical Air Force. Once the invasion forces had gained a foothold in Normandy, they used a landing strip during their sorties to carry out additional patrols before returning to England. *The National Archives: DEFE 2/502*

The railway bridge over the river Seine at Oissel, 8 miles south of Rouen, was one of those wrecked in the campaign by the Allied Expeditionary Air Force to destroy the enemy's transportation system in France. The photograph was taken on D-Day. *The National Archives: AIR 34/240*

CHAPTER THREE

ENLARGING THE BEACH-HEAD

The Allied commanders were gratified by the success of their deception measures and the consequent slow response of the Wehrmacht to the invasion of Normandy. The assault had caught the Oberkommado der Wehrmacht by surprise, partly because the weather conditions seemed to be unfavourable. The possibility of any attack had been dismissed until the heavy seas subsided and the skies cleared.

The immediate reaction of the Commander-in-Chief West, Feldmarschall von Rundstedt, was that the Allied landings were not a major operation, although his opinion was not shared by the Chief of Staff of the Seventh Army, Major-General Max Pensel. The commander of von Rundstedt's Army Group B in the north of France, Feldmarschall Erwin Rommel, was absent from the scene of action on D-Day. He had also made the assumption that there would be no invasion in the prevailing weather conditions and taken the opportunity to visit his family in Germany. But he rushed back to France as soon as the news was conveyed to him. With von Rundstedt's approval, his course of action was to order divisions from the Seventh Army and Panzer Group West to head north and help form another strong line which might eventually push the invaders back into the sea. On 7 June, the Germans took some American prisoners and captured their orders. These confirmed Rommel's suspicion that the Americans intended to cut off the Cotentin peninsula. He ordered an infantry division and a Panzer division to move to the area, followed by a parachute division, to form part of LXXXIV Corps under General Erich Marcks.

Of course, strategic or even tactical decisions were not wholly the province of either von Rundstedt or Rommel. At the time of the landings, Hitler had gone to bed late and was asleep in his mountain retreat at the Berghof. Nobody dared to awaken him or inform him of the development until he had risen and had his breakfast. Even then, he regarded the invasion as no more than a diversionary attack, believing that the main assault would take place in the Pas de Calais on 15 June from the FUSAG (First United States Army Group). This was the imaginary formation which had been concocted by the Western Allies to deceive him.

But any movement of the German formations was not easy, for much of the transport system in northern France had been destroyed and the columns had to endure frequent attacks from the air during daylight or were harried by the French Resistance. The Luftwaffe was powerless to prevent these air attacks. It made spasmodic attempts under cover of darkness to bomb the Allied bridgeheads and to drop mines on the anchorages, but with little effect. One minor success was achieved in the early hours of 7 June. A fighter direction ship which had been converted from an armed merchant cruiser, HMS *Bulolo*, was hit by a 250lb phosphorous bomb which caused damage and casualties. By comparison with this small effort, the RAF's Bomber Command despatched nearly 1,100 aircraft during the night, mainly against lines of communication behind the Normandy battle area. These bombardments caused considerable damage to railway and road centres but inevitably there were civilian casualties.

The US Eighth Air Force took over these targets in daylight on 7 June, despatching over 1,000 heavy bombers, plus about 1,500 fighters either as escorts or engaged on strafing enemy columns. The Luftwaffe made little

Bomber Command despatched 1,065 aircraft on the night of 6/7 June to bomb lines of communications near French towns behind the Normandy beach-heads. Among them was the railway near Argentan, running diagonally across this photograph. The weather was very cloudy and most of the bombs appear to have fallen in nearby fields. *The National Archives: AIR 37/1231*

response to these massive forces. The American fighter escorts tended to avoid combat on the outer flights, when they were carrying drop-tanks, but hunted enthusiastically on the return journeys and achieved a ratio of three to one 'kills' in their favour.

The Allied Expeditionary Air Force also swung into action during daylight. Lieutenant-General Leonard T. Gerow, who commanded the American divisions which had landed on the Omaha beaches, requested 'continuous fighter-bomber support' to suppress German artillery which was still firing on his troops. The IX Fighter Command of the US Ninth Air Force responded by sending thirty-five squadrons of fighter-bombers during the day, dropping 1,000lb bombs on enemy gun positions. Behind the American positions on Utah and Omaha, medium bombers of the Ninth struck at road bridges while other fighters maintained mastery of the skies or carried out low-level bombing attacks. An example of their effectiveness was recorded by part of the German 275th Infantry Division which left St Nazaire in two trains in the early hours of 7 June, bound for Bayeux. One train was destroyed near Avranches, with all the vehicles and equipment, and causing numerous casualties. The other was halted by a cut line and similarly attacked. The surviving infantry had the problem of trudging over 50 miles to their destination, still under air attack.

Meanwhile, Typhoon squadrons of the RAF's Second Tactical Air Force, supported by Mustang squadrons of the Air Defence of Great Britain, were given the task of hunting and destroying enemy movements towards the British sector. These were almost entirely along roads, since the railway system had already been shattered. Thick low cloud forced the aircraft to fly low and suffer some losses from ground fire. But an example of their successes may be judged from the records of the Panzer Lehr Division. This had moved up from south of the river Loire and was spotted at dawn near Falaise, heading north in five columns towards the British and Canadian forces. The RAF aircraft knocked out as many as eighty-four half-tracks, some of which were carrying 88mm guns, as well as ninety trucks carrying ammunition and forty others carrying fuel. Such air operations set a pattern which would be followed until the Wehrmacht was cleared out of France.

Apart from these devastating air attacks, the German ground forces faced another insuperable problem, for when reaching the battle area they came within range of tremendous fire from Allied warships. This fire knocked out much of their artillery and there was no way they could retaliate against the warships. Nevertheless, the position of the Allied invaders remained precarious. Their footholds were still isolated, they were short of military supplies, and they were heavily outnumbered by enemy divisions. Before the end of August, the Allies would encounter ten Panzer Divisions, three motorised divisions and thirty-eight infantry divisions in France. If sufficient of these had been brought against them in the early stages of the invasion, the outcome might have been very different.

The Allied troops had had little sleep on the night of D-Day, in whatever shelters they could find, and faced the prospect of close combat soon after dawn. Their main tasks for the next few days were to consolidate the gains already made, to wipe out pockets of enemy resistance behind their forward lines and to coalesce into a unified force.

The Americans had to join up their two bridgeheads as well as to probe westwards across the base of the Cotentin peninsula, in order to establish strong links with their airborne forces and cut off enemy access to the port of Cherbourg before assaulting it. The British and Canadians also had to link up their bridgeheads, maintain contact with the Americans on their right flank, probe towards the cities of Caen and Bayeux, and strengthen their defences on their left flank along the river Dives against potential attack from the German Fifteenth Army. They found much of the countryside increasingly difficult when they tried to penetrate southwards. Apart from the area north of Caen, the roads were narrow and winding, set low between banks, hedgerows and wooded hills. This was the 'bocage' country, which favoured defence rather than attack, and it was to hinder operations in the next few weeks.

The RAF's Bomber Command despatched over 450 aircraft on the night of 7/8 June, finding weather conditions improved and bombing enemy positions behind the lines with considerable accuracy. The US Eighth Air Force resumed these attacks in the morning, despatching over 1,100 bombers and 1,350 fighters or fighter-bombers. The Wehrmacht had little answer to these merciless attacks, or to those of the Allied Expeditionary Air Force which were also resumed in daylight. These attacks continued throughout each day and night, although weather conditions were unfavourable on 8 June. The RAF's Bomber Command scored a notable success on the night of 8/9 June when the first streamlined 'Tallboy' bombs of 12,000lb were dropped with pinpoint accuracy on the entrance of a railway tunnel near Saumur on the Loire, blocking it for two months and seriously hindering a Panzer unit from reaching the front.

Von Rundstedt complained that it was easier for the Allies to bring reinforcements over the Channel by sea than it was for his forces to reach the

Extremely accurate bombing took place on the night of 8/9 June when the first 'Tallboy' bombs of 12,000lb were dropped by twenty-five Lancasters of No. 617 Squadron on a railway tunnel at Saumur, south of the Normandy battle area. The target was illuminated by four other Lancasters and three Mosquitos. The bombs created 'earthquake' effects and craters of between 100 and 120ft diameter, and the mouth of the tunnel was blocked for a considerable period. No aircraft were lost. This photograph was taken by a reconnaissance Spitfire on the following day. *The National Archives: AIR 25/792*

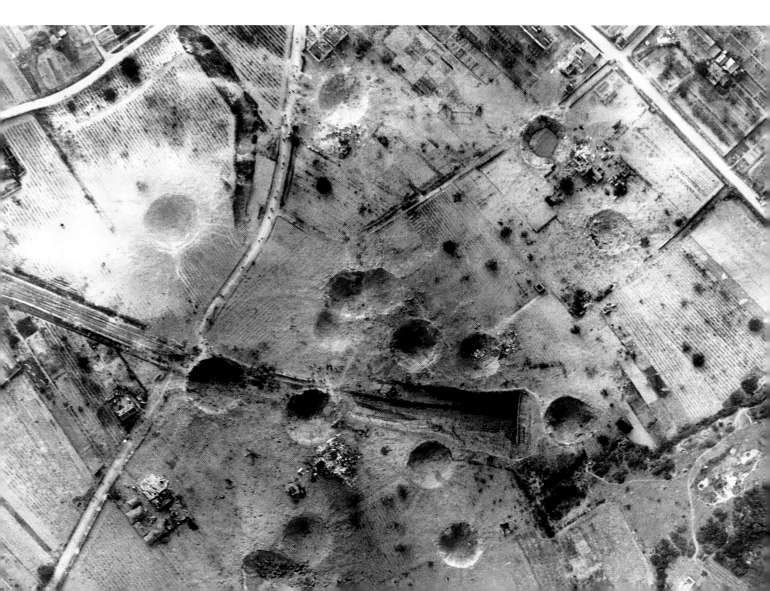

front by road or rail. In fact, however, the unseasonable weather was hindering this Allied supply route and the military build-up was falling behind schedule. The Kriegsmarine did its best to interfere with this process, although the results were almost nil. The three destroyers despatched from the Gironde estuary were mauled by rocket-firing Beaufighters of the RAF's Coastal Command on D-Day and put into Brest for repair as well as to bring their dead and wounded ashore. The holes caused by the rockets were rapidly plated over and they slipped out again on the evening of 7 June, together with a torpedo boat, but were brought to action by eight destroyers of the 10th Destroyer Flotilla. The torpedo boat and one destroyer were damaged and turned back to Brest, but another destroyer was sunk. The third destroyer was forced to beach on the Ile de Batz, where it was finished off the next day by the Beaufighters.

Meanwhile, U-boats were approaching the Channel from the west but the Admiralty was monitoring their movements from Enigma decrypts. Allied warships and aircraft were waiting for them. There were losses at sea from other causes. The minesweeper USS *Tide* hit a mine and sank off Utah beach on 7 June. The US destroyers *Meredith*, *Glennon* and *Rich*, were lost from mines on the following day, while the frigate HMS *Lawford* sank after an air attack. The French destroyer *Mistral* was sunk by coastal gunfire off Le Havre on 10 June. In the early hours of 11 June, the frigate HMS *Halsted* was torpedoed by Schnellboote; she returned to Portsmouth but was never repaired. Some merchant ships and landing craft were also sunk by these fast motor torpedo-boats, but four of the attackers were sunk in the four days up to 13 June while ten others were damaged.

By 9 June, the British, Canadians and Americans had consolidated their bridgehead into a continuous line stretching from the river Orne in the east to the Vire estuary in the west, at the corner of the Cotentin peninsula. The Vire estuary still separated the Americans of V Corps who had landed on the Omaha beaches from those of VII Corps who had landed on the Utah beaches. These were being reinforced by XIX Corps on Omaha and VIII Corps on Utah.

The junction of these American forces was effected on 10 June by V Corps, which overcame the German garrison at Carentan near the mouth of the estuary. Advancing north in the Cotentin peninsula, VII Corps closed on the town of Montebourg, about halfway to the port of Cherbourg. Fearing this Channel port could not hold out, von Rundstedt ordered the destruction of the dock facilities, apart from those which might be used by the Kriegsmarine. This fear was accentuated on 14 June when the Americans entered St Sauveur-le-Vicomte, more than halfway across the peninsula. Three days later they had reached the west coast, cutting off two German divisions, while their rear was guarded by the newly arrived VIII Corps. Rommel intended to withdraw these divisions to Cherbourg, where they could form a strong defence, but Hitler had already decreed that there was to be no retreat. Instead they must hold their line at all costs, and launched a counter-attack.

Meanwhile, forces from the American V Corps pushed inland and on 12 June fought their way into Caumont, about 15 miles south of the Omaha beaches and adjoining the British XXX Corps. In this British sector, General Montgomery intended to assault southwards from the Gold and Juno beaches. His objective was to advance through the towns of Villers-Bocage and Noyers and then to occupy high ground to the south-west of Caen. As it happened, enemy forces attacked first, on 10 June against the eastern positions, after infiltrating the bocage country. This attack was repelled, but the British 7th Armoured Division which attempted to advance through the bocage at Tilly-sur-Seulles made little progress. The tanks were unable to manoeuvre in the narrow lanes and were easily waylaid by a determined enemy, the Panzer Lehr Division. The attempt was resumed on the following day, 11 June, but again was stalled. The 3rd Canadian Division, on the left of the British, was also repulsed, with its armoured regiment suffering heavy losses of tanks.

It became apparent that the area east of Tilly-sur-Seulles was firmly held by the Germans and that it might be preferable to sweep round near the American sector at Caumont and outflank these enemy defences. This assault was led by the 22nd Armoured Brigade on 13 June but the columns met Tiger tanks near Villers-Bocage which destroyed many of their tanks and armoured trucks. On their right, the 50th Division attacked Tilly-sur-Seulles, with assistance from RAF Typhoons, and there was heavy fighting on 14 June. Then it was learnt that the 2nd Panzer Division was approaching from the south. This was unexpected, since Montgomery believed that it was being held in reserve by von Rundstedt for the expected Allied landing in the Pas de Calais. He ordered a withdrawal of the 7th Armoured Division, which was in a vulnerable position, and this took place in the early hours of 15 June.

Events on the far left flank of the British sector were influenced by the activities of double agents in Britain, who continued to pass false information to the Abwehr with considerable success. On 9 June, the double agent GARBO (known by the codename of ARABEL by the Abwehr) sent an important message to the Germans. After 'consultation with his sub-agents', he was able to inform them that there were seventy-five Allied divisions available on D-Day (the true number was fifty) and the main attack would take place along the Pas de Calais. This message gave an 'order of battle' for the FUSAG formation, which included the Guards Armoured Division, as well as some true details of the regiments in the Normandy 'diversionary' force. The Germans were able to check the latter from Allied prisoners, providing evidence of the accuracy of the report. Thus the majority of Rommel's Fifteenth Army remained in positions east of the river Orne and was not committed to assisting the Seventh Army in its efforts to repulse the invaders in Normandy.

Nevertheless, elements of this Fifteenth Army began determined attacks on 7 June against the left flank of the British Second Army, sending in the 346th and 711th Infantry Divisions, part of the 716th Infantry Division, and a battle group from the 21st Panzer Division. These were all part of the German LXXXI Corps. Some fierce fighting ensued. On 9 June, the German forces came up against the British 3rd Division at Ranville, south of Ouistreham, but were beaten off by accurate defensive fire and a counter-attack. The 51st (Highland) Division was brought in to reinforce the defenders. The German forces came in again on the following day but were heavily shelled by the cruiser HMS *Arethusa* and then counter-attacked by the 3rd Parachute Brigade. One battalion of the German 346th Division was almost wiped out. On the other hand, the Black Watch suffered severe losses when it attempted to attack German positions on 11 June. The Germans attacked once more on the following day and there were very heavy losses on both sides, but the British line held and was not seriously attacked again.

While the Allied armies were striving to make headway, American and British engineers were busy constructing forward airstrips in the territory already occupied. Units of the Engineer Aviation Battalions, US Ninth Air Force, had landed on the Utah beaches on D-Day and on the Omaha beaches the following

day. They began constructing airstrips immediately. An emergency strip at St-Laurent in the Omaha sector was begun two days after D-Day and completed on 10 June, capable of taking Dakotas and evacuating the wounded to England. The first of the RAF's Servicing Commandos and Construction Wings had come ashore on 7 June and begun their work with bulldozers, excavators and rollers. At first, this was carried out under shellfire, although the men dug trenches for their protection. The first fighter airstrip, B.3 at St Croix-sur-Mer between the Gold and Juno sectors, was completed on 10 June, supplied with fuel taken mainly from DUKWs. Such airstrips enabled aircraft, mainly fighters, to refuel and carry out more operations, but squadrons soon began to base themselves on these temporary landing grounds. Eventually thirty-one airstrips were constructed in the British sector and fifty in the American. They were protected by light anti-aircraft guns, those in the British sector being manned by detachments of the RAF Regiment.

On the night of 12/13 June, the Wehrmacht made its first attempt to fire V-1 flying bombs against London from some of the launching sites located in woods between the Seine estuary and Cap Gris-Nez. Ten of these pilotless devices were fired but only four reached England. Two exploded in the London area, one in Sussex and one in Kent, killing four people and injuring nine. Then the pace

Amphibious DUKWs moving inland, some loaded and some empty, along a road to a transit depot, after the British beach-head had been secured. These American vehicles were built on the chassis of a GMC truck of 2½ tons. They were powered by a six-cylinder engine and had a speed of about 50mph on land and about 6mph on water. *The National Archives: DEFE 2/502*

quickened. By 16 June, 144 had been seen crossing the English coast and 73 exploded in the London area. They were inaccurate weapons which cut out at a predetermined time and fell almost haphazardly to explode on impact.

The existence of these weapons was already well known to the British, who had taken countermeasures under the codename of operation 'Crossbow'. Attacks on the launching sites had been made from December 1943 by the RAF's Bomber Command, the US Eighth Air Force and the Allied Expeditionary Air Force, and it was estimated that 103 sites had been destroyed out of 140 located by photo-reconnaissance. Meanwhile, belts of anti-aircraft batteries and balloon defences had been prepared in south-east England. When the flying bombs began to arrive, the faster fighters such as the new Hawker Tempest of the Air Defence of Great Britain were given the task of bringing them down in flight.

But German engineers had designed and built pre-fabricated ramps which were more mobile and could be easily assembled and camouflaged in the Pas de Calais. Some of the bombing offensive against enemy forces in Normandy had to be diverted to meet this new threat to the civilian population of England. The RAF's Bomber Command began by sending over 400 aircraft to bomb the sites on the night of 16/17 June. The US Eighth Air Force followed with over 500 bombers escorted by fighters on 20 June. Such attacks continued until the sites were overrun in early September.

The U-boats ordered to attack the Allied invasion fleet ran into serious problems. Seventeen which left Brest were hunted relentlessly by the RAF's Coastal Command, equipped with anti-surface vessel radar and depth charges. Some aircraft were fitted with the ingenious 'Leigh Light', a brilliant searchlight to be used in the hours of darkness. Unknown to both the RAF and the U-boat crews, the Admiralty Tracking Room was able to monitor the progress of these boats from decryption of German Enigma signals. By 10 June, five U-boats had been sunk while seven others had been so badly damaged or had suffered such defects that they were forced to return to port. Three of the remaining five had to put into St Peter Port in Guernsey to recharge their batteries after a long period underwater and enable their exhausted crews to rest.

Four other U-boats based in Norway and on patrol off Iceland were diverted to the Channel, together with five from French bases on war cruises in the Atlantic. Only two of these nine U-boats managed to penetrate the Allied naval and air screens to begin attacks, joining the campaign with the five from Brest. On 15 June, *U-767* sank the frigate HMS *Mourne* near Ushant and on the same day *U-764* damaged the frigate HMS *Blackwood* so badly that she sank when under tow to Portland harbour. But three of these seven U-boats were sunk in the Channel.

Nineteen other U-boats based in France had been ordered to form a patrol line in the Bay of Biscay, for the Oberkommando der Wehrmacht believed the report from the double agent BRONX in Britain that the Allies would mount another invasion on that coastline. One of these U-boats was sunk by air attack and another returned damaged. The remainder were recalled from their fruitless operation on 12 June, to shelter in the concrete bunkers of Lorient, St-Nazaire and La Pallice against air attack.

During all these developments, Allied engineers and naval personnel had been intensely busy trying to facilitate the movement of reinforcements of men and supplies from England. The small harbours of Port-en-Bessin and Courseulles were opened on 12 June and able to handle limited quantities, but most of the men and supplies continued to arrive at the beaches through the surf. The main effort centred on the construction of artificial Mulberry harbours in the American and British sectors. This work had begun on 7 June with the sinking of the first blockships by explosive charges, to provide breakwaters off the five main assault beaches. Two of these were intended to be expanded into complete harbours, one off Omaha near St-Laurent and the other off Juno near Arromanches. For this purpose, concrete caissons fitted with flooding valves were towed over the Channel and began to arrive on 8 June. They were duly sunk, while being held in position by tugs. Then came the work of building piers into the harbour from the shore. These were formed from floating steel tanks of about 180ft in length, carried from England slung on the sides of tank landing craft.

It is estimated that by 16 June a total of 278,000 Americans and 279,000 British had been brought over by sea. In addition, some 81,000 vehicles and 183,000 tons of stores had been landed. But the herculean task of constructing the artificial harbours had not been completed when disaster struck on 19 June. A raging storm sprang up, with gale force winds, fiercer than any for over forty years in the Channel during June. It lasted for four days and the destruction was enormous. Most of the breakwater at Arromanches held, but that at St-Laurent was wrecked. Only ten of the thirty-five caissons remained intact in this American sector, blockships were driven on to the beaches and broke up, while the piers were completely destroyed. In both harbours and in the other three sheltered anchorages, the seas and beaches were littered with over 800 sunken or

The artificial Mulberry harbour near Arromanches in the British Gold sector, about 2½ miles long and 1 mile wide. The first 'Phoenix' caisson arrived at dawn on 6 June 1944 to begin the construction of this harbour. Nine days later, 115 of these caissons were resting on the sea bed at Arromanches and near St-Laurent in the American Omaha sector. About 60 disused ships were also brought across and sunk with small explosive charges to reinforce these two artificial harbours. A fierce storm blew up on 19 June and destroyed the American harbour but the one in the British sector was less damaged and remained operational. *The National Archives: AIR 37/1231*

wrecked small craft. The arrival of men and military equipment was seriously delayed and a planned campaign had to be postponed.

General Montgomery believed that the main purpose of the invasion at this stage was the destruction of the German armies in Normandy. The acquisition of territory was a secondary objective, although this would also be necessary. Of course, he had the immense advantage of knowing the disposition of enemy forces, from decrypts of Enigma signals and from air reconnaissance. The Allied Expeditionary Force also possessed overwhelming air and sea power, although its land forces were not yet built up to the strength he required.

On the other hand, von Rundstedt and Rommel had false ideas about the Allied forces and intentions. By 17 June it had become obvious that the Germans were on the defensive and could not push the Allies back into the sea without huge reinforcements. The German field commanders also suffered the immense handicap of an inept commander-in-chief, Adolf Hitler, whom they met on that day at his *Führerhauptquartier* (named *Wolfsschlucht 2*) at Margival, near Soissons in France, well behind the battle front. Hitler's concept of military strategy seems to have been rooted in his experiences as a corporal on the western front in the First World War. The field commanders were told to hold their lines everywhere, never make any strategic withdrawals and to order counter-attacks. They were also to rely on Hitler's new 'wonder weapons' in the form of flying bombs and rockets, which would bring their enemy to his knees.

Montgomery's next objectives were the capture of Cherbourg and Caen, as soon as possible after the great storm subsided and further troops and supplies could arrive. The first was achieved with conspicuous success by the Americans. While the newly arrived VIII Corps took over the front facing south, leading towards the difficult bocage country, the VII Corps resumed its attack northwards in the Cotentin peninsula. It was supported at all stages by RAF and USAAF fighters, fighter-bombers and bombers of the Allied Expeditionary Air Force.

By 20 June, the Americans were within 5 miles of the port, but then there was a delay while the storm raged in the Channel. This began to abate two days later and the Americans broadcast a message to the German commander-in-chief, giving him until 09.00 hours to surrender. There were about 21,000 German troops penned in the area and there was no response, even though their position was hopeless and without prospect of relief. Accordingly, the final assault was begun with an immense air attack by the Allied Expeditionary Air Force on enemy fortifications. These were then overcome one by one by the advancing Americans, who took thousands of prisoners from the survivors. The port was entered on 25 June, but the remaining defenders still fought on, street by street. General Bradley called for a naval bombardment of the heavy coastal guns in the port, and this was begun by three US battleships accompanied by two US and two British cruisers, screened by eleven American destroyers. A thunderous gun battle ensued, lasting for three hours. One battleship, one cruiser and three destroyers received hits, but the enemy guns were silenced and the ships withdrew.

The American troops then continued their assault until the Germans surrendered on the following day. There remained other positions to be taken along the coast, but the whole of the Cotentin peninsula fell into American hands. The port of Cherbourg was in a shambles, with the dock facilities destroyed and the harbour littered with blockships and mines, but recovery work began immediately. After this victory, it was possible to begin

withdrawing some of the Allied heavy warships from the Channel for duties elsewhere, marking the end of operation Neptune but leaving many smaller vessels to escort the transports.

The second objective, the capture of Caen by the British Second Army, proved a tougher problem. The task fell to VIII Corps, which had newly arrived from England, with support from the British and Canadian troops of XXX Corps who had landed on the Gold beaches. It was originally intended to start on 22 June but the storm caused delays. This bad weather also hindered air operations over the battle front, which enabled the Germans to bring up some reinforcements.

The British 51st Division began a diversionary attack east of the Orne on 23 June, but the main thrust was launched two days later to the west of Caen. The latter was codenamed operation 'Epsom' and the forces involved amounted to about 60,000 men with 700 guns and 600 tanks. The tactics were to punch a salient through the German lines and capture bridges over the river Odon, which flowed into the Orne south of the city. The attackers of VIII Corps would then be able to wheel to the east and take the German defences from the rear, while their right flank was protected by XXX Corps.

The assault achieved some success on the first day, opening a gap of about 4 miles wide in the enemy positions. Both corps were strongly supported from the air by the RAF's Second Tactical Air Force, which was still based mainly in England although some fighter squadrons were stationed at forward airstrips in Normandy. The enemy consisted of the 12th SS Panzer Division on the left. Although advances were made, the Odon bridges were not reached by nightfall.

The second and third days, 26 and 27 June, were marred by extremely bad weather in England which prevented the tactical aircraft from taking off. Almost equally bad weather in Normandy resulted in heavy going over sodden ground, and the defenders fought back tenaciously. The squadrons based in Normandy

American infantrymen working their way through the ruins of Cherbourg, while keeping their eyes open for snipers who had delayed them for several hours. The port fell to them on 3 July. *The National Archives: CAB 106/1004*

did their best to provide support but were hampered by low cloud and ground mist while the reinforced Luftwaffe put in an appearance. Nevertheless, the attackers captured intact a bridge over the Odon near Tourmauville and formed a bridgehead on the other bank. The weather improved in the afternoon of 27 June, giving Mosquitos and Mitchells of the RAF's Second Tactical Air Force an opportunity to attack enemy positions during the night.

No further advances were made on 28 June, but much fighting took place and the bridgehead over the Odon was strengthened in anticipation of a counter-attack. They reached the lower slopes of a large and flat-topped mount which they labelled Hill 112. There were signs that the enemy was being reinforced on both sides of the salient they had won. On this day the commander of the German Seventh Army, General Friedrich Dollmann, died unexpectedly and suddenly of a heart attack. On Hitler's directive, General Paul Hausser took over as acting commander.

On the evening of the same day both von Rundstedt and Rommel set off for a private interview with Hitler at Berchtesgaden. On the following day this was enlarged into a general conference with other Nazi leaders. Von Rundstedt's request for greater freedom of action was denied but the conference was to give rise to a directive which Hitler would issue on 8 July, having given what he doubtless believed was profound thought to the current strategic problems.

The weather over the battle front had cleared by the morning of 29 June and the RAF's Second Tactical Air Force resumed intense activity, inflicting much

This photograph of one of the concealed V-1 flying bomb sites at Vignacourt, near Abbeville, showed how the German prefabricated buildings were merged with surrounding farm buildings. Launching pads were constructed in orchards, woods and hedges, and camouflaged when not in use. The launching ramp on top right was hidden in an orchard, above the square building on bottom right. The photograph was taken on 12 June 1944 from 5,500ft by a keen-eyed pilot in an RAF reconnaissance Spitfire. On 2 July 1944, twenty-four B-24 Liberators of the US Eighth Air Force dropped 58 tons of bombs on this site. *The National Archives: AIR 25/792*

damage on the enemy's armour. There were reports of large enemy reinforcements approaching the front and indeed these began counter-attacks all around the salient in the early evening. These were repulsed with heavy losses, by British artillery fire and the RAF's Typhoons. They were resumed on 30 June, with much the same result, and many German prisoners were taken. But by this time the situation on the front had become more static.

At the beginning of July there were over 850,000 Allied troops in Normandy, with the Americans forming the slightly greater proportion. Battle casualties amounted to almost 8,500 killed and 42,500 wounded. About 11,000 men were missing, of whom many were probably prisoners of war. Although serious, they were far less than had been feared when the invasion was planned. The USAAF and the RAF had lost about 5,250 men, some of whom were also prisoners of war. Allied shipping losses had amounted to twenty-four warships and thirty-five merchant vessels, of all types, with fifty-nine warships and sixty-one merchant vessels damaged.

Supplies were still pouring over the Channel, with the backlog caused by the great storm being steadily cleared. The main life blood for this great force was fuel. Much of this was being brought ashore by the 'Tombola' system, whereby storage depots built on the coast were fed by pipelines from moored tankers. A more ambitious scheme, the laying of a 'pipe line under the ocean' from England to France (codenamed 'Pluto') was in hand. Meanwhile, eleven new airfields had been constructed in the American sector and twelve in the British.

In early July, the wrath of Hitler descended on von Rundstedt and the commander of Panzer Group West, General Geyr von Schweppenburg, both of whom had dared to recommend a withdrawal from Caen to form a line further south, thus querying his earlier ruling. Von Rundstedt was superseded on 2 July, although it was officially stated that he had retired, and replaced by Feldmarschall Günther von Kluge. Three days later, von Schweppenburg was replaced by General Heinrich Eberbach. Rommel retained his command, although he had shared the views of his two erstwhile comrades. On 8 July, Hitler issued his 'Directive for the conduct of the war in the West'. In this, he accepted that the Allies had seized the Cotentin peninsula 'with astonishing speed' and then forecast that the next landing would be in the Pas de Calais, partly to eliminate the flying-bomb sites. Thus the Fifteenth Army should be ready to repel this assault. He also forecast, correctly in this instance, that the Allies would eventually land in the south of France. He ordered that under no circumstances must the Allied bridgeheads be allowed to increase in size, confirming his original order that there should be no strategic withdrawals. German casualty figures are available for this date. From D-Day to 7 July, the armies had suffered over 81,500 killed, wounded and captured.

In this period, Montgomery launched his final assault on Caen. It began in the morning of 4 July with an attack on the major airfield of Carpiquet, to the east of the city. This was the task of the 8th Canadian Infantry Brigade, which had landed in the Juno sector on D-Day, supported by tanks and artillery as well as the RAF's rocket-firing Typhoons. The assault opened with fire from the 16in guns of the battleships HMS *Rodney* and HMS *Warspite*, at a range of almost 15 miles while directed by spotter aircraft. The airfield was defended by the 26th Panzer Grenadier Regiment plus tanks of the 12th SS Panzer Division. A fierce battle ensued, with attack and counter-attack. There were heavy casualties on both sides, and the airfield was only partially captured on the first day.

The main ground attack on Caen began on 8 July. The British and Canadian I Corps, strongly reinforced and consisting of about 115,000 men, was ordered to clear the enemy from the city, while VII Corps on its right flank was to be ready to sweep round to the south. The enemy had made extensive preparations for defence, the positions being held by the 16th Luftwaffe Field Division of LXXXXVI Corps with tanks from the 21st Panzer Division, the 1st and 12th SS Panzer Divisions, I and II SS Panzer Korps, and the 7th Werfer Brigade.

As a prelude, heavy bombers of the RAF's Bomber Command were employed for the first time on tactical support. Over 450 aircraft attacked in the evening of 7 July, their targets being enemy defences about 3 miles behind the enemy front line, to avoid any bombs dropping on the British troops. These were delivered with complete accuracy, but there were very few German losses. The northern suburbs of the city were devastated and there were civilian casualties. Then the British artillery and naval guns opened up on the enemy front-line defences.

The British moved forward early the following morning, strongly supported by artillery fire and the Allied Expeditionary Air Force. The RAF's Second Tactical Air Force strafed the enemy positions first. It was then followed by 250 medium bombers of the US Ninth Air Force while American fighter-bombers attacked further south. The British battleships and two cruisers also joined in the assault, setting enemy tanks on fire and destroying bridges from ranges of over 18 miles, while guided by spotter aircraft exposed to intense flak.

Despite this enormous firepower, the German forces fought back stubbornly and in some cases attempted counter-attacks. The two wings of the British and Canadian forces made steady progress through the rubble of the suburbs but had not entered the centre of the city by nightfall. The attack was resumed early the next morning. Rommel had ordered the withdrawal of all the German heavy weapons during the night, leaving infantry and engineers to hold the positions; if forced to retreat they were to form a new line between the rivers Odon and Orne south of the city.

The British and Canadians fought their way into the centre of the city, obstructed as much by stone blocks and other rubble choking the streets as by enemy defences. Mopping up was required and then the cost could be counted. About 20,000 French inhabitants had remained during the fighting. They had suffered severe losses and much of their beautiful city had been reduced to ruins. Total casualties in I Corps were about 3,500 killed, wounded or missing. The German casualties are not recorded but are known to have been far heavier, with much of their heavy weaponry destroyed. The way was clear for the next phase of Montgomery's strategy, with the aim of destroying the whole of the German forces in northern France.

An electric flash-bulb known as a D-2 was used successfully by the US Ninth Air Force on the night following the D-Day landings. This photograph was taken from 900ft by an A-20 Havoc in the vicinity of St-Lô. Fires were burning in the centre of the town, which was brought out in sharp detail. *US National Archives and Records Administration # 342-FH-3A-18306-60146*

Omaha Beach after the initial landings on D-Day, showing landing craft on the shore and ships lining up to form a breakwater as part of an artificial harbour. *The National Archives: AIR 37/865*

Supplies streamed ashore at Omaha Beach after D-Day. During one period of about a week, a daily average of 1,970 vehicles, 7,670 tons of supplies and 11,430 soldiers were landed. LCT 974 is unloading its cargo on the left of this photograph. *The National Archives: CAB 106/1004*

An American Rhino Ferry photographed from an LCT on one of the Normandy beaches. These huge ferries provided a shuttle service between the ships and the beaches. *The National Archives: DEFE 2/502*

A heavy American truck pulling a field kitchen up the bow ramp of an LST (Landing Ship Tank), watched by sailors of the US Navy. This large vessel could transport 18 tanks or 27 trucks with 8 Jeeps and 177 soldiers. *The National Archives: DEFE 2/502*

Below: For the first time in history, an invading army took its own harbour to a shore held by the enemy. Huge concrete caissons, each weighing 7,000 tons, were towed 100 miles across the Channel, together with floating piers and pierheads. Fifteen obsolete ships were sunk to form a preliminary harbour arm. The operation began a few hours after D-Day and thirteen days later this Mulberry harbour was completed at Arromanches in the British sector, in spite of a storm of winter strength. Another was completed in the American sector. The two harbours were protected by about 600 guns. This photograph shows lorries rolling ashore along the causeway. *The National Archives: DEFE 2/502*

American Air Force engineers laying down one of the landing strips in northern France on 14 June 1944. These were built rapidly to give tactical air support to the ground forces. *US National Archives and Records Administration # 342-FH-3A-17250-123081*

Men of an Aviation Engineer Battalion, US Ninth Air Force, pouring concrete grout onto steel mats, before covering these with pierced steel planking to form a semi-permanent runway on an airfield in France. It was estimated that a runway of 3,000ft length and 150ft width could be laid in about 90 hours by 100 unskilled men. *The National Archives: AIR 37/865*

A wounded American soldier being lifted aboard a Douglas C-47 Skytrain of the US Ninth Air Force in June 1944, for transfer from France to a hospital in England. *The National Archives: AIR 37/865*

A party of about 300 German prisoners from Normandy arriving at an English port in a tank landing craft. *British Official*

The Handley Page Halifax was the second of the RAF's heavy bombers to enter service, No. 35 Squadron being the first to receive the new machine in December 1940. The Mark II, such as the example of No. 78 Squadron shown here, entered service about a year later. This was powered by four Merlin XX engines of 1,390hp, carried up to 13,000lb of bombs, and was armed with two Browning .303in machine-guns in nose and dorsal turrets plus four more in the tail turret. Later variants served with Coastal Command while others were modified for glider towing or paratroop duties. *British Official*

The RAF provided constant fighter and balloon cover over the D-Day beaches during the invasion and while the troops moved inland. This RAF sergeant and leading aircraftman are inspecting a German Flak 30 gun of 2cm calibre installed in a pit near one of the beaches. *The National Archives: DEFE 2/502*

B-26 Marauders of the US Ninth Air Force attacking the transportation system behind the German lines after D-Day. The photograph shows bomb bursts, as well as some train cars beneath the starboard wing of the Marauder in the centre. *US National Archives and Records Administration # 342-FH-3A-18224-51981*

The Avro Lancaster was the RAF's most successful heavy bomber to serve in the Second World War. The Mark I, such as serial R5689 of No. 51 Squadron shown here, was powered by four Merlin XX engines of 1,280hp, armed with twin Browning .303in machine-guns in nose and dorsal turrets, plus four more in the tail turret, and could carry up to 14,000lb of bombs. The operational sorties began in early March 1942, and variants of this famous machine continued throughout the war. *British Official*

A Boston A-20 Havoc of the US Ninth Air Force, with black and white AEAF recognition stripes, supporting the US First Army in June 1944 by bombing the railway station at Domfront, east of Mortain. *The National Archives: AIR 34/240*

The 4th, 9th and 79th Infantry Divisions of the US 7th Army Corps, commanded by Major-General J.L. 'Lightning Joe' Collins, began a drive towards Cherbourg on 22 June 1944, but the port did not fall until 3 July. This group of Germans was captured near Cherbourg. The two soldiers on the left are an Obergefreiter (corporal) and a Kanonier (gunner) of a Luftwaffe flak unit. The wounded soldier on the right is also an Obergefreiter. *US Official*

On 15 June 1944, the US Eighth Air Force despatched 747 B-17 Flying Fortresses and 614 B-24 Liberators against targets in France, Holland and Germany, escorted by 742 fighters. Of these, 59 Liberators attacked enemy communications near Tours in France, as shown here from smoke markers over the target, bombs falling and smoke from a hit on a bridge. The attackers lost only two Fortresses and four fighters on this day. Author's Collection

British Commandos pushing inland after the beach-heads had been secured, welcomed by French civilians in the streets of a town near Caen. *The National Archives: DEFE 2/502*

Much destruction was caused on 20 June 1944 when 290 B-17 Fortresses attacked Hamburg, with fighter escorts. This was a day when the US Eighth Air Force despatched the huge total of 3,076 heavy bombers and escorts against targets in Germany, mainly synthetic oil refineries. This photograph of burning storage tanks and refineries at Hamburg was taken from 29,000ft by a Lockheed F-5. Most of the devastation shown was caused by the terrible attacks made earlier by RAF Bomber Command and the US Eighth Air Force. *The National Archives: AIR 25/792*

Another target attacked on 20 June 1944 was the Volkswagenwerke (People's Car Factory) at Fallersleben, about 16 miles north-east of Braunschweig, which had been turned over to war production and aircraft repairs. The US Eighth Air Force despatched 137 B-17 Fortresses to this factory on this day. This photograph of the resulting fires was taken from 35,000ft by a reconnaissance Spitfire flown by an American pilot. *The National Archives: AIR 25/792*

The seas were calm on 24 June 1944 when unloading on the Normandy beaches continued. The front had been established and the process of getting equipment ashore was in full swing, with little interference from the enemy. This photograph shows British Army lorries being brought ashore in an LCT. *The National Archives: DEFE 2/502*

A German pillbox being blasted by pole charges, otherwise known as Bangalore Torpedoes, when the US First Army advanced towards Cherbourg. After D-Day, this port was the main objective for the 7th Army Corps, reinforced by the 90th and 91st Divisions, together with the 2nd Armoured Division. *The National Archives: CAB 106/1004*

This dead German soldier was photographed in a
doorway in Cherbourg on 27 June 1944. He was one
of those who made a last stand against the Americans.
Captain Earl Topler, who led one of the first sections
into the port, removed his helmet as homage to a
brave enemy. He estimated that he had killed three of
his men before he fell. *US National Archives and Records
Administration: War & Conflict # 1050*

Following a request from the British First Army for help in eliminating an enemy strongpoint in the steelworks of the Société du Normandie, on the south bank of the river Orne near Caen, 70 Mitchells and Bostons were despatched on 22 June 1944 by the Second Tactical Air Force. The photograph above shows bombs falling from the first wave and the one below shows the tremendous effect of other waves. The operation was very successful and a warm message of thanks was received from the Army. *The National Archives: AIR 34/240*

Opposite page: During daylight on 30 June 1944, Bomber Command despatched 266 aircraft to bomb a road junction at Villiers Bocage, 14 miles west-south-west of Caen, through which the 2nd and 9th SS Panzer Divisions were expected to pass and attack the junction of the British and American Armies in Normandy. About 1,100 tons of bombs were dropped with great accuracy from 4,000ft, as shown in this photograph of explosions with Lancasters flying above them. Two aircraft were lost but the German attack was thwarted. *British Official*

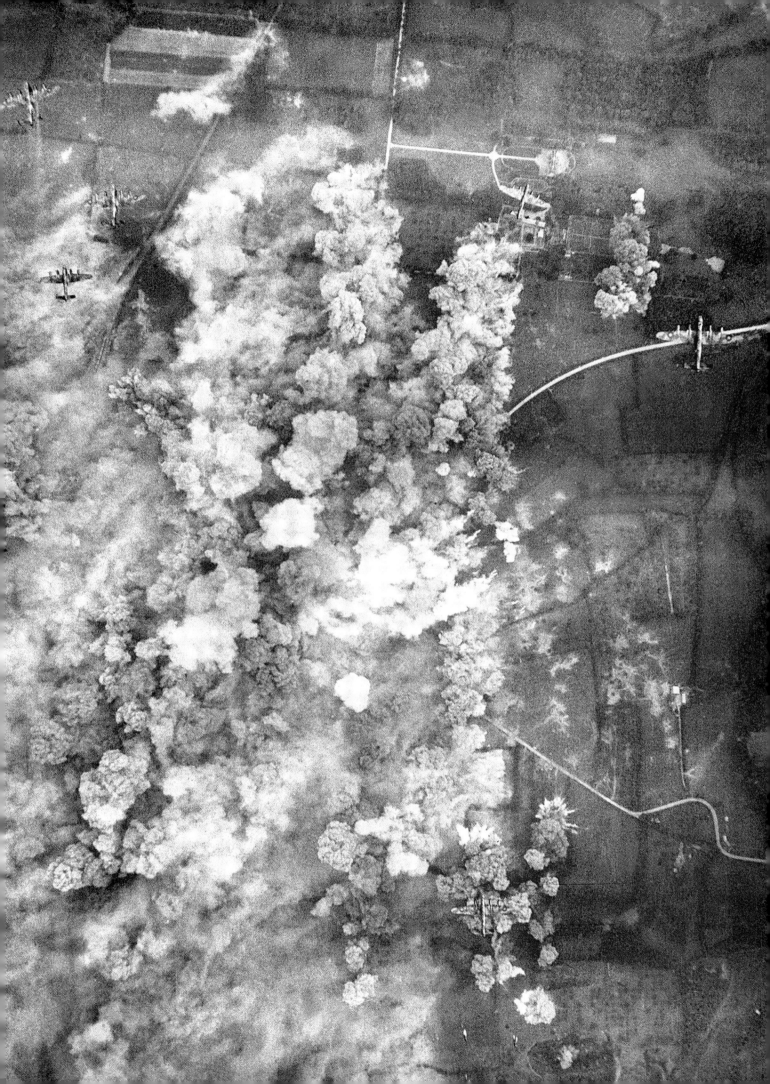

All was peaceful over Utah and Omaha Beaches at 11.00 hours on 27 June 1944 when this photograph was taken from 25,000ft. Convectional upcurrents from the land surface in warm weather had caused small alto-cumulus clouds to form, while above there were cirrus and cirro-stratus clouds. There was no convection out to sea and the sky was blue and cloudless. *The National Archives: AIR 34/839*

The railway bridge at Champtoceaux over the river Loire, 16 miles east-north-east of Nantes, was photographed at an unrecorded date by a Lockheed F-5 of the US Ninth Air Force, as a potential target. The camera shot also took in the shadow of the aircraft on the surface of the river. *The National Archives: AIR 37/1231*

A demolished Würzburg-Reise (Giant Würzburg), or Fu MG 65, at Fermanville, facing the Channel about 7 miles east-north-east of Cherbourg. This radar installation, of which about 1,500 were built, was a bowl-shaped structure about 25ft in diameter. It was designed for use with stationary flak batteries but also earned a reputation as a system for directing night-fighters. *The National Archives: AIR 20/2207*

The entrance to a Morrison shelter in a house in Shillingford Street, Islington, hit by a V-1 flying bomb on the night of 28/9 June 1944. *The National Archives: AIR 20/4376*

A London bus completely destroyed by the V-1 flying
bomb which exploded at Aldwych on 30 June 1944.
The National Archives: AIR 20/6185

Opposite page: The effect of a V-1 flying bomb on a
block of buildings. The date and place are not
recorded, but it was probably in the London area. *The
National Archives: HO 338/27*

A very unlucky cyclist knocked down by the blast of the V-1 flying bomb which exploded at Aldwych on 30 June 1944. It seems that someone has given him a cigarette. This was the normal wartime
practice, in the belief that smoking helped the wounded to recover from shock. *The National Archives: AIR 20/6185*

A V-1 flying bomb fell on Aldwych in London on
30 June 1944. This photograph was taken looking east,
with the Air Ministry's Adastral House, the BBC's Bush
House and a Post-Office on the right, and a branch of
the Westminster Bank on the left. *The National
Archives: AIR 20/6185*

The effect of a lunar landscape was created at Marquise-Mimoyecques, a hamlet in Landrethun-le-Nord, when Bomber Command despatched 551 aircraft in daylight on 6 July 1944 to attack V-1 flying bomb sites, mainly in the Pas de Calais. The largest craters were caused by 12,000lb bombs dropped by No. 617 Squadron. In fact, this site did not contain V-1 weapons but two long-range guns known as the V-3 'Tausendfüssler' (Millipede). These had been ordered by Hitler in 1943 and were smooth-bore guns of over 400ft in length. The 15cm shell was breech-loaded with a normal propelling charge, but there were side chambers along the barrel containing charges for additional acceleration, giving a final velocity of about 5,000ft per second. The intention was to fire shells 95 miles to London, but it was probably impractical and the project was abandoned after this attack. *The National Archives: AIR 25/792*

A-20 Havocs of the US Ninth Air Force on a cloudless but hazy day in July 1944, bombing V-1 flying-bomb sites in the Pas de Calais. US National Archives and Records Administration # 342-FH-3A-19069-52868

CHAPTER FOUR

BEFORE THE BREAKOUT

By July 1944, the more experienced soldiers and airmen of the Wehrmacht must have looked back with nostalgia to the heady days of four years before, when their Blitzkrieg swept irresistibly through the Low Countries and France, sending Belgian and Anglo-French forces reeling back in confusion and dismay. The modern war of mobility was indeed a German concept, with Junkers Ju87 Stukas acting as long-range artillery for fast-moving columns of tanks and mechanised vehicles which were far superior to those of their adversaries. These dive-bombers struck fear and fury into the hearts of soldiers and civilians alike, with their terrifying 'screamers' switched on to herald the explosions of bombs delivered with pinpoint accuracy. The German artillerymen and infantry accompanying the Panzers were well trained and confident, sure of a quick victory, while the French, British and Belgians were still fighting a war based on a false belief in the impregnability of fixed defences such as the Maginot Line on France's border with Germany.

But in the summer of 1944 the exponents of mobile warfare would receive a lesson which demonstrated that their prowess had been greatly surpassed by that of their enemies. The Allied air forces were supreme in the skies, not only in numbers but in quality of aircraft and weaponry. The outdated Stukas were nowhere to be seen, having been abandoned long since after becoming easy and welcome targets for Allied fighters. Huge numbers of Allied fighter-bombers (called 'Jabos' by the Germans) were equipped with bombs or rockets, wreaking havoc among German armoured columns. Three weeks after D-Day, thirty-one such squadrons of the Allied Expeditionary Air Force were operating from forward airstrips in France, and this number was growing steadily.

However, it is an ironic fact that German production of new aircraft was increasing steadily in 1944 under the guidance of Albert Speer, the Minister for Armaments and War Production. He had introduced new methods of mass production, with the aid of slave labour. But the Luftwaffe suffered from severe disadvantages. It had to fight on three fronts, Russian, Italian and in the West. It had lost many of its best pilots and other aircrew, and there were not enough competent instructors to train newcomers. It was also extremely short of aviation fuel. Without supplies of natural oil, apart from the wells of Romania which were by then under immediate threat from the advancing Soviet forces, the

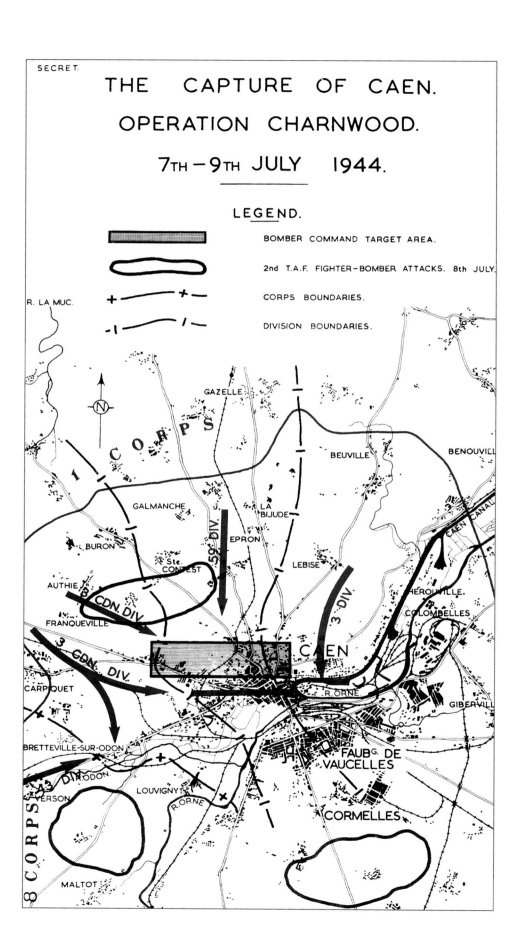

The capture of Caen; operation Charnwood
7–9 July 1944. *The National Archives: AIR 41/67*

Germans were largely dependent on synthetic fuel produced from coal deposits. Shortage of oil was the Achilles heel of their huge war machine.

Fortunately for the Allies, the biggest hydrogenation plants producing this synthetic fuel were few in number, as were the crude-oil refineries. From April 1944, they had received close attention from Allied strategic bombers, especially from the US Eighth Air Force in England and the US Fifteenth Air Force in Italy. Damage to the plants could be repaired, but the bombers frequently returned to the same targets. A shortage of diesel oil was almost equally acute in the German armies, which remained heavily dependent on horse-drawn vehicles, unlike the Allied mechanised divisions.

The main question for the Western Allies was how to exploit their technical superiority and break out of the large bridgehead already created. The bocage country continued to favour defence and made the going extremely difficult for the attackers. They needed to find a way through this to the more open country beyond, from where they could encircle and eliminate the German armies. The American First Army under General Omar Bradley was fighting hard to reach the objective of St-Lô, a town about 20 miles south of the western edge of the Omaha beaches, but it was meeting stiff resistance and could not find a 'soft spot' in the enemy's lines. On its right flank, the American VIII Corps was attempting to reach the town of Coutances but finding similar difficulties.

After more than a month since the D-Day landings, there seemed to be something akin to a stalemate along the whole of the Allied front, resulting in queries among the national newspapers of Britain and the USA. The public euphoria at the success of the initial landings had been replaced by doubts about the subsequent conduct of the land campaign. This disquiet also extended to the Allied High Command, for both Air Chief Marshal Sir Arthur Tedder and Air Chief Marshal Sir Trafford Leigh-Mallory had never approved of the extension of the D-Day landings to a broad 50-mile front. They had contended that the front should have been narrower, with the objective of ensuring the immediate capture of Caen. The delay in entering this strategic city seemed to vindicate their opinion. Of course, their views were known to General Eisenhower and some doubts must have entered his mind about the generalship of Field-Marshal Sir Bernard Montgomery.

If Montgomery was fully aware of this dissent, it had no effect on him. On 10 July, he conferred with his senior British, Canadian and American commanders and expressed broad objectives which remained unchanged. He intended to order the British and Canadian Second Army to advance from Caen in a southerly direction towards Falaise, about 20 miles away. This would exert strong pressure on the German Army Group B and Panzer Group West. The American First Army would also continue to push southwards and attempt to reach the port of Avranches on the Channel coast, from where one corps and one armoured division could sweep into the Brittany peninsula and capture the Atlantic ports. The remainder of the First Army should be prepared to fight towards the south and then sweep east of the bocage country, encircling the German forces.

The initial effort by the British and Canadians was codenamed operation 'Goodwood'. This was intended to do as much damage as possible to the enemy troops and armour, relieving pressure on the American front. Here the push by the American First Army, once it had reached St-Lô, was codenamed operation 'Cobra'. Both these operations were to become epics in the story of the breakout of the Allied forces.

Although the British and Canadian Second Army was at maximum strength, with five corps available, its opponents had also been reinforced. Apart from the

Allied commanders discussing plans in a small orchard in Normandy before operation 'Goodwood', the attack by British forces on the high ground south of Caen which began on 18 July 1944. Left to right: Lieutenant-General Omar Bradley, commanding the US First Army Group; General Sir Bernard Montgomery, commanding the British and Canadian 21st Army Group; Lieutenant-General Sir Miles Dempsey, commanding the British Second Army; Air Marshal Sir Trafford Leigh-Mallory, commanding the Allied Expeditionary Air Force. *British Official*

German infantry divisions, it was faced with six German armoured divisions and three heavy-tank battalions, arranged in depth behind minefields covered by numerous anti-tank guns and mortars. Thus operation Goodwood was to be made against the enemy where he was strongest, not where he was weakest. Moreover, the Germans were well aware of the Allied preparations, for these were being made within view of their vantage points. The Germans assumed that there would be a push towards Paris and were ready to repel it. Of course, they did not have the advantage of air power, which the Allies possessed in abundance.

On 17 July, the day before the British and Canadians launched their assault, Feldmarschall Erwin Rommel was seriously wounded when travelling in a car strafed by Spitfires of the RAF's Second Tactical Air Force near the hamlet of St-Foy-de-Montgommery. The car overturned and Rommel's skull was fractured when he was flung out. His command of Army Group B was taken over by Feldmarschall von Kluge, who had already replaced von Rundstedt and thus assumed a dual function.

The thrust to the south under operation Goodwood was made to the east of Caen by three corps of the British and Canadian Second Army. It began at dawn on 18 July with an immense attack by 942 aircraft of the RAF's Bomber Command, mainly against two enemy positions through which the Canadian II Corps and the British I Corps had been ordered to advance. The bombing was extremely accurate and there were heavy casualties with loss of equipment among the defenders, particularly on an eastern position which was defended by units of the 346th Infantry Division, the 16th Luftwaffe Field Division, the 21st Panzer Division and part of the 711th Infantry Division. There was also a third position which Bomber Command attacked, in the centre behind the front line through which the British VIII Corps was to advance, but this was less effective.

This was followed by a bombardment from two British cruisers and a monitor, coupled with a great barrage of artillery fire all along the front. In the course of this, 658 B-24 Liberators of the US Eighth Air Force arrived with an escort of fighters to bomb three other positions, one in the enemy front line on the far left of the attackers and two in the centre behind the front line. Medium bombers of the US Ninth Air Force also arrived to bomb enemy front-line positions in the centre. There was so much smoke and dust from exploding shells that the crews of many of these medium bombers could not see their targets and had to return with their bomb loads. Then fighter-bombers of the RAF's Second Tactical Air Force swept in at low level, attacking enemy gun positions and fortifications which had been detected from air reconnaissance. These squadrons provided a continuous 'cab rank' presence, being available on call via the Air Support Signal Units of each army corps, brigade or division. Meanwhile, protection from any interference from the Luftwaffe was maintained by squadrons of fighters from the RAF's Air Defence of Great Britain.

Under a renewed and sustained artillery bombardment, the advance began with II Canadian Corps on the right, VIII British Corps in the centre and I British Corps on the left. All went well with VIII Corps at first, with the troops fighting their way through shattered enemy front lines. Most initial objectives were

The breakout operations, 25 July–4 August 1944. *The National Archives: AIR 41/67*

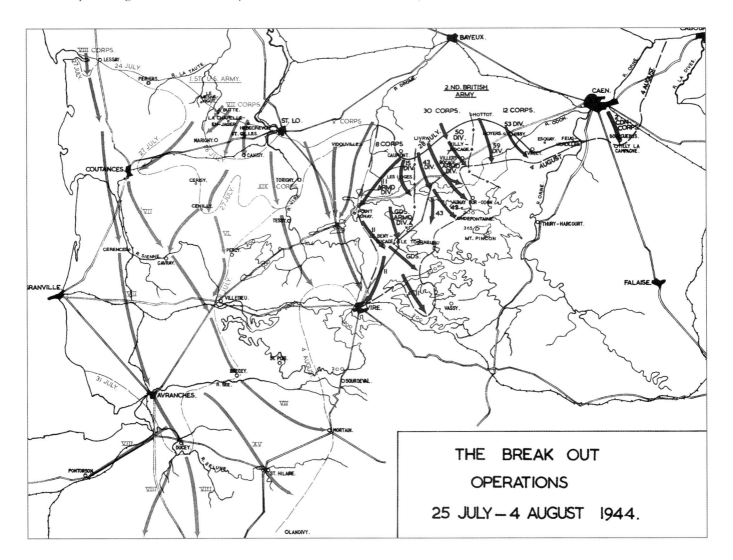

THE BREAK OUT
OPERATIONS
25 JULY – 4 AUGUST 1944.

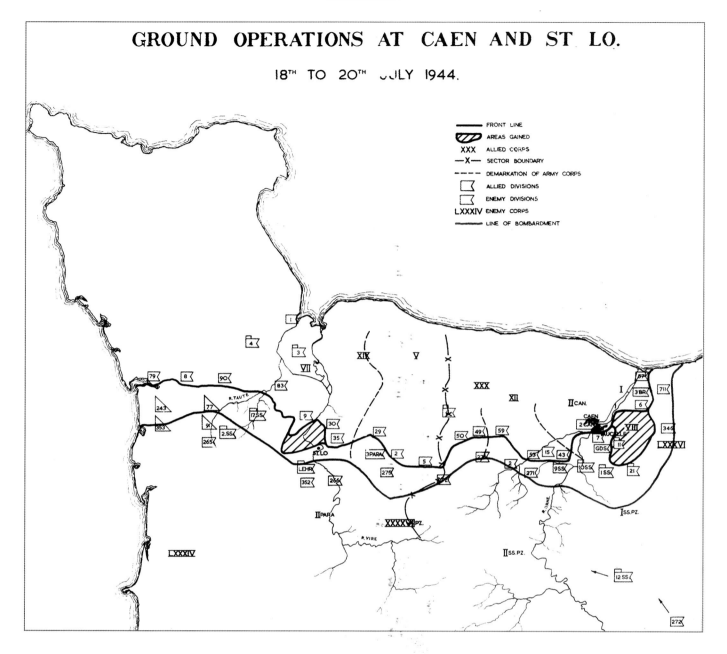

Ground operations at Caen and St-Lô, 18–20 July 1944.

The National Archives: AIR 41/67

gained by mid-morning but then there were delays in bringing up supplies and reinforcements through congested roads. Enemy resistance began to stiffen, and both the 1st and 21st Panzer Divisions launched a counter-attack against the British 11th Armoured Division.

The 21st Panzer Division had lost many tanks in the attack by Bomber Command on the left flank but enough were left to begin this counter-attack. The 1st Panzer Division had been further to the rear and suffered less severely. Together, they could muster forty-six tanks and a number of assault guns. Most of the tanks were Mark I Tigers and Mark II King Tigers, more heavily armoured and with a more powerful gun than the American Sherman tank with which the British were equipped. Although the Shermans were mechanically more efficient, they suffered badly in this battle, many being knocked out by Tiger tanks and Jagdpanther self-propelled anti-tank guns. The battlefield became littered with burning Shermans. Meanwhile, rocket-firing Typhoons did their best to destroy the German armour.

On the far left flank, the British I Corps had mixed fortunes. Some of their initial objectives had been heavily hit by Bomber Command and the defenders were too dazed to offer much resistance. The British took many prisoners, particularly from the 16th Luftwaffe Field Division and the 346th Field Division. Others had escaped more lightly and were able to hold out until nightfall, reinforced by the 711th Infantry Division, which arrived on bicycles.

On the right flank, II Canadian Corps attacked with its usual determination. Bomber Command had caused much destruction on the eastern side of their sector and the Canadians were able to surround and overcome the defenders, although these fought tenaciously. The enemy counter-attacked in the early evening, but this was beaten off. Canadian engineers began building Bailey bridges over the river Orne, on their right flank, to facilitate the arrival of supplies from the city of Caen.

Operation Goodwood had not been a complete success. The advance in the centre by VIII Corps had not reached its objectives of Vimont or Tilly-la-Campagne, to the south-east of Caen. On the other hand the bridgehead had been extended to the east and for about 6 miles to the south, while the suburbs of Caen were now clear of the enemy. The day had cost the British and Canadians about 1,500 killed, wounded or captured, plus about 200 tanks. Moreover, the Wehrmacht had not escaped lightly. Its casualties are not recorded but the two Panzer divisions had lost 109 tanks, mainly from air attacks. The 21st Panzer Division suffered so many casualties that it was reduced to no more than a single battalion. The 16th Luftwaffe Field Regiment had been almost wiped out. The commander of the Seventh Army, General Eberbach, admitted that the territory lost would provide the British with a jumping-off ground for a breakout. He ordered reinforcements to be sent to I Panzer Korps. Von Kluge ordered Panzer Group West to launch counter-attacks to push back the enemy. He also requested permission for the 116th Panzer Division to be brought over from the Fifteenth Army to reinforce the position. The Germans still believed that an Allied invasion would be carried out in the area it was helping to guard, the Pas de Calais, but its movement westward was authorised.

The British and Canadians devoted most of the next two days to mopping-up and consolidation. Inclement weather over the battlefields prevented all but limited operations by the Allied Expeditionary Air Force, while heavy rain reduced tracks and fields to mud and restricted movement on the ground. But in the interim, the American First Army gained an important objective. Its advance troops reached the outskirts of St-Lô on 18 July and occupied the centre on the following day. The town had been shattered by bombardment from the air and artillery fire, but it would provide a jumping-off point for the American breakout from the west of the Allied bridgehead.

On 20 July, an event occurred which came close to ending the war in Europe. This was the attempt to assassinate Hitler together with two of his leading Nazis, Hermann Goering and Heinrich Himmler. Not everyone in Germany was besotted with the philosophy of National Socialism and its brutal consequences. The leading dissenters were senior officers in the Wehrmacht, who by 1944 were led by Colonel Claus von Stauffenberg, a war hero who fought in the Polish, French and North African campaigns and been severely wounded. Dissent had been stifled during Germany's initial successes in the war but the military defeats at Stalingrad and North Africa had convinced the conspirators that Hitler was leading his country to disaster.

As many as six plans had been made since 1943 to eliminate Hitler and other Nazis, but they had not come to fruition for various reasons. It was intended that on their death the codeword 'Valkyrie' would be relayed. The Army would act immediately to form a new government with the former Chief of the General Staff, General Ludwig Beck, as its head. This plan was backed by other senior officers, although not all participated in its implementation. Some of them would occupy the top positions in the new government, which would depose all leading Nazis and try to negotiate peace with the Western Powers.

The attempt was made in one of Hitler's 'Wolf's Lairs', a headquarters at Rastenburg in East Prussia, where a discussion took place concerning the Eastern Front. In his position as Chief of Staff for the General Army Office in Berlin responsible for recruitment and training, von Stauffenberg was present. He carried a briefcase containing a time bomb and passed through the security without difficulty. To his disappointment, Goering and Himmler were not there. Leaving the briefcase close to Hitler under an oak map table, he left the room to answer a supposed telephone call.

The bomb duly exploded, killing four of those present. Von Stauffenberg witnessed the explosion and managed to escape temporarily, believing Hitler to be dead. But the Führer had been shielded by the table while the blast had blown out the wooden structure of the building. Had this been concrete, the devastation might have been complete. Hitler staggered out with his trousers shredded, injured, shocked and deafened, but still alive and vowing revenge. The conspirators were rounded up by the Gestapo and subjected to appalling tortures before being executed. A wave of terror was unleashed on the German people, with the arrest of thousands of soldiers and civilians suspected of opposing the dictatorship. All internal resistance in Germany was stifled by vicious brutality and the war continued.

With the capture of St-Lô and the pressure being maintained on the British and Canadian front, the American First Army could launch operation Cobra. It was intended to begin on 21 July but the pouring rain inhibited the air support on which the ground assault depended.

The First Canadian Army came into being on 23 July with the arrival in France of its headquarters under Lieutenant-General Henry D.G. Crerar. It was destined to occupy the left flank of the British Second Army but this was not immediately possible. Instead, Crerar commanded the British I Corps in this sector while for the time being II Canadian Corps remained under the Second Army. As a deception during the beginning of the American operation Cobra, II Canadian Corps began a limited advance towards Falaise on 23 July, during weather which had begun to improve. This advance confirmed General Eberbach's belief that the main Allied thrust would take place from the east of their lines, and he had used the period of bad weather to bring up reinforcements to this sector.

On the following day, nearly 1,600 Fortresses and Liberators of the US Eighth Air Force were despatched to soften up enemy defences on the American front but were recalled since the weather was unsuitable for accurate bombing. Some did not hear the recall until too late and mistook their targets in the ground haze. Bombs were dropped among American troops, resulting in twenty dead and sixty wounded.

After these losses from 'friendly fire', which was only one of many during the Second World War, operation Cobra began on 25 July. In the area of St-Lô, the American VII Corps under the command of Lieutenant-General J. Lawton Collins, supported by XIX and V Corps, was to advance southwards through defences devastated by air bombardment. On their far right flank, VIII Corps was to advance from its positions on the west of the Cotentin peninsula to capture the port of Avranches. The left flank of the sector was protected by the British VII and XXX Corps.

The weather was now fine and the first attack was made by a stream of eight fighter-bomber groups of the US Ninth Air Force on a narrow strip of the enemy defences ahead of VII Corps. Most dropped 250lb and 500lb bombs, but one group carried deadly napalm fire-bombs. They were followed immediately by about 1,600 heavy bombers of the US Eighth Air Force, escorted by over 500 fighters, which dropped over 3,400 tons of bombs in a concentrated area. Then came seven more groups of the Ninth's fighter-bombers, adding to the murderous devastation. Finally, eleven groups of the Ninth's medium bombers struck at strongpoints and other targets behind the enemy front line. Overall, about 3,000 American aircraft participated in these attacks. Unfortunately in some of them, more bombs had fallen into the American lines, killing 102 and wounding 380.

In spite of this additional disaster, the American infantry of VII Corps began their advance in mid-morning, followed by their armour, while other fighters of the US Ninth Air Force attacked targets under the direction of the 'air support parties' which accompanied the troops. The Americans advanced into a great pall of smoke rising to over 2,000ft above the German lines. These were held by Panzer Lehr Division commanded by General Fritz Bayerlein, and had been shattered by the air bombardment. The attackers did not know the extent of this at the time, but General Bayerlein later described his front line as like a lunar

Winston Churchill paid a surprise visit to Caen on 22 July 1944, after it had fallen into Allied hands. He drove to the ruined city in an open car, crossing two bridges built over the river Orne by the Royal Engineers. Here he is talking to General Sir Bernard Montgomery (right) and the commander of the British Second Army, Lieutenant-General Sir Miles Dempsey. *British Official*

landscape from the bomb craters, with 70 per cent of his troops out of action and only isolated pockets holding out.

On the following day, General Collins ordered his armoured forces to penetrate further, with the close support of the Ninth Air Force. Advances were made and the ground gained was firmly held. At the same time, XIX Corps made good progress on the left flank, while VIII Corps on the far right flank drove the Germans down the coast towards Avranches. By 28 July the German troops of LXXXIV Infantry Corps in this coastal sector began to disintegrate and the Americans took over 4,500 prisoners. Most of the Panzer divisions which might have supported them had been moved to the British and Canadian sector, while much of the German Fifteenth Army was still waiting fruitlessly in the Pas de Calais to repel an invasion force which never arrived. Remnants of LXXXIV Corps were trapped near the town of Coutances and their columns subjected to intense attacks from the US Ninth Air Force. Avranches was captured on 30 July and a major breakthrough on the west of the Allied line was achieved. The remaining German forces in this sector had lost most of their heavy equipment and had broken up into small and disorganised groups of stragglers, with badly shaken morale and little hope of reinforcement. Without rations, they were attempting to forage for food and live off the land, becoming prey to the French Resistance.

Seizing the opportunity to exploit the enemy's weakness, Montgomery shifted some of the British Second Army's formations westwards to the centre of the Allied lines, relieving some of the positions held by the Americans on their right flank. The British moved via roundabout routes, to avoid detection, until five infantry and three armoured divisions, together with four armoured brigades and three groups of artillery, formed a line west of the river Orne. They were faced by the German LXXXIV Infantry Corps, which was backed by armour only about a third of its strength. However, the country through which they had to advance was a form of bocage particularly difficult for tanks, with narrow lanes sunk between high hedgerows and hills covered with trees. It was scenically delightful but ideal for defence.

A British assault towards the south began in the early morning of 30 July, supported by two major air attacks. The RAF's Bomber Command despatched 692 aircraft in daylight to bomb six enemy positions near Villers-Bocage, facing the British XXX Corps on the left flank. Heavy low cloud hampered the operation and only 377 aircraft bombed their targets, using 'Oboe' radar methods. Two of these enemy positions were hit, very effectively. The other attack was carried out by medium bombers of the US Ninth Air Force, against three areas south of the British VIII Corps near Caumont on the right flank. This experienced similar difficulties with the weather conditions.

These air attacks were made about an hour after the ground forces began to advance, leaving some armoured divisions in reserve. Fighter-bombers of both the RAF's Second Tactical Air Force and the US Ninth Air Force stood by awaiting orders to support the attack, but it was almost midday before the skies were clear enough for their low-level work. The troops were met by heavy fire when they began their advance and also encountered thickly sown minefields, for the Germans had had plenty of time on this front to prepare their defences.

South of Caumont, VIII Corps made good progress in the direction of the town of Vire. Flail tanks managed to clear paths through the minefields sown in rough ground, spraying hedgerows and orchards with machine-guns as they drove forward. Some of the Churchill tanks in the advance were knocked out but most of the German infantry fell back, leaving only a few defenders and snipers to be mopped up. By the end of the day, the British had advanced about 6 miles. On hearing of this, von Kluge ordered the 21st Panzer Division, which by then was in reserve, to move towards the line south of Caumont.

On their right, XXX Corps had less success. It was to advance southwards in the direction of Villers-Bocage and then towards a massive ridge of hills in which Mont Pinçon was situated. This ridge could have been used by the enemy for defensive purposes if forced to withdraw. The line was held by the German 276th and 326th Infantry Divisions, which put up a stiff fight behind fields which were full of anti-personnel and anti-tank mines. Only limited gains were made before nightfall.

The British resumed their attack on the following morning. On this occasion, the thrust of VIII Corps was synchronised with the American V Corps on their right flank and further advances were made. The 21st Panzer Division assembled enough armour to attempt a counter-attack during the morning, but was met with artillery fire and devastating rockets from five squadrons of Typhoons of the RAF's Second Tactical Air Force. About thirty German tanks were destroyed, according to their records. Others tried again on the next day, 1 August, but these were repelled. By this time, the British VIII Corps had punched a salient to within 2 miles of the town of Vire, creating a worrying situation for von Kluge.

On the left flank, the British XXX Corps made less progress. Royal Engineers worked during the night of 30/1 July to clear the minefields but the advance

Two bridges built by American engineers over the river Sienne at Gavray, 19 miles south-west of St-Lô in the region of Cotentin, to facilitate the movement of the US First Army. The photograph was taken from the air on 29 July 1944. *The National Archives: AIR 37/865*

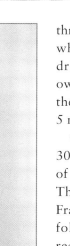

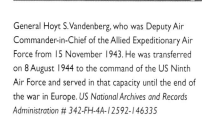

General Hoyt S. Vandenberg, who was Deputy Air Commander-in-Chief of the Allied Expeditionary Air Force from 15 November 1943. He was transferred on 8 August 1944 to the command of the US Ninth Air Force and served in that capacity until the end of the war in Europe. *US National Archives and Records Administration # 342-FH-4A-12592-146335*

through the cleared area was met with a counter-attack which developed into close quarters before it was driven off. Movement remained extremely difficult owing to the absence of roads leading south through the bocage. By 1 August the troops were still about 5 miles from their objective of Mont Pinçon.

On the day the British first launched their attack, 30 July, Hitler was handed a draft order by the Chief of Operational Staff of the OKW, General Alfred Jodl. This recommended a withdrawal from the front in France, to be considered at a conference to be held the following day. By this time, Hitler had partially recovered from his injuries sustained in the assassination attempt eleven days before and was able to deliver pronouncements. He still complained of dizziness and an inability to withstand noise, as well as trembling in his left leg. It is clear from a transcript of his speech that his mind was dominated by an acute fear of treachery among his high commanders. He blamed these generals for military disasters on all fronts and contended that Germany's problem was primarily one of low morale which they had created. So far as the west was concerned, an Allied breakthrough in France must be avoided at all costs, since vital U-boat bases would be lost and moreover the Allies would use the ports to bring in their own supplies. They must be turned into 'fortresses' which could hold out indefinitely. Strategy could not be left to von Kluge, who must be made to understand that no withdrawal would be tolerated. Despite these orders, it is known that Hitler did have contingency plans for a partial withdrawal from the front lines in France.

On 1 August the American land forces in France were formed into two Armies, under the 12th US Army Group (TUSAG) commanded by General Omar N. Bradley. Command of the First US Army (FUSA) was taken over by Lieutenant-General Courtney H. Hodges while the new Third US Army (TUSA) was commanded by Lieutenant-General George S. Patton. The latter had arrived in Normandy some weeks before but had remained incognito to preserve the fiction that he still commanded FUSAG in the south-east of England, the dummy formation that had been created to fool the Abwehr. Patton was the ideal commander of the mobile warfare to be launched, both by temperament and his experience as an Army commander in North Africa and Sicily. Most of his troops admired him, perhaps grudgingly, if only because he exemplified the assurance and drive which characterised their nation. But they knew there would be heavy casualties under his forceful leadership and nicknamed him 'Blood and Guts'.

These rearrangements in the American Army were also accompanied by others in the US Ninth Air Force. Command was taken over by Major-General Hoyt S. Vandenberg, replacing Lieutenant-General Lewis H. Brereton who was withdrawn somewhat unwillingly to command the new First Allied Airborne Army being formed in England for forthcoming major operations. The Ninth was then formed into two commands. The IX Tactical Air Command under Major-General Elwood R. Quesada supported the First US Army, while the XIX Tactical Air Command under Brigadier-General Otto P. Weyland supported the new Third US Army. This close collaboration was necessary for the war of movement envisaged by SHAEF for the American forces.

The British Second Army continued its attacks from the centre of the Allied bridgehead on 2 August. Once again, VIII Corps was able to advance and overcome the resistance of enemy infantry. The 9th SS Panzer Division which had arrived to try to restore the situation was repelled with heavy losses. Meanwhile, XXX Corps managed to advance about 3 miles, but was engaged in heavy fighting with the 21st Panzer Division and the newly arrived 10th SS Panzer Division.

On the American front, VIII Corps (by then part of the Third US Army) had succeeded in penetrating beyond Avranches in the coastal zone of the Cotentin peninsula. It was originally intended that the whole of Patton's Third Army would sweep west and capture the Brittany ports of St-Malo, Brest, Lorient and St-Nazaire, but the pressure on the enemy being exerted from the widening bridgehead produced a more favourable situation. Generals Montgomery, Bradley and Dempsey decided that Patton need use only 'minimum forces' for this purpose. On 3 August he was ordered to advance with the majority of his Third Army south towards the north bank of the Loire

Major-General Lewis H. Brereton, who commanded the US Middle East Air Force from 28 June 1942, then the US Ninth Air Force in the Mediterranean from 12 November 1942, then the latter when it was reactivated in England on 16 October 1943. On 7 August 1944, he was transferred to command the newly formed First Allied Airborne Army. *US National Archives and Records Administration # 342-FH-4A-6863-148795*

and then he prepared to swing east through the open and undefended country south of the bocage, towards Le Mans. Patton sent his VIII Corps into Brittany while his XV Corps began to advance south-east towards Le Mans and his XX Corps south towards the Loire. At the same time, Hodges was ordered to advance with his First Army south-east towards the town of Mortain. All the American formations began to make gains against crumbling resistance.

These advances in the American sector alarmed Hitler. On 3 August, von Kluge received firm orders from him. The front between the Orne and the Vire (the sectors held by the British and Canadians) was to be defended almost entirely by infantry divisions. Armoured divisions on this front were to be moved to the west and used to cut through the American lines and recapture Avranches on the west coast of the Cotentin peninsula. Thus the American formations would be cut off and annihilated, or so Hitler believed. His order was to lead to one of the major defeats suffered by the Wehrmacht in the west.

Von Kluge acted immediately to obey Hitler's instructions. The German Seventh Army was ordered to provide the 2nd SS Panzer Division as well as the 17th SS Panzer Grenadier Division, while Panzer Group West would contribute the 1st SS Panzer Division. These would join the 116th Panzer Division already facing the American front. The attack would be made in the general direction of Mortain and come under the command of General H. von Funck. Panzer Group West was renamed the 'Fifth Panzer Army' two days later.

The armoured attack against the American front began in the early hours of 7 August, after the arrival of the divisions from the east. Small advances were made during the hours of darkness, although bazookas and artillery fire from the Americans knocked out some Panzers and forced others to take cover. The Allied Expeditionary Air Force was grounded in the morning, owing to low cloud and mist, but the fighter-bombers were able to take off shortly before midday.

C-47 Skytrains of the Troop Carrier Command, US Ninth Air Force, dropping supplies by parachute on the edge of an airfield in the Cherbourg peninsula in mid-June 1944. *US National Archives and Records Administration # 342-FH-3A-18056-52035*

The Douglas C-47 Skytrain, such as this example photographed on 22 February 1944, was the most famous Allied transport aircraft of the Second World War. Known as the Dakota in the RAF, it was powered by two Pratt & Whitney Twin Wasp R-1830-92 engines of 1,200hp and carried a crew of three. It could accommodate over 8,000lb of freight and up to twenty-eight troops. *US National Archives and Records Administration # 18-WP-23-137013*

Rocket-firing Typhoons of the RAF's Second Tactical Air Force swept at low level over the battlefield while Thunderbolts and Mustangs of the US Ninth Air Force attacked enemy transport behind the front line and hunted for any Luftwaffe fighters. The result was devastating. The Typhoons flew nearly 300 sorties during the afternoon against about 260 tanks or other armoured vehicles and destroyed approximately half of them. German soldiers could be seen scampering away. Anti-aircraft fire was only desultory, the main problem for the pilots in this massacre being the dust and smoke which rose from the battlefield. The Panzer assault ground to a halt and its small initial gains were lost to American counter-attacks and more attacks from the air during the next day. A path leading to the encirclement of the German Army in Normandy had been opened.

The city of Rouen, an important inland harbour on the river Seine, was heavily bombed by the Germans before its capture on 9 July 1940 and was also attacked by the US Eighth Air Force before the D-Day invasion. The road bridge on the left was destroyed while the road bridge on the right was damaged. The old Opera House below the bridge on the right was a victim of the bombing. Ruins surrounded the cathedral. The Tour de Beurre (far right), built from the proceeds of butter, appeared to be undamaged, but the Tour St Romain (near right) had lost its Viollet-le-Ducal roof. The air photograph was taken on 25 September 1944, when the citizens were trying to resume normal conditions. *The National Archives: AIR 34/845*

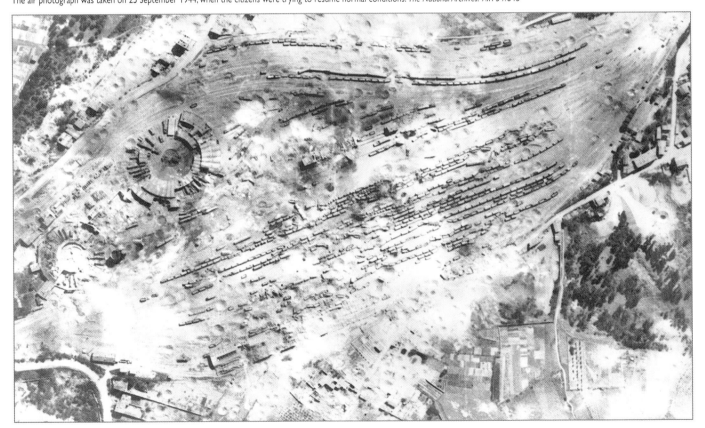

On the night of 26/7 July 1944, Bomber Command despatched 178 Lancasters and 9 Mosquitos to the railway yards at Givors, 16 miles from Lyon, causing immense damage for the loss of five aircraft. The attack was repeated on the night of 11/12 August 1944, when 179 Lancasters and 10 Mosquitos were despatched, without loss. One roundhouse in the yards was obliterated and the other badly damaged, while all the tracks were cut and many wagons wrecked. These attacks were in support of the advancing Allied armies. *The National Archives: AIR 37/1231*

An American 105mm howitzer shelling German troops near Carentan on the river Douve on 11 July 1944. The weapon had a range of over 6 miles. *US National Archives and Records Administration: War & Conflict # 1047*

The industrial city of Caen paid a terrible price for freedom from German rule, after being bitterly defended by the Wehrmacht. Concentrated bombing by the Allied Air Forces destroyed 60 per cent of the houses and damaged 36 per cent of the remainder. Countless art treasures were lost for ever. British forces finally entered the city on 9 July 1944, to find the streets choked with rubble. *The National Archives: AIR 37/1231*

La Poissonière railway bridge over the river Loire, 16 miles west-south-west of Angers, was partly destroyed by B-26 Marauders of the US Ninth Air Force during an attack on German communications on 18 July 1944. The inset shows the direct hit which caused the damage. *The National Archives: AIR 37/1231*

A Frenchman waving encouragement on 20 July 1944
to the pilot of an Allied reconnaissance aircraft as he
flew over a country road in enemy-occupied territory.
Aircrews frequently reported such incidents, although
bitter fighting was still devastating parts of the country.
The National Archives: AIR 34/241

The large storage building for V-1 flying bombs in
Eperleques forest near Watten, 6 miles north-north-
west of St-Omer, was bombed repeatedly by RAF
Bomber Command and the US Eighth Air Force from
the night of 18/19 June 1944 to 4 August 1944.
No. 617 Squadron dropped 'Tallboy' bombs during a
daylight raid on 19 June, with the nearest exploding
50yd from the concrete structure. The site was
overrun by Canadian troops in November 1944. *The
National Archives: AIR 37/1231*

American infantrymen on 3 August 1944 in a deserted house in Tessy-sur-Vire, about 9 miles south of St-Lô. They complained that all the kegs were empty in the beer cellar which was their 'foxhole' for the night. *US National Archives and Records Administration: War & Conflict # 1048*

A Lancaster flying over the oil storage depot of Bec d'Ambes near Bordeaux in France, in daylight on 4 August 1944. Bomber Command despatched 288 Lancasters to this target and the nearby depot at Pauillac, scoring direct hits without losing any aircraft. *British Official*

The exact location of this photograph is not recorded, but it was taken in early August 1944 when the First Canadian Army was advancing from Caen towards Falaise. The soldiers are taking cover in a ditch while bombing takes place ahead of them, probably by fighter-bombers of the Second Tactical Air Force. *British Official*

The marshalling yards at Hazebrouk in France, about 12 miles east of St Omer, were attacked in daylight on 6 August 1944 by sixty-two aircraft of Bomber Command. Serious damage was caused for the loss of one aircraft. This was part of the campaign to prevent supplies reaching the V-1 flying-bomb sites. *British Official*

The Hawker Typhoon, fitted with a Napier Sabre IIA engine of 2,180hp and armed with four 20mm cannons in the wings, suffered numerous engine failures and accidents when it first entered service with the RAF's Fighter Command in September 1941. Once the teething troubles were overcome, however, it earned fame as one of the most formidable fighters in the RAF. With a top speed of 412mph, it was a match for the Focke-Wulf Fw190. As a fighter-bomber, carrying eight rocket projectiles or two 1,000lb bombs under the wings, it became a deadly ground attack against the Wehrmacht when the squadrons formed part of the Second Tactical Air Force. The undersurfaces of the wings in this example were painted with black and white stripes to distinguish it from enemy aircraft. *British Official*

Three rocket projectile warheads from an attacking aircraft penetrated the wall of this enemy building and caused considerable destruction but did not damage a dugout below. *The National Archives: AIR 20/2207*

On 2 August 1944 the Second Tactical Air Force despatched forty-eight Mitchells and thirty Bostons to attack an enemy ammunition dump at Montreuil-Belfroi, east of Nantes. These dropped about 100 tons of high-explosive bombs, much of which fell exactly on the target. *The National Archives: AIR 34/241*

In the early morning of 6 August 1944, the British 129th Brigade, together with the 13/18th Hussars and the 4th and 5th Wiltshires, began an attack on Mont Pinçon, 1,200ft, south-west of Caen. The gunners in this photograph are giving supporting fire during the advance. *British Official*

CHAPTER FIVE

ALLIED BLITZKRIEG

The crushing defeat of the German counter-attack in the Mortain area did not have an immediate parallel in the British sector. The going was even tougher for those troops in the centre of the Allied lines who were attempting to break through the woods and valleys of the bocage to open country beyond. However, advances in this sector formed part of Montgomery's plan to encircle the German Seventh Army or force it to retreat to the Seine, over which all bridges had been destroyed by Allied bombing. Another part of the plan was being achieved by pressure from the First Canadian Army on the left flank. The action of these two armies would facilitate a rapid enveloping movement by the American First and Third Armies through the gap created by the crushing of the German forces at Mortain.

Montgomery ordered the British Second Army to continue pushing southwards, and advances were made. The withdrawal of the German armoured divisions in the area of Mortain enabled the British XII and XXX Corps in the centre of the Allied line to fight their way past minefields and booby traps to occupy the shattered town of Villers-Bocage on 4 August. After a stiff fight against strong resistance from eight battalions of the German 276th and 326th Infantry Divisions, the tactical advantage of Mont Pinçon, about 1,200ft high, was stormed and won on 6 August at the cost of heavy casualties. On the right flank, the British VII Corps made further advances to the south but was having to fight hard against counter-attacks.

On the left flank of the British Second Army, the First Canadian Army began the difficult task of reaching the town of Falaise. This army was not composed entirely of Canadian nationals, for its II Corps was joined by the British 51st Division, the British 33rd Armoured Brigade and the newly arrived 1st Polish Armoured Division. Their advance was being made through fairly open country but against two very strong German lines of mortars and anti-tank guns, forming part of the 1st SS Panzer Korps, the 89th Infantry Division and the 12th SS Panzer Division.

The Canadian assault was preceded by an unusual and potentially hazardous operation, a heavy air bombardment *at night* of enemy positions immediately in front of the lines. The RAF's Bomber Command despatched over 1,000 aircraft for this purpose on 7/8 August. The attacks against five aiming points on the flanks of the battlefield were so carefully controlled by master bombers, guided by artillery marker shells, that only 600 aircraft were allowed to bomb.

The results were extremely accurate, and the other aircraft returned with their bomb loads. Ground artillery then opened fire and the infantry moved forward in vehicles specially adapted with bullet-proof plates, before dismounting to begin attacking their objectives on foot.

As the sky lightened, swarms of Typhoons of the RAF's Second Tactical Air Force arrived to attack forward enemy targets picked out by the Canadians and British, while Spitfires and Mustangs identified and strafed other enemy formations. The commander of the 2nd Panzer Division, General Heinrich Freiherr von Lüttwitz, reported that the Typhoons arrived in their hundreds, firing rockets against tanks and other vehicles, and that his troops could not retaliate against this onslaught. Soon after midday, about 500 B-17 Fortresses of the US Eighth Air Force arrived to bomb enemy positions, although tragically some of their loads fell on Canadian and British positions.

The Allies managed to advance up to 7 miles on that first day, taking them to about 12 miles from Falaise. Von Kluge reported despairingly that both his 89th Infantry Division and his 12th SS Panzer Division had been almost wiped out by air attack, and that Feldmarschall Hugo Sperrle, the commander of the Luftwaffe's Third Air Fleet in the area, could do nothing to defend his forces.

The German 47th Panzer Korps began an attack towards the American forces in Avranches in the early misty morning of 7 August 1944. They captured the town of Mortain, which became the centre of one of the fiercest and most important battles of the Normandy campaign. This photograph shows the destruction of a German column at St Barthélemy, a village north of Mortain, after a rocket attack by Typhoon IBs of No. 121 Wing, Second Tactical Air Force. *The National Archives: CAB 106/1010*

Although this report was exaggerated, there is no doubt that his troops had suffered appalling casualties.

Nevertheless, the remaining Germans were determined to protect Falaise and formed another line with a strong defensive screen against tanks. There was fierce fighting and this line was not breached on 9 August. It was not until the following day that more advances were made, after enemy counter-attacks had been repelled. The Germans also brought up the additional defence of the 85th Infantry Division from their Fifteenth Army.

While these critical battles were in progress along the British and Canadian sectors, the Americans achieved a major breakthrough in the west. The US First Army cleared out the remainder of the depleted German forces in the Mortain area while VIII Corps of the US Third Army pushed west towards the Atlantic ports of Brest and Lorient. Then General Patton saw a prime opportunity of encircling the German Seventh Army behind the Allied lines with the other two corps of his US Third Army. His XV Corps sped almost unopposed about 70 miles in that direction, reaching Le Mans on 8 August. At the same time, his XX Corps raced south to the Loire, reaching Nantes on 9 August and Angers two days later.

In these extraordinary achievements, Patton relied on advance arrangements with the US Ninth Air Force to provide cover for the flanks of his armoured columns. The Ninth already consisted of a Bomber Command, a Fighter Command and a Troop Carrier Command. On the formation of the new US Third Army on 1 August, its Fighter Command was split and enlarged into IX Tactical Air Command to support the US First Army and XIX Tactical Air Command to support the US Third Army. Patton arranged with Brigadier-General Otto P. Weyland, the commander of the new XIX Tactical Air Command, for all nine Fighter Wings to support the three Army Corps of the US Third Army. With an American Wing the equivalent of an RAF Group, P-51 Mustangs, P-38 Lightnings and P-47 Thunderbolts were constantly in the skies above the advancing troops, maintaining air supremacy over the Luftwaffe and ready to strafe enemy troops and armour as required. The outcome was similar to the German Blitzkrieg of 1940, but the American attackers were even more powerful and the roads were free of streams of terrified civilians fleeing an advancing enemy. Instead, French people everywhere welcomed the Americans as liberators, not as remorseless conquerors.

These startling breakthroughs resulted in a stream of orders from Hitler to von Kluge, mainly requiring him to resume an attack westwards. Such orders were quite impracticable, since any counter-attacks in daylight would have been met with overwhelming Allied air power, while at night there was a bright moon. An even worse situation for von Kluge developed when Patton's XV Corps left Le Mans on 10 August and suddenly struck northwards, as directly by Montgomery. This Corps was led by the 5th US Armoured Division, plus the 2nd French Armoured Division under General J. Philippe Leclerc. The latter had earned a high reputation during the fighting in North Africa, and now his division was the first composed of French nationals to engage the enemy in the liberation of their country.

The American XV Corps neared Argentan three days later, having covered a distance of about 50 miles. This brought it to the rear of the German Seventh Army and the Panzer Group opposing the First Canadian Army which was continuing its push towards the south. At the same time, the British Second Army had also made further progress on the right flank of the Canadians. Thus the Germans were being squeezed into a salient with a single opening in the east, the gap being only about 25 miles. Nevertheless they resisted the Americans and

French fiercely, managing to hold them a few miles south of Argentan. A single American corps was not able to make a serious impression on the German army. The gap towards the east, enabling the Germans to escape, was not closed although it became narrower.

The RAF's Bomber Command despatched 144 aircraft on the night of 12/13 August and made a very effective attack on German troop positions north of Falaise. The Canadians resumed their attack in the following morning and achieved further progress. But the pressure on the German positions in the south was lessened, for General Omar N. Bradley ordered XV Corps of the Third Army to cease this advance and leave the French 2nd Armoured Division plus one American Infantry Division to hold the positions south of Argentan. Meanwhile, other elements of the US Third Army were to speed to the east in the direction of Paris. These were the remainder of XV Corps plus the whole of XX Corps arriving from the direction of Angers and Le Mans. At the same time, the newly arrived XII Corps headed in the direction of Orleans on the Loire.

On 14 August, the Canadians continued their advance on Falaise, supported in the morning by bombers and rocket-carrying fighters of the RAF's Second Tactical Air Force. During the afternoon, the RAF's Bomber Command despatched over 800 aircraft to support the troops. Most of the heavy bombing was very accurate but unfortunately some crews mistook Canadian flares for target indicators and bombed these forces, causing considerable casualties. Despite this setback, the First Canadian Army made good progress.

Lieutenant-General George S. Patton, commander of the United States Third Army. *Author's Collection*

Hitler was reported as saying that the following day, 15 August, was the worst of his life. Not only did the Canadians reach the outskirts of Falaise, with some of the defending German divisions almost wiped out, but the Allied landing that he had anticipated took place on the French Riviera, between Le Lavandou and St-Raphael. This operation was codenamed 'Dragoon' and came under the authority of General Sir Henry Maitland Wilson, the Supreme Allied Commander in the Mediterranean theatre. Of course, it was mounted with the full approval of General Eisenhower, with the purpose of creating another front against the German forces occupying France. It would also secure working ports for supplying the Allies, which would be welcome after the destruction of one of the Mulberry artificial harbours in the great storm of mid-June.

Operation Dragoon had been preceded by five days of attacks by the Mediterranean Air Force along the area between Marseille and Toulouse. The aircraft cut railway lines and destroyed road bridges, knocked out coastal batteries and destroyed radar stations. Some 5,000 aircraft were available for these purposes, compared with only about 220 which the Luftwaffe could muster in the south and south-west of France. The latter had been overwhelmed and the survivors forced to withdraw from the area.

During the night of 14/15 August, these Allied air forces dropped a task force of US paratroopers in the early morning, carrying some 9,000 airborne troops with about 220 jeeps and over 200 artillery pieces as well as supplies of other war material. Within these airborne troops were a British brigade, a Canadian-American Special Service Force and French Commandos.

The seaborne forces were supported by five battleships, twenty-four cruisers, nine escort carriers and over a hundred destroyers, under the command of Vice-Admiral H. Kent Hewitt of the US Navy. These escorted numerous landing craft and other vessels, providing for them a heavy naval bombardment of German positions. The first troops consisted of three American infantry divisions forming VI Corps, together with an American Special Service Force and French Commandos. These were followed by a French Armoured Brigade and a French Infantry Division with an Algerian Infantry Division. They formed the US Seventh Army under Lieutenant-General Alexander M. Patch.

The landings were successful everywhere, against opposition which was only slight by comparison with Normandy. They were also accompanied by intense air activity from the Mediterranean Air Force, which made concentrated attacks against the German beach defences. Moreover, the Allies had the benefit of tactical air support from seven British and two American carriers which remained in the vicinity for over a fortnight, assisting with the advance of the land forces.

By the end of the first day, some 60,000 men had landed, as well as 6,000 vehicles and 50,000 tons of supplies, at the cost of about 300 casualties. Within the first few days the Allies secured a large bridgehead and took over 2,800 German prisoners from Army Group C's Nineteenth Army. Apart from a

The massive U-boat shelter at Brest, which was battered on 12 and 13 August 1944 by Lancasters of Bomber Command with 'Tallboy' 12,000lb bombs. Some of these penetrated the roof, which had previously been impregnable to bombing. The photograph was taken on 31 August 1944, but the German garrison in Brest held out until the afternoon of 19 September 1944, when it surrendered to the US Third Army. *The National Archives: AIR 34/241*

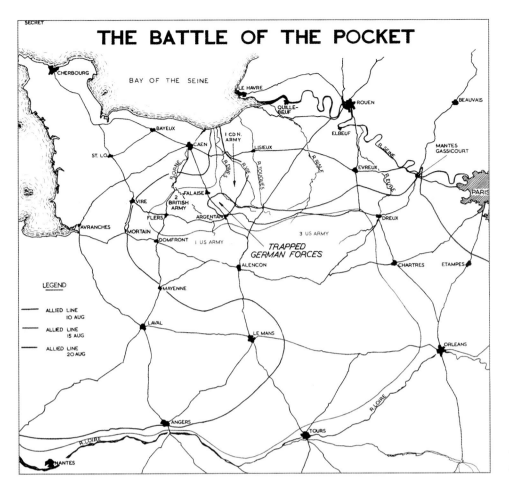

THE BATTLE OF THE POCKET

The Battle of the Pocket. *The National Archives: AIR 41/67*

subsequent advance northwards, the US Seventh Army threatened German forces in western France. Three days after these landings, Hitler was forced to order the evacuation of his forces on the west coast of France, leaving 'fortresses' in Brest, Lorient, St-Nazaire, La Rochelle and an area near Bordeaux. Grossadmiral Karl Dönitz, who commanded the Kriegsmarine, ordered sixteen of the U-boats remaining in French ports to head for Norway, with eight others to cover them by operating off the Bristol Channel and the North Channel between Scotland and Ireland. Nine U-boats had to be left behind and were either scuttled or broken up, while nine others were sunk before the end of August in transit or on operations, by air attacks, warships or mines. Meanwhile, the RAF's Coastal Command and the Royal Navy destroyed all the German naval vessels stationed at ports along the Atlantic coast of France. Marinegruppe West ceased to exist.

When he was presented with so much unwelcome news on 15 August, Hitler also had to consider withdrawing his Seventh Army from Normandy, as well as the accompanying Panzer Army. To add to the flood of adverse reports, it appeared that von Kluge was missing. Of course, Hitler suspected that he had gone over to the enemy to discuss a surrender. He instructed the commander of the Seventh Army, SS-Obergruppenführer (General) Paul Hausser, to act temporarily in his place, and on the following day appointed Feldmarschall Walther Model permanently in that position. But then von Kluge turned up unexpectedly, explaining that all his wireless sets had been put out of action by Allied air attacks. Learning of his replacement, he wrote a long letter to Hitler justifying his absence and swearing loyalty. He committed suicide on 17 August by swallowing a cyanide pill.

By this time, the Canadians were entering Falaise. Hitler had ordered the troops defending the town to resist tenaciously while the main bulk of Army Group B and the Panzer Army withdrew to the east through the gap still available, which by then had shrunk to about 15 miles. This retreat began after darkness on the evening of 16 August. Throughout the campaign, German signals were monitored by the British 'Y' Service and then decrypted by the Government Code and Cypher School at Bletchley Park. Thus Montgomery and other high-ranking Allied commanders had accurate information about the disposition of enemy forces and even their probable intentions.

The weather was unsuitable for air attack during 17 August but the skies cleared the following day, when the retreating enemy columns offered splendid targets to the RAF's Second Tactical Air Force. From the afternoon of that day the two main roads leading to the Seine became killing grounds for the Spitfires, Typhoons and Mustangs. The pilots could see German troops waving white handkerchiefs in desperate attempts to surrender as they fled, but there were no Allied troops near enough to take prisoners. Nevertheless, attempts by the First Canadian Army and the XV Corps of the US Third Army to close the gap were beaten off by a determined German resistance on the flanks of the retreat.

The massacre continued on the following day, with the Germans sometimes attempting to hide in woods. They began to move only at night, but could not conceal their vehicles during daylight. These were up to four abreast on the main roads, many having burst into flames from bombs or rockets fired from the air. Some of the survivors had turned off the roads into country lanes but they could not escape the relentless RAF pilots. Fighter groups of the US Ninth Air Force also joined in these attacks, while others warded off those fighter pilots of the Luftwaffe who were desperately trying to support their comrades on the ground.

Other Allied tactical fighters headed for the Seine, attacking barges and other river transport which were being used to convey German survivors to a safer area. All the bridges over the river had already been destroyed by air attack. Medium bombers of the Second Tactical Air Force, Mitchells and Mosquitos, joined in the slaughter by both day and night. The retreat turned into a rout, leaving a litter of wrecked military vehicles as well as civilian cars and vans commandeered by the Germans, all clogging the roads and lanes. Much of this transport was horse-drawn, presenting the distressing sight of dead animals. Lifeless soldiers could be seen inside smashed and burnt-out vehicles, while others were sprawled outside. When the survivors drove forward, some of the soldiers lay with their backs on the mudguards, scanning the skies above for their relentless attackers. Eventually, there appeared to be no vehicles left, with the remaining German soldiers continuing on foot. Unfortunately a few of the air attacks were made in error on Canadian I Corps, which was closing on the rear of the enemy and taking large numbers of prisoners.

On 20 August two armoured divisions of the 2nd SS Panzer Korps, assembled near Vimoutiers to the east of the retreating troops, attempted a counter-attack, but this was beaten off. SS-Obergruppenführer Paul Hausser, who commanded the Panzers, was badly wounded on this day and his function was taken over by SS-Oberstgruppenführer (Lieutenant-General) Sepp Dietrich. It was estimated by the Germans that under half the soldiers of Army Group B who attempted to reach safety were able to do so. By this time, the British and Canadian divisions in the forefront of the pursuit had taken about 20,000 prisoners, and the Americans

American infantrymen on 20 August 1944 at Chambois in France, in front of a wrecked Panzerkampfwagen 5 Panther and a captured Nazi flag. This was the last German stronghold in the Falaise area, about 34 miles south-east of Caen. *US National Archives and Records Administration: War & Conflict # 1049*

had taken about the same number. If the Allies had been able to close the narrow gap through which the Germans passed, the figure would have been far higher. But the future of those who managed to escape by 21 August was still uncertain.

The British, Canadian and American armies continued to pursue these fleeing German forces. On the left was the British 21st Army Group commanded by General Sir Bernard Montgomery. This consisted of the First Canadian Army on the left flank, commanded by Lieutenant-General Henry Crerar, and the British Second Army on its right, commanded by Lieutenant-General Sir Miles Dempsey. On their right was the US 12th Army Group commanded by General Omar N. Bradley. This consisted of the First Army on the left, commanded by Lieutenant-General Courtney H. Hodges, and the Third Army on the right flank, commanded by Lieutenant-General George S. Patton. Close support from the air was provided by the RAF's Second Tactical Air Force for the British and Canadian armies, while the US Ninth Air Force supported the American armies, apart from those periods when aircraft were unable to take off in bad weather.

General Montgomery intended to employ these four armies on the destruction of all German forces in north-west France. Of course, Hitler issued orders for defensive lines and reinforcement of his Seventh Army, as well as instructions regarding the defence of Paris, which he directed should be 'fought regardless of the city's destruction'. He ordered that any revolt within the city should be put down by the severest measures, such as the public execution of ringleaders and the demolition of blocks of buildings. Such measures were not practicable, since there were only about 5,000 Germans in scattered pockets of the city and these were already in armed clashes with the French Resistance, known as the French Forces of the Interior (FFI).

The commander of the German forces in Paris, General Dietrich von Choltitz, prudently decided to ignore Hitler's orders. As soon as the SS security personnel vanished from the city, he made a truce with the FFI. The French then sent envoys to the Americans asking them to occupy the capital with all possible speed. The advancing force was the French 2nd Armoured Division under General Leclerc, part of the US Third Army, which had fought its way past German outer defences at the cost of considerable casualties. The French troops arrived in the city on 24 August and von Choltitz surrendered on the following day. Citizens of Paris went wild with joy as the liberators rolled through beautiful and largely unscathed boulevards, except those few nationals who had collaborated willingly with the German occupiers. General Charles de Gaulle also made a triumphal entry into the capital after his arrival in France.

This dramatic and welcome event was of only incidental importance to the main campaign. The Canadians, British and American armies had pushed forward to the Seine on both sides of Paris. From 20 to 24 August, survivors of the defeated Seventh Army and Fifth Panzer Army used whatever ferries were available to cross the meandering but broad and fast-flowing river. The British 21st Army Group arrived at the Seine in the evening of 24 August and immediately began building bridges on the stretch between Vernon and Rouen, to enable about 4,400 vehicles and artillery to cross and continue the pursuit. At the same time, the RAF's Second Tactical Air Force continued to attack the fleeing Germans.

Allied advances were also being made in the west of France, until the troops came to ports which had been designated 'fortresses' by Hitler. On 6 August, the US Third Army's VIII Corps overran the outer defence of St-Malo, on the north coast of Brittany, but the defenders fought bitterly until the old port was captured six days later, with most of its historic buildings destroyed. The major military port of Brest was invested by VIII Corps on 25 August, in the course of repeated bombardments by the RAF's Bomber Command and the US Eighth Air Force. The port was also shelled by the 15-in guns of the battleship HMS *Warspite*. But the garrison still held out until it finally succumbed on 19 September, by which time the port and the city were in ruins.

On 26 August, Montgomery ordered his 21st Army Group to destroy all enemy forces in the Pas de Calais and Flanders. It was then to capture Antwerp and eventually advance on the Ruhr. The US First Army was ordered to provide support on the right flank. His plan of advancing on such a narrow front was not accepted by Eisenhower, who changed this policy three days later by ordering a broader advance by the Allied forces in northern France, including both sides of the Ardennes in both France and Belgium. At the end of the month, Eisenhower assumed direct command of the Allied forces while Montgomery was promoted to field-marshal and retained his position as commander of the 21st Army Group.

In the meantime, the US First and Third Armies had swept beyond Paris to the south of the city, advancing some 40 miles north-east towards Soissons. On their left, the British and the Canadians began crossing the Seine on 25 August, with considerable air support. Feldmarschall Model decided that withdrawal was his only option and Hitler agreed reluctantly that another line should be formed along the river Somme, with the city of Amiens as its centre.

On the far left flank, the Canadians continued to progress along the coast of France. There was a tragic accident on 27 August when the RAF's Second

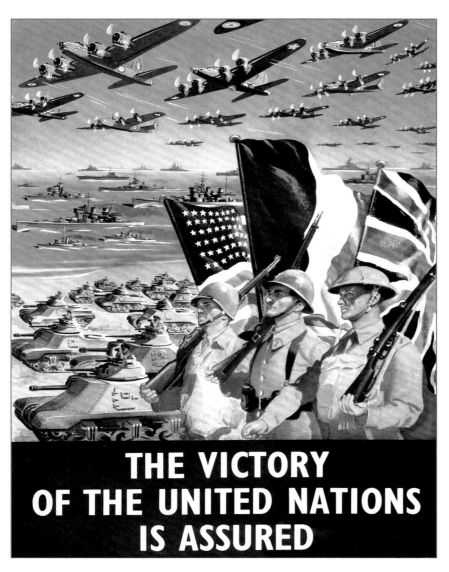

A general publicity poster issued by the Central Office of Information. The artist is not recorded. *The National Archives: INF 2/3*

**THE VICTORY
OF THE UNITED NATIONS
IS ASSURED**

THIS IS THE YEAR!

IT'S UP TO US TO LET 'EM HAVE IT!

A general publicity poster issued by the Central Office of Information. The artist was Clive Uptton. *The National Archives : INF 13/122*

Lightning, Camera, Action by Charles Thompson GAvA, ASAA, GMA, EAA

Lockheed F-5 of the 31st Photographic Reconnaissance Squadron, 10th Photographic Group, US Ninth Air Force, over the beaches between Le Tréport and Berck-sur-Mer on 6 May 1944. It was flown by Lieutenant Albert Lanker from Chalgrove in Oxfordshire, who recorded that he was understandably apprehensive before take-off but found that he enjoyed himself immensely in the four minutes over the target area. He dived on groups of workmen to make them scatter, then scaled a cliff with his wingtip only 6ft from the top. Very surprisingly, the only opposition encountered was when a German soldier fired a rifle at him.

Action Scene from Superstructure of Battleship on D-Day by unknown war artist. *The National Archives: INF 3/1651*

'Johnnie' Johnson over the D-Day beaches in Spitfire IX by Mark Postlethwaite GAvA
Wing Commander J.E. 'Johnnie' Johnson was one of the most popular and highly respected of the RAF's war aces. He commanded No. 144 (RCAF) Wing of the Second Tactical Air Force during the Normandy invasion, consisting of Nos 441 (RCAF), 442 (RCAF) and 443 (RCAF) Squadrons, all equipped with Spitfire IXs. Johnnie Johnson flew his personal machine, serial MK392. His Wing was able to operate from the newly constructed B3 airfield at St-Croix in France as early as 10 June 1944.

. . . And Rockets Blazed by Charles J. Thompson GAvA, ASAA, GMA, EAA

Hawker Typhoon IB serial MN526 of No. 198 Squadron, Second Tactical Air Force, based at B.7 airstrip at Martragny in France, firing rockets with 60lb high-explosive warheads at German troops who had taken cover with their armour in a roadside copse. The incident took place during the Battle of the Falaise Gap in the third week of August 1944, before the German defences finally broke and enabled the Allied armies to sweep through northern France to Belgium and the Netherlands.

Alpine Armada by Charles J. Thompson GAvA, ASAA, GMA, EAA

On 17 August 1943, the US Eighth Air Force despatched seven Bombardment Groups of B-17 Fortresses from its 4th Bombardment Wing to attack the German aircraft industry at Regensburg on the river Danube in Bavaria. There were 146 bombers escorted by 240 P-47 Thunderbolts. An epic air battle ensued with Focke-Wulf Fw190s and Messerschmitt Bf109s from the time the coast of Holland was crossed until the target was reached. Nevertheless the attack was pressed home and the surviving bombers then headed over the Alps towards North Africa. Some 24 B-17s and the 3 P-47s were lost in the operation, with 203 US airmen missing in action. Many of the aircraft which reached North Africa were so badly damaged that they could not be repaired. The American airmen who survived claimed heavy losses among the German fighters.

Infantry and Tanks by unknown war artist. *The National Archives: INF 3/1670*

Soldiers Emerging from Aircraft by war artist Oliphant. *The National Archives: INF 3/1663*

***Opposite:* Soldiers Descending by Parachute** by war artist Oliphant. *The National Archives: INF 3/1664*

Focke-Wulf Fw 190D-12 of JG26 over B-17s in January 1945 by Mark Postlethwaite GAvA

One of the variants of the Focke-Wulf Fw190D was the D-12, which first began to enter squadron service in early 1945. The fuselage was lengthened and it was powered by a Jumo 213F engine of 2,060hp. It was fitted with a 30mm Mk108 cannon firing through the spinner, in addition to the standard MG151 cannons of 20mm in the wing roots. With a maximum speed of 453mph at 37,000ft, it was a formidable adversary for the formations of American bombers and fighters which appeared almost daily in the skies over Germany.

Messerschmitt Me 262s led by Adolf Galland of JV44 about to intercept Mustangs in 1945 by Mark Postlethwaite GAvA

After falling out with Reichsmarschall Herman Goering in January 1945, the fighter ace Generalleutnant Adolf Galland was relieved of air staff duties and assumed command of Jagdverband 44, which he led in action until the end of the war. This elite unit was equipped with the Messerschmitt 262A-1a Schwalbe (Swallow), the first jet-propelled fighter in the world to enter squadron service. It was powered by two Jumo 109-004B turbojets of 1,980lb static thrust and fitted with a basic armament of four 30mm Mk108 cannons, although rockets could be fitted in some sub-types. Other variants of the Me262 were employed as fighter-bombers and for fighter-reconnaissance. By the end of the war, Galland had been credited with 104 victories.

Tactical Air Force ordered a strike against vessels believed to be *Schnellboote* (fast torpedo boats) off Cap d'Antifer. Typhoons attacked and sank two British minesweepers and damaged another so badly that it had to be scrapped. The loss of life among Royal Navy personnel was heavy.

The Canadians invested Le Havre but this port had been declared a 'fortress' by Hitler and the well-armed defenders of 11,300 men under Oberst Eberhard Wildermuth resisted stubbornly. These were subjected to a bombardment from the monitor HMS *Erebus* on 5 September as well as a heavy attack in daylight by the RAF's Bomber Command on that day. These were followed by more air attacks on 8, 10 and 11 September. The last was particularly effective and the Germans surrendered on the following day.

Meanwhile, Le Havre was bypassed temporarily while the Canadians continued their advance along the coastal area. In contrast to Le Havre, Dieppe was left undefended and the Canadians were able to enter it on 1 September, to find the harbour little damaged. In the course of these advances, the Canadians eliminated bases from which German *Kleinkampfverbände* (Small Battle Units) had been operating in the Channel against the western flank of the Allied invasion fleet. These were small carriers to which were clamped a single standard torpedo, which could be aimed at a target and then fired. They operated almost entirely on the surface but could dive for short periods. There were two types, the *Neger* and the slightly larger *Marder*. All the pilots were volunteers and they were unquestionably extremely courageous, for the chance of survival of a single operation was rated as no more than 50 per cent. They had succeeded in sinking two minesweepers of the Royal Navy on 5 July and damaging a cruiser two days later. This was followed by the sinking of a minesweeping trawler on 2 July and a barrage balloon vessel on the night of 17/18 August. But these midget submarines were hunted remorselessly by the

One of the ferries west of Rouen used by the Germans in their retreat across the river Seine was photographed on 26 August 1944. Vehicles were seen waiting and at least two were burning furiously after an attack by the Allied Expeditionary Air Force. *The National Archives: AIR 34/542*

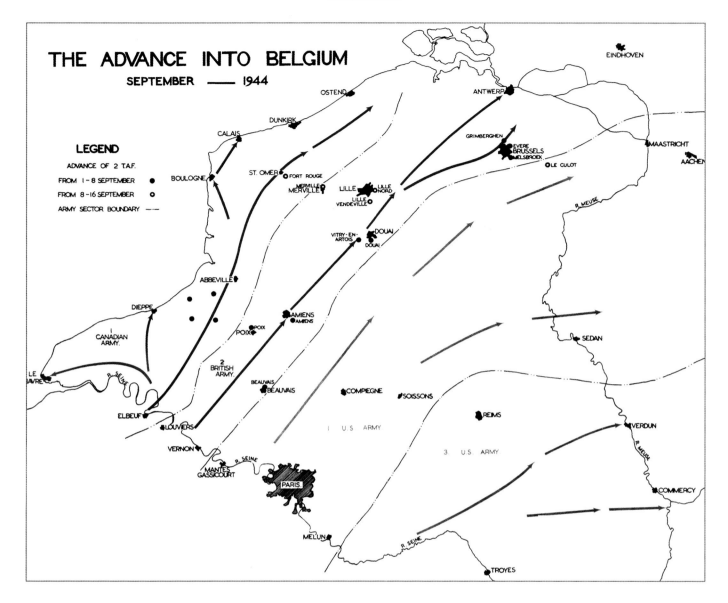

The advance into Belgium, September 1944. *The National Archives: AIR 41/67*

Royal Navy and the RAF, while others succumbed to the elements. The few survivors and their craft were withdrawn to Dutch ports.

The British Second Army freed Amiens on 30 August and on the evening of that day the 29th Armoured Brigade captured General Heinrich Eberbach, who had arrived to take over from SS-Oberstgruppenführer Sepp Dietrich, who managed to avoid capture. By then, the gateway to Belgium could be kicked open and the pace of the advancing British and Canadian armies quickened. The Somme was crossed and advanced guards of the British Second Army crossed the Belgian border on 2 September. Throughout these advances, assistance with information was given by both the French and Belgian Resistance movements, who were desperately anxious to witness the crushing of their German occupiers. They knew, often accurately, the positions and strength of the rearguards of both the fleeing Fifteenth Army and the remnants of the Seventh Army. Moreover, they were able to relieve the Allies of the difficult task of guarding numerous German prisoners.

On the right flank of the 21st Army Group, British forces either overcame opposition or bypassed groups of the enemy and reached Brussels on 3 September. The 1st Battalion of the Welsh Guards was the first to enter the capital in force, headed by scout cars of the Household Cavalry. The liberators were greeted with an ecstatic welcome from Belgian citizens. On the following day, the British 11th Armoured Division entered the strategic port of Antwerp and found the docks almost undamaged, for the Germans had not had time to complete its demolition. Nevertheless, this essential port could not be used immediately, for it lay on the river Scheldt, about 60 miles from the sea, and the approaches were heavily mined as well as overlooked on the north bank by German artillery.

The US 12th Army Group made similar advances to the south of the Canadians and the British, following shattered remnants of the German Seventh Army. The US First Army also reached the Belgian border, when its VII Corps was ordered to turn north. The troops managed to cut off a large and mixed group of retreating Germans in the region of Mons. In the first few days of September these unfortunate Germans were subjected to attacks from American spearheads, tanks and Belgian Resistance groups. The US Ninth Air Force delivered devastating attacks, destroying huge numbers of motor transport and horse-drawn vehicles. Short of ammunition and without hope of rescue, about 25,000 Germans were forced to surrender. They were the remnants of twenty divisions. On 8 September, the US First Army arrived at the approaches to Liège in Belgium.

On the right flank, the US Third Army sped across France to reach Verdun on 1 September, the scene of some of the most appalling slaughter of the First World War. It then crossed the Meuse and approached Metz and Nancy. It seemed probable that the Germans would attempt to make a stand along their Siegfried Line, built before the war for such a purpose.

By this time, the US Seventh Army in the south of France had also made considerable advances. The French divisions which formed a major part of this army had captured the naval port of Toulon on 27 August after a long, fierce and bloody battle. Over 2,700 French soldiers had died but they had inflicted severe casualties on the German Army Group G and taken over 27,000 prisoners. The French had also liberated Marseille. The US Seventh Army then advanced up the Rhône and through the mountainous region in the east, in pursuit of the retreating German Army Group G. On 15 September the advanced American troops linked up with their comrades in the east of France and their Seventh Army then came under the command of General Eisenhower of Supreme Headquarters Allied Expeditionary Force.

The swift pace of the Allied advances from Normandy had not been completely anticipated. Both the RAF's Second Tactical Air Force and the USAAF's Ninth Air Force had difficulty in bringing enough of their fighter squadrons forward by as much as 150 miles to provide continuous support for the forward elements of the armies. Some established airfields used by the Luftwaffe were occupied but needed to be made serviceable. Other airstrips had to be constructed. The airfield service teams of both air forces worked heroically in these endeavours but they too had to be supplied with bombs, ammunition, fuel and food. Fortunately the temporary reduction in the strength of Allied fighter cover was tolerable since the Luftwaffe had been reduced almost to impotence in the preceding months.

But carrying supplies to the forward elements of the armies and air forces remained a problem. The scale of the Allied enterprise had become colossal. By the end of August about 440,000 vehicles and 3,100,000 tons of supplies had been shipped across the Channel, and much needed to be transported to the forward lines. By this time, about 1,220,000 Americans and 830,000 British servicemen had arrived in Normandy for their respective armies, the great majority by ships or landing craft. These included nationals of other countries serving within the armies. About 20,800 servicemen in the US armies and 16,000 in the British or Canadian armies had been killed. The wounded amounted to about 95,000 in the US armies and 10,000 in the British or Canadian, the majority having been taken back to England by ship or air. About 10,000 Americans and 9,000 British or Canadians were missing, but some of these must have been captured by the Germans. The combined air forces had flown over 480,000 sorties, many of these from French airfields, and had lost over 4,100 aircraft and about 16,700 aircrew, some of the latter becoming prisoners.

Everywhere in France the broken German armies were in retreat towards their homeland, apart from those still holding out in coastal 'fortresses'. Although Hitler instructed them to 'contest every foot of land in a stubborn delaying action', they could not achieve the impossible. The badly mauled Fifth Panzer Army had reached the Saar but was in need of reinforcement and re-equipment. In the north, the German Fifteenth Army was in retreat towards the north coast of the Scheldt and the Netherlands, pursued by the First Canadian Army. To the south, what was left of the German Seventh Army was nearing the Ardennes and the German border town of Aachen, harried by the British Second Army and the US First Army. Most of the German First Army was in retreat from south of the Loire and its positions along the Atlantic coast of France; it was heading for the Siegfried Line while in combat with the US Third Army. The German Nineteenth Army from the south had reached Dijon, pursued by the US Seventh Army which had landed on the Riviera, as well as the new French First Army under General de Lattre de Tassigny, formed from divisions which had accompanied the Americans.

Within SHAEF, the means of invading Germany itself were being discussed and planned. Both Eisenhower and Montgomery had their ideas on the best way this could be accomplished, and perhaps bring the war in Europe to an end before December.

Elements of the 30th Division, US First Army, entering the battered streets of Mortain on 12 August 1944. *The National Archives: CAB 106/1010*

On the night of 11/12 August 1944, thirty-three Mosquitos of Bomber Command dropped their 4,000lb bombs on Berlin. One aircraft was lost in the operation, which was partly intended as retaliation for the V-1 flying-bomb attacks against London. This night photograph shows a burning target indicator and tracks of searchlights. The main road running diagonally on the bottom left is the Charlottenburger Chaussée, which continues through the Tiergarten district and joins the Unter den Linden at the Brandenburger Tor. *British Official*

Bomber Command despatched twenty-eight Lancasters and one Mosquito to Brest in daylight on 13 August 1944, to attack the U-boat pens and sink vessels which the Germans might use as blockships before capture by the US Third Army. Hits were claimed on the pens and the ship arrowed in the photograph. One Lancaster was lost on the operation. *The National Archives: AIR 37/1231*

Bomber Command despatched 113 aircraft on the night of 18/19 August 1944 to attack the 'Purlina' oil depot at Rieme in Belgium, south-west of Zelgate and near the Ghent-Terneuzen canal. No aircraft were lost in the operation, but the area was reduced to a mass of craters, with widespread damage to the installations. The foundations of the railway bridge over the canal, which was destroyed by Belgian military engineers on 20 May 1940, can be seen on the left of this photograph. *British Official*

An American soldier looking at the remains of a German horse-drawn column shattered by artillery fire in August 1944. This vehicle is a so-called 'Gulaschkanone', the German nickname for a horse-drawn field kitchen. *The National Archives: CAB 106/1010*

By the time the Battle of Mortain ended on 25 August 1944, the commander of the LXXIV Corps, Lieutenant-General Otto Elfeldt (centre), had been captured by the US First Army. The LXXIV Corps had fought bitterly and bravely but had been almost wiped out. The German general and his staff were able to enjoy American cigarettes with their captors. *The National Archives: CAB 106/1010*

The US 7th Army Corps entered the French town of Laon on 30 August 1944, as shown here with an American soldier capturing a German who had been hiding in one of the houses. The Americans then advanced towards Belgium and crossed the border, entering the town of Bergen in the evening of 2 September 1944. *The National Archives: CAB 106/1010*

The Typhoon IBs of the Second Tactical Air Force operated from airfield B5, near La Fresnoy Camilly, during the Battle of Mortain. They created havoc among the German Panzer Divisions, being credited with the destruction of 162 tanks. This German Hanomag Sd.Kfz 251/1d (half-track armoured car) was left knocked out by air attack in the vicinity of Mortain, with a dead crew member lying alongside it. *The National Archives: CAB 106/1010*

This air photograph of eerie shadows cast by the ruins of Falaise in Normandy was taken on 21 September 1944, a month after the fierce battle for the town came to an end. Such destruction occurred in French towns where the Germans put up strong resistance, but fortunately many others remained unscathed when they passed through them in full retreat. *The National Archives: AIR 34/545*

British and Canadian troops driving through an avenue of fir trees during their rapid advance towards Belgium in late August 1944. *British Official*

This Hanomag Sonderkraftfahrzeug, SdKtz 251/1, was caught in the open and destroyed by rocket projectiles fired by an RAF fighter. This type of vehicle became standard equipment for the German Army in 1942. There were many variants, such as a carrier for ten soldiers with a crew of two, ambulance staff car or self-propelled gun. It was underpowered and difficult to steer, but supply never satisfied demand. *The National Archives: AIR 20/2207*

Opposite page: British armour entering Brussels after the advanced elements of the troops reached the capital in the evening of 3 September 1944. *British Official*

The Panzerkampfwagen P IV (PzKpfw) tank had a crew of four and a weight of 24 tons. Its maximum speed was 25mph and the radius of action about 130 miles. The armament consisted of a 7.5cm gun and two 7.92mm machine-guns. This tank was caught by a rocket projectile fired from an aircraft, probably a Typhoon, which blew off the engine cover plate. The rear plate is covered with 'Zimmerit' coating, a rough cement plaster designed to prevent magnetic anti-tank charges sticking to the metal. *The National Archives: AIR 20/2207*

General Charles de Gaulle received an ecstatic welcome when he toured Paris on 26 August 1944. After laying a wreath on the tomb of the Unknown Warrior in the Arc de Triomphe, he walked down the Champs Elysées, cheered wildly by a huge crowd of exuberant Parisians. Then he visited the Hôtel de Ville before attending a service at Notre Dame Cathedral. *British Official*

A wild welcome given by cheering crowds to British troops as they passed through Lannoy, a suburb of the French industrial town of Roubaix on the border with Belgium. The troops crossed this border on 2 September 1944. British Official

The Palais de Justice in the centre of Brussels, set on fire by the Germans as they fled the capital. *British Official*

Belgium's great port of Antwerp was captured by the British on 4 September 1944. A delighted woman joined a British soldier in escorting German prisoners, at the intersection of Britse Lei and Anselmostraat. The tall building on the top left now houses the Bell Telephone Company but the Excelsior Hotel is no longer there. *British Official*

Overjoyed citizens of Brussels, cheering wildly and welcoming British troops as their transport passed through the streets, verifying that liberation had at last arrived. *British Official*

British troops in a tank-buster crossing the Albert Canal over a Bailey bridge on 7 September 1944, near Beringen, while Belgian refugees make their way back into a safer area. *British Official*

Rockets with 60lb explosive warheads, fired by a Typhoon III of No. 174 Squadron, streaking towards a German transport vessel near Terneuzon on the Scheldt estuary of the Netherlands on 10 September 1944. The squadron was part of the Second Tactical Air Force and based at Vitry-en-Artois in France at the time. The transport vessels, including barges, were crammed with German soldiers. The Typhoon pilots caught them in the middle of the estuary. *British Official*

CHAPTER SIX

THE NORTHERN SECTOR

Differences of opinion between General Dwight D. Eisenhower and Field-Marshal Sir Bernard Montgomery as to the best method of continuing the attack against the Wehrmacht do not appear to have been marked by acrimony. Eisenhower's view that the Allied advance should be made on a broad front probably rested on his knowledge of the enormous military and industrial strength of his country and his confidence in its ability to support such an endeavour. Montgomery's proposal was based on his experience with the British armed forces, which usually faced a far more powerful and numerous enemy. His preference was for a single well-directed thrust which might result in a quick kill. His view also seemed to be substantiated by the difficulties of supplying the Allied front lines in the late summer of 1944.

Both high commanders hoped that the Western Allies and the Soviet forces could bring the war in Europe to an end before the winter set in. The rapid advances on the Eastern and Western Fronts since June, combined with the thrust northwards by the Allied armies in Italy, appeared to hold out this possibility. In early September, Field-Marshal Montgomery and General Dempsey of the British Second Army Group met Lieutenant-Generals Bradley and Hodges of the US 12th Army Group and its First Army. They discussed a plan devised by Montgomery of seizing bridges over the Rhine between Wesel and Arnhem in the Netherlands, thus enabling the attackers to skirt round the north of the Siegfried Line. This would employ the new First Allied Airborne Army under the American Lieutenant-General Lewis H. Brereton. The airborne forces would be joined by an advance of the British Second Army from Belgium. Then the troops would cut off all the German forces in western Holland and also be able to sweep round to the south, where they would link up with the US First Army after it had crossed the Rhine south of Cologne. Thus the Allies would capture the great industrial heartland of the Ruhr and commence an advance on Berlin. At this stage, the operation was codenamed 'Comet', but this was later changed to 'Market Garden', with 'Market' representing the airborne part and 'Garden' the ground part.

Montgomery met Eisenhower in Brussels on 10 September for what was described as a friendly and amiable meeting. By this time, SHAEF had moved to France and was based on the west side to the Cotentin peninsula with a forward unit being established at Versailles. The plan was approved, although Montgomery did not obtain priority for all the supplies he required. Eisenhower wrote to his Army Group commanders on 15 September stating that Berlin was their main prize, provided the Russians did not get there first. The two means by which this might be achieved were the Northern Group of Armies via the Ruhr and Hannover, or the Southern Group of Armies via Frankfurt and Leipzig.

The airborne forces for the forthcoming operation in the north consisted of the American XVIII Corps under Major-General Matthew Ridgeway and the British I Corps under Lieutenant-General Frederick A.M. Browning. The former consisted of the 82nd and 101st Divisions, while the latter was composed of the 1st and 6th Divisions together with the 1st Special Air Service Brigade and the 1st Polish Independent Parachute Brigade. These were to be carried or towed in gliders by the American IX Troop Carrier Command and Nos 38 and 46 Groups of the RAF's Transport Command.

The airborne forces would coordinate with the British Second Army's XXX Corps, commanded by Lieutenant-General Brian Horrocks, pushing northwards from Belgium towards the Zuider Zee. This Corps consisted of the Guards Armoured Division with the 43rd and 50th Infantry Divisions, which had already experienced a hard fight to gain a bridgehead over the Meuse-Escaut canal, just south of the Dutch border. It would have to fight its way forward for 65 miles to reach the airborne troops in the most northerly position of Arnhem. This involved crossing the Wilhelmina canal, the Willems canal, the river Maas, the Maas-Waal canal, the river Waal and the Lower Rhine. About 9,000 sappers joined XXX Corps, providing great quantities of bridging material in case the Germans managed to destroy the existing bridges.

It was thought that the German forces opposing this operation would be scattered and irresolute, following their recent defeats. This assumption was over-optimistic. On 5 September, Hitler had recalled Feldmarschall von Rundstedt to resume his previous appointment as Commander-in-Chief West, while Feldmarschall Walther Model retained his command of Army Group B. These commanders made strenuous efforts to stabilise the front in this area. Enigma decrypts on 6 September established an order from Hitler making the First Parachute Army under the charismatic General Kurt Student responsible for the defence of the Albert canal between Antwerp and Maastricht. This Army included the 3rd, 5th and 6th Parachute Divisions, acting as infantry, reinforced by the 1st Luftwaffe Training Division, as well as LXXXVIII Corps's 719th and 344th Infantry Divisions. It was supported with ten flak battalions equipped with heavy weapons which were also effective against tanks. The British troops in the front line identified elements from other divisions withdrawn from the region north of the Scheldt. Perhaps most ominous of all, on 14 September the Dutch Resistance reported that the 9th Hohenstaufen and the 10th Frundsberg SS Panzer Divisions were re-forming near Arnhem and that Feldmarschall Model was based nearby. Two days later came the information that they were being re-equipped with new Mark IV tanks.

These reports were treated with some scepticism by the British commanders. Morale continued high after their successes against the German armies in the west, not only among those in command but throughout the airborne troops and those on the ground. There was a general belief that they were about to deliver a

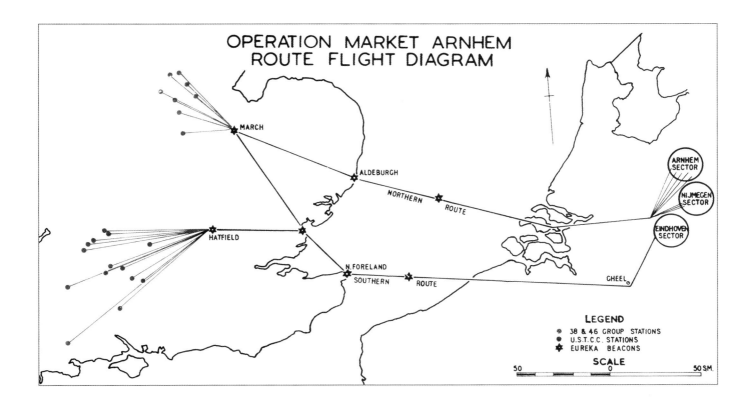

OPERATION MARKET ARNHEM
ROUTE FLIGHT DIAGRAM

LEGEND
⦿ 38 & 46 GROUP STATIONS
● U.S.T.C.C. STATIONS
✦ EUREKA BEACONS

SCALE
50   0   50 SM.

Operation Market, Arnhem, route flight diagram. *The National Archives: AIR 41/67*

knock-out blow and bring the war in Europe to an end, while the Wehrmacht was still reeling from the shock of its earlier defeats. But the Germans had had time to regroup and re-equip their forces.

Unfortunately the weather was unfavourable for flying on 15 September and not much better the following day, so the intelligence reports were not confirmed by air reconnaissance. There was, moreover, the erroneous impression that there were strong flak batteries around some bridges scheduled for capture, so that landing points for gliders were arranged for several miles away.

The operation began on the night of 16/17 September when the RAF's Bomber Command despatched 282 aircraft against airfields and flak positions in the Netherlands. These were followed in daylight by over 800 B-17 Fortresses of the US Eighth Air Force, escorted by almost 150 of its fighters, attacking similar targets. Then came about 1,400 bombers and fighters of the Allied Expeditionary Air Force, making further attacks against German positions.

A thunderous barrage was opened at 13.30 hours in front of XXX Corps, and the British troops began to move forward, making good progress at first. Meanwhile, the airborne forces headed accurately for their positions. These took off from twenty-two airfields in England and consisted of over 1,500 transport aircraft and almost 500 towed gliders, escorted by about 400 fighters of the Air Defence of Great Britain and 500 fighters of the US Eighth Air Force. General Kurt Student viewed these enormous air armadas with amazement, but he guessed they were making for bridges and ordered counter-attacks.

The US 101st and 82nd Airborne landed successfully south of Arnhem, in the areas of Eindhoven, Grave and Nijmegen. Their objectives were to capture and hold the bridges between the British XXX Corps and Arnhem. The Guards Division and a battalion of the 50th Division broke out of their bridgehead over the Maas-Scheldt canal and, after initial problems with German anti-tank guns, advanced 15 miles and made contact with the US 101st Airborne south of Eindhoven on the following day. The Americans in this Division had captured the bridges over the Willems canal, but the bridge over Wilhelmina canal had been blown by the Germans. To their north, the US 82nd Airborne had also landed accurately and captured bridges over the Maas-Waal canal, but the

Halifaxes towing Horsa gliders while flying over the Rhine en route to the Arnhem area on 17 September 1944. *British Official*

A Douglas C-47 photographed on 11 April 1944 while making a double tow pick-up of two Waco CG-4A gliders. *US National Archives and Records Administration # 18-WP-63-141682*

bridges over the river Maas at Nijmegen, a few miles south of Arnhem, had not been taken.

Events went less well with the British Airborne Corps in the far north of the zone. Elements of the 1st Airborne Division landed 6 miles outside Arnhem, on the north bank of the Lower Rhine, and guided in the remainder, consisting of about 5,700 men. More arrived later. But they were separated from Arnhem by forested and difficult country, through which they had to advance in order to seize road and railway bridges. The 1st Parachute Brigade managed to reach the main bridge at Arnhem during the night, but then the fortunes of war swung heavily against the airborne forces. Fog blanketed England and only a handful of the 1st Polish Brigade, which was due to reinforce the division, managed to reach the dropping zone. Even worse, radio communication within the 1st Airborne Division failed almost completely. The commanders had to make use of runners to communicate with other units, and few of these got through. Unfortunately, supplies carried with great determination on 19 September by 163 aircraft of the RAF's 38 and 48 Groups, through an immense barrage of flak, fell straight into German hands.

When the British XXX Corps fought its way to form a bridgehead over the Waal at Nijmegen, General Browning had no way of knowing the position at Arnhem with any accuracy. Meanwhile, the Germans brought up reinforcements, including light flak units, and no aircraft were able to make contact with the beleaguered 1st Airborne. By 21 September, these troops were overrun by the 9th and 10th SS Panzer Divisions, after fighting for three and a half days with insufficient ammunition and little food.

The only option for the survivors in the Arnhem area was to withdraw if possible, following huge casualties. The British 1st Airborne lost over 7,500 men killed, wounded or captured from its total strength of 10,000. To the south, the US 82nd Airborne lost about 1,400 from over 7,500 dropped, while the US 101st lost over 2,100 from about the same number. The RAF and the USAAF lost 261 aircraft, in addition to all the gliders. Precise German casualties are not known but they must have been heavy. This was the largest airborne operation the Allies had ever mounted and it had ended in failure.

The prospect of ending the European war in 1944 had disappeared, but the bridgehead at Nijmegen was held despite determined attempts by the Germans to retake the position. Attacks by the Luftwaffe on the bridges over the Waal were unsuccessful but German frogmen managed to blow up parts of both the railway and road bridges during the night of 28 September, by using floating demolition charges. Royal Engineers repaired the road bridge almost immediately and also built a Bailey bridge over the river.

While these events were taking place, the First Canadian Army was battling its way along the French coast of the English Channel and the southern part of the

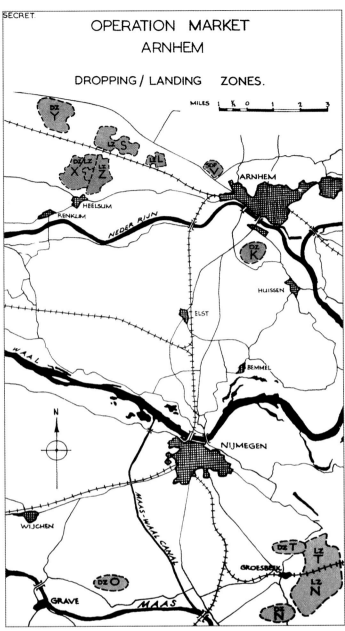

Operation Market, Arnhem. *The National Archives: AIR 41/67*

North Sea. Its task was to either capture the ports or invest them, and then to clear the Germans out of their positions on both sides of the Scheldt estuary. This would enable the port of Antwerp, already in British hands, to be brought into full use for the purpose of supplying the Allied armies pressing against the German frontier.

The Canadian Army consisted of two armoured and four infantry divisions, but one of the latter was immobilised since its transport was being used by other forces. The next task was to capture the heavily defended port of Boulogne, which was first invested on 5 September. As with Le Havre, the RAF was called in to soften up the enemy defences. The RAF's Second Tactical Air Force made a series of attacks with medium bombers from 8 September, and the Germans allowed about 8,000 French civilians to leave the city. A massive attack was also made in daylight by the RAF's Bomber Command on 17 September, when 688 aircraft dropped 3,391 tons of bombs. These continual air attacks, combined with the shelling from the Canadians and their advances into the outskirts, resulted in the surrender on 22 September by the commander, General Ferdinand Heim. Over 9,500 Germans were taken prisoner but the capture of Boulogne had cost the Canadians about 650 casualties, primarily from artillery fire. The port had been largely destroyed and could not be brought into operation for about three weeks.

The next objective was the port of Calais, which had also been invested by the Canadians on 5 September. This threatened the narrow Strait of Dover with its coastal batteries guns and the huge long-range guns on Cap Gris-Nez. These needed to be eliminated, if only to ensure that Boulogne could be used. The port was well defended by about 7,000 troops and part of the approaches had been flooded. Some advances into the outskirts had already been made by Canadian infantry, but now it required the same treatment as Boulogne. The RAF's Bomber Command despatched 188 aircraft on 24 September, but low cloud prevented some bombing. Eight aircraft which descended below cloud were shot down by accurate flak.

Low cloud also hampered 872 bombers sent out on the following day, and only 287 could release their loads through breaks below. A very effective attack followed on 26 September, when 722 aircraft dropped accurately on targets in Calais and on Cap Gris-Nez. The RAF's Bomber Command despatched 341 aircraft on 27 September and they came down low to bomb visually below the cloud. Yet another attack by 494 aircraft took place on the following day, but once again low cloud prevented most of the bombers from releasing their loads. These attacks were supplemented by medium bombers of the Second Tactical Air Force. At the same time, the Canadians made steady advances and were nearing the inner line of defences. On 29 September the German commander, Oberst Ludwig Schröder asked for an armistice to evacuate civilians and this was granted for twenty-four hours. The German defences collapsed when the Canadians resumed their attacks and over 9,000 of their troops were rounded up.

The next port geographically was that of Dunkirk, near the Belgian border, which was another of Hitler's 'fortresses'. But the Canadians had more important business elsewhere, further along the coast. On 16 September, they had left their 4th Special Service Brigade to invest the port and moved enough forces to begin taking over the Antwerp area from the British Second Army. Dunkirk was the port from which most of the British Expeditionary Force and some of their allies had withdrawn to England in June 1940, after their defeat in the German Blitzkrieg. In October 1944, a strong German garrison was left there to contemplate a reversal of roles, except that their only means of escape were by a handful of midget submarines. They remained bottled up, in increasing hardship, until the end of the war.

By the end of September, the Canadians had cleared the Germans from the coast of Belgium apart from a large pocket around the harbour of Breskens, on the south bank of the Scheldt estuary. This was held by German forces in an area where much of the land was below sea level and criss-crossed with canals and ditches. Tracts had been flooded by the Germans and the Canadian armour had difficulty in moving through them. But the Allies were now experiencing acute problems in bringing up supplies to their front lines and the clearance of the approaches to Antwerp had become a vital necessity.

By this time General Crerar needed to return to England for medical treatment and Lieutenant-General Guy G. Simonds took over his position temporarily as commander of the First Canadian Army. His II Corps, with I Corps of the Second British Army pushing northwards on its right, fought for the whole of October to clear the Germans from the area south of the Scheldt, against a determined and skilful resistance from the 64th Infantry Division commanded by General K. Eberding. This division had been formed mainly from about 11,000 experienced soldiers returned from the Russian front, plentifully supplied with arms and equipment from the German Fifteenth Army.

Eberding had been given independent authority by Hitler as a 'fortress commander' and his men fought with great resolution, constantly reinforced from German forces north of the Scheldt. RAF Bomber Command took a hand in this operation on 11 October by making a heavy raid against gun batteries at Breskens. However, it was not until 22 October that this port was captured by the Canadians and then more than another week before the remaining area was overrun. The RAF's Second Tactical Air Force provided support throughout the protracted fighting. Eventually about 12,700 Germans were taken prisoner, including Eberding himself. It is true that the terrain over which they fought favoured defence, but the Germans had succeeded in delaying for several weeks the opening of the port of Antwerp, the largest in the European mainland, and seriously hampered the advance of the Allied armies towards the Rhine. Canadian casualties in this operation numbered about 2,000.

During this period, the RAF's Bomber Command also made a series of attacks against the German forces occupying the island of Walcheren and its port of Flushing (Vlissingen) on the north entrance to the Scheldt estuary. Much of this island was reclaimed 'polder' lying below sea level. It was reluctantly decided by the Allies to breach the sea wall at Westkapelle on the west of the island and flood many of the German positions, in spite of the damage this would cause to the properties of Dutch residents. The first of these operations took place with over 250 aircraft of the RAF's Bomber Command on 3 October when a breach was made in the great sea wall, which was over 200ft wide, from the earthquake effect of a mass of bomb explosions. Another breach was made on 7 October at Veere on the eastern side of the island.

The two breaches caused the sea to enter and flood most of Walcheren, but the gun batteries were not

In the course of extensive operations by the Allied Expeditionary Air Force over Belgium and the Netherlands on 11 September 1944, Mitchells and Bostons of the Second Tactical Air Force bombed the Breskens end of the ferry to Flushing. This was being used by the Germans as an escape route during their retreat. The bombing was well concentrated, causing damage to jetties, craft used as ferries, buildings and motor transport. *The National Archives: AIR 34/843*

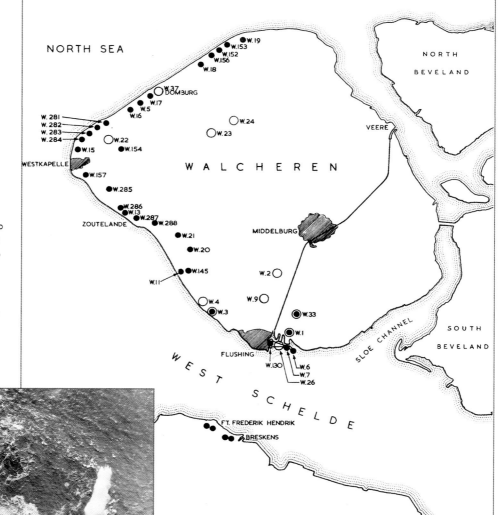

PRE-ARRANGED AIR ATTACKS ON WALCHEREN

17 SEPT. — 30 OCT. 1944

LEGEND

● AMMUNITION DUMP

○ BATTERY (ATTACKED BY 2ND. T.A.F.)

● BATTERY (ATTACKED BY BOMBER COMMAND)

● STRONGPOINT

● RADAR STATION

NORTH SEA

NORTH BEVELAND

W.19
W.153
W.152
W.156
W.18
W.37 DOMBURG
W.17
W.5
W.16
W.281
W.282
W.283
W.284
W.22
W.154
W.24
W.23
W.15
W.157
WESTKAPELLE
W.285
W.286
W.13
W.287
W.288
ZOUTELANDE
W.21
W.20
W.145
W.11
W.4
W.3
W.9
W.2
W.33
W.1
W.30
W.6
W.7
W.26
FLUSHING
WALCHEREN
VEERE
MIDDELBURG
SLOE CHANNEL
SOUTH BEVELAND
WEST SCHELDE
FT. FREDERIK HENDRIK
BRESKENS

Bomber Command despatched 252 Lancasters and two Mosquitos in daylight on 3 October 1944 to attack the sea wall at Westkapelle in Walcheren Island, in order to flood the German coastal batteries which dominated the approaches to Antwerp. They attacked in waves, dropping high-explosive bombs which eventually breached the wall and caused the sea to pour through. This photograph was taken by a Lancaster of No. 115 Squadron based at Witchford in Cambridgeshire. No aircraft were lost in this operation. *The National Archives: AIR 14/3677*

silenced. German coastal artillery could still fire on the Scheldt estuary from both Walcheren and South-Beveland to its east. The two were connected by a causeway reclaimed from the sea, over which ran a railway and a road from the mainland to the port of Flushing. South-Beveland was equal in size to Walcheren but linked to the mainland by a narrow isthmus. Both areas were defended by the 70th Infantry Division, manned principally by soldiers who were considered physically unfit to serve in more active theatres. There were also three battalions manning the 'fortresses' plus a number of naval and flak units. Their defences, which included numerous gun emplacements, formed serious obstacles. The whole area needed to be cleared before supply vessels could sail through the Scheldt and reach Antwerp.

An attempt by the Canadians to storm South-Beveland began on 24 October. A brigade advanced up the isthmus from the mainland, preceded by an artillery barrage and an attack by the RAF's Second Tactical Air Force. The men made steady progress despite craters, road blocks, anti-tank guns and slithery conditions along narrow pathways. Two days later seaborne forces landed on the south coast ahead of them, transported about 9 miles from the south bank of the Scheldt in 'Buffalo' landing craft. Reinforcements arrived in more Buffaloes, LCAs (Landing Craft Assault) and 'Terrapins' (the British equivalent of the American DUKW). DD (duplex-drive) amphibious tanks also came ashore. A bridgehead was established while more troops crossed the isthmus and support was provided by the RAF's fighter-bombers. By 31 October, the whole of South-Beveland was in Canadian hands and many prisoners taken, but Walcheren was still occupied by the Germans.

The causeway connecting South-Beveland with Walcheren presented difficulties for an assault, being long, narrow, open and straight. Nevertheless the Canadians made attempts on 31 October but were beaten back by strong enemy fire. A further attempt on the following day made more progress but the enemy counter-attacked and the outcome remained in doubt, despite support from RAF Typhoon fighter-bombers. The German defences were then outflanked by seaborne landings and both Canadian forces linked up to advance on Middelburg, in the centre of Walcheren.

At the same time, seaborne landings were mounted against Flushing and Westkapelle. Gun batteries had been targeted by the RAF's Bomber Command, on 21, 23, 29 and 30 October. Those at Flushing were attacked by Mosquitos of the RAF's Second Tactical Air Force before dawn on 1 November, shortly before British Commandos from Breskens harbour began landing on nearby beaches. These secured a bridgehead and enabled the British 155th Brigade to land. The defenders were taken by surprise and initial casualties were fairly light, but then began the more difficult task of clearing the port strongpoint by strongpoint and house by house.

The batteries at Westkapelle were shelled shortly after these landings by the battleship HMS *Warspite* with the monitors HMS *Erebus* and HMS *Roberts*, timed to precede the arrival of a seaborne force of over 150 landing craft from Ostend. They approached under intense fire and many craft were hit, but the troops landed under cover fire from rocket craft and support from Typhoons of the RAF's Second Tactical Air Force. Commandos and Royal Marines stormed ashore and after a stiff fight managed to subdue the defenders and capture the batteries.

Fighting at Walcheren continued, the most difficult part being clearing of the enemy from warehouses and shipping at Flushing. The remaining 2,000 Germans at Middelburg under General Wilhelm Daser surrendered on 6 November but

THE BATTLE FOR THE APPROACHES TO ANTWERP

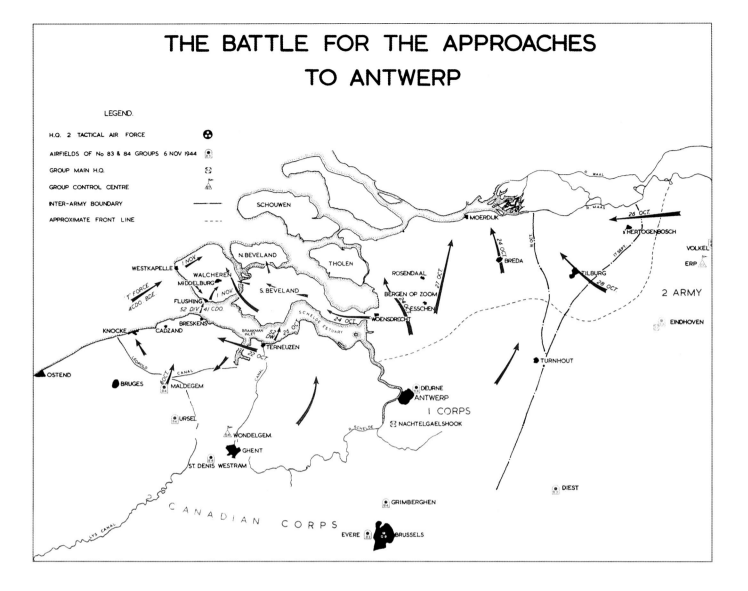

The battle for the approaches to Antwerp. *The National Archives: AIR 41/68*

survivors in other strongpoints fought on for another two days. The British and Canadians were welcomed with wild enthusiasm by Dutch citizens, despite the privations and destruction they had suffered. Apart from those who lost their lives, about 8,000 Germans were taken prisoner.

The achievements of the First Canadian Army in the previous two months had been at the cost of about 17,000 casualties, of whom about 3,000 had been killed in action. But now that both banks of the Scheldt had been cleared, the work of clearing about 80 miles of the approaches to Antwerp could begin. This was an enormous task, involving ten squadrons of minesweepers, and it was not until 26 November that it was completed to the satisfaction of the Royal Navy. The first coasters reached Antwerp on that day and a huge convoy of nineteen Liberty ships arrived two days later.

The British Second Army also made progress during the period when the north bank of the Scheldt was being won from the enemy. It had been ordered by Field-Marshal Montgomery on 16 October to make a strong thrust westwards towards the Dutch towns of 's-Hertogenbosch and Breda. This task fell to the XII Corps with two armoured divisions, two infantry divisions and the 6th Guards Armoured Brigade, plus other specialised units. The advances were strongly supported by the RAF's Second Tactical Air Force, which attacked bridges over the Maas and German positions. The towns of 's-Hertogenbosch and Tilburg were taken by 27 October, after fierce house-to-house fighting, and counter-attacks by the German Fifteenth Army beaten back. The advances also coincided with an advance by I Corps of the Canadian First Army, which included the US 104th Infantry Division on temporary detachment as well as the 1st Polish Armoured Division. These forces reached Breda on 29 October and managed to clear the town of its defenders. Feldmarschall von Rundstedt wished to withdraw his forces to behind the Waal but as usual Hitler ordered them to stand fast south of the Maas. They were pushed back gradually, under devastating air attack and losing more than 8,000 prisoners, until the survivors were forced behind the Waal.

Up to this period, the British 21st Army Group could rely on about 11,000 tons of supplies arriving daily, mostly brought across the Channel in small coasters. This was roughly sufficient for maintenance but far more was required if a major assault was to be mounted. The railways in north-east France and Belgium, so badly devastated during the Allied air campaign, were being repaired and coming back into service with all possible speed. Coal was required for the engines and for many other civilian purposes, and much of this had to be imported from the United Kingdom. Before any major advance into Germany could be made, great supplies of fuel, ammunition and other resources needed to be built up in rear maintenance areas.

Some relief with petrol supplies arrived by means of PLUTO (Pipe Lines under the Ocean). One of these pipes had come into operation on 18 September from the Isle of Wight to Cherbourg but there were teething troubles and it did not perform well. Three more were laid between Dungeness and Boulogne by 1 November, providing 300 tons a day, and others were being laid which eventually increased the supply tenfold. But of course the petrol still needed to be transported to advanced areas.

The position with the US 12th Army Group, with twenty divisions in forward areas, was even less favourable than the British. At the beginning of October, some divisions had less than two days of supplies, with only paltry amounts in rear maintenance areas. Some of these supplies were being brought via the British Mulberry artificial harbour, but transport from there to the forward divisions was slow and laborious. The ports on the Atlantic coast were of little

A British soldier covering a German member of a flak unit, wearing a paratrooper's helmet and trousers, who had run out of a burning house in the Dutch village of St Michielsgesel, on 24 October 1944. The nearby city of 's-Hertogenbosch (Bois Le Duc), which was the main objective of the British forces, was liberated three days later. *British Official*

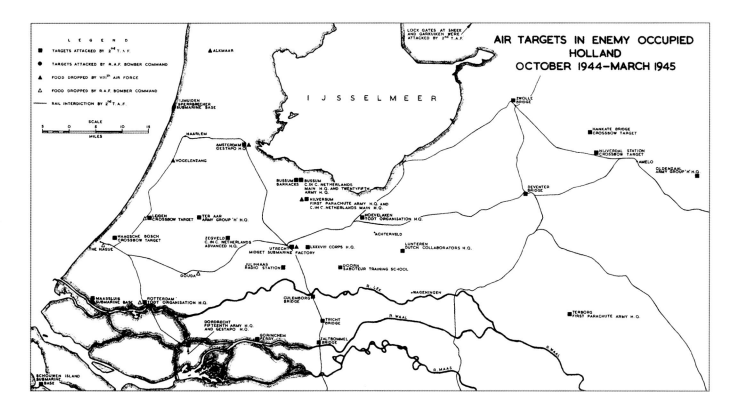

Air targets in enemy-occupied Holland, October 1944–March 1945. *The National Archives: AIR 41/68*

use at this stage. Bordeaux had surrendered in early September and Brest on 18 September, after much destruction of their facilities. Those of Lorient and St-Nazaire were left invested by the Allies until the end of the war.

The port of Marseille had been blocked by sunken ships but was cleared fairly rapidly and the first stores were offloaded on 15 September. From this time, Marseille and Toulon became of increasing importance in supplying the US 6th Army Group. Le Havre and Rouen were allocated to the Americans but the improvement in supplies was only gradual. It was not until late November that the supply situation for the US 12th Army Group was eased.

It had been hoped in September that German morale was beginning to crack and that the Wehrmacht did not have the strength or resolution to withstand another major assault. By the following month, it had become clear that this optimism was unfounded. The Germans had been able to stabilise many positions along their western front and were using civilian labour, from the occupied territories and their own nationals, to build more entrenchments and engage in industrial work. These workers included women as well as young teenagers.

Nevertheless, with the opening of the great port of Antwerp, the Allies could look forward to a far more favourable situation and plan the prosecution of the war with more confidence. In anticipation of this benefit, General Eisenhower and his deputy Air Chief Marshal Sir Arthur Tedder had met Field-Marshal Sir Bernard Montgomery and General Omar Bradley in Brussels on 16 October to discuss future operations. At that time, the activities of the British 21st Army Group in clearing the approaches to Antwerp were known and approved. It was decided that the US 12th Army Group should attempt to gain a bridgehead over the Rhine south of Cologne in early November. For this to be achieved, the US Ninth Army would strike northwards between the Rhine and the Maas (Meuse), while the British Second Army fought its way south-west to link up with it. Then the crossing of the Rhine would be made further south by the US First Army, protected on its right flank by the US Third Army.

Of course, the Germans could not fail to be aware of the importance of Antwerp to the Allies. One way they could try to hinder its usefulness was by their

V-weapons. When the launching sites for the V-1 rockets along the Pas de Calais were overrun by the Canadians in September, these weapons were directed against England from sites in the Netherlands or from specially adapted Heinkel He111s flying at night over the North Sea. But there was a deadlier weapon which also came into German service. This was the larger V-2 rocket, which was launched almost vertically, had a greater range, and flew at a height and speed which made it impossible to shoot down. The first had been fired against England on 8 September and many others continued to arrive until almost the end of the war.

Both these V-weapons could be directed against Continental targets and Antwerp was a prime objective. The first V-2 exploded there on 13 October, followed by the first V-1 on the same day. Thereafter, Antwerp underwent frequent bombardments from these inaccurate weapons, which exploded almost entirely in civilian areas rather than on port installations. The worst incident occurred in the afternoon on 16 December 1944 when a V-2 exploded in the packed Cinema Rex in the central De Keyserlei district, killing 576 civilians and soldiers and wounding 291 others. The last V-1 came down in an eastern district of Antwerp on 30 March 1945 and the last V-2 on 27 March 1945 at Mortsel, near Antwerp. It is estimated that 2,448 V-1s and 1,261 V-2s exploded in the Antwerp district before the end of the war, resulting in the deaths of 3,653 civilians or military personnel and 6,205 wounded.

Meanwhile, there had been two high-level policy decisions concerning Allied air operations. On 12 September 1944, the 'Octagon' conference had opened in Quebec, attended by Roosevelt, Churchill and their Chiefs of Staff. The meeting

The interior of the booking office at Wimbledon station, Southern Railway, after the station was hit by a V-1 flying bomb on 15 September 1944. *The National Archives: AIR 20/4376*

reflected the optimism that was felt at the time by the high commanders in the European theatre. One result, however, was a change in command. It was decided that Air Chief Marshal Sir Trafford Leigh-Mallory's position as Air Commander-in-Chief was becoming redundant and he was posted to Southeast Asia from 16 October. The RAF's Second Tactical Air Force under Air Marshal Sir Arthur Coningham and the US Ninth Air Force under Major-General Hoyt S. Vandenberg would then report directly to the Deputy Supreme Commander, Air Chief Marshal Sir Arthur Tedder.

The other decision had been made on 25 September by the Combined Chiefs of Staff and concerned strategic bombing against Germany by both the US Eighth Air Force and the RAF's Bomber Command. Up to this period the campaign had concentrated mainly on the area bombing of German cities, with the objective of destroying manufacturing capacity within them and reducing the ability to wage war. This policy, initiated by the British War Cabinet, had been implemented for

On 6 October 1944, Bomber Command despatched 254 Halifaxes, 46 Lancasters and 20 Mosquitos on a daylight attack against synthetic oil plants at Sterkrade and Scholven in Germany. Accurate results were obtained, although seven Halifaxes and two Lancasters failed to return. This photograph was taken from 18,000ft over Sterkrade by a Halifax III of No. 578 Squadron based at Burn in Yorkshire. *The National Archives: AIR 14/3677*

Part of the Krupps Armaments Works at Essen, showing extremely heavy damage after a night raid by 1,035 aircraft of Bomber Command on 23/4 October 1944, followed by a daylight raid by 771 aircraft on 25 October 1944. Twelve aircraft were lost, but the two attacks caused many casualties and so much destruction that much of the surviving industry was dispersed to various locations. *The National Archives: AIR 37/1231*

over two years by the RAF's Bomber Command, commanded by Air Chief Marshal Sir Arthur Harris. It had caused enormous destruction and many civilians had been killed or injured, but German output of war material had nevertheless increased substantially, under the guidance of Reichsminister Albert Speer. He had dispersed the industries, introduced flow production and employed forced labour from the occupied territories.

The new directive to the two strategic bombing forces instructed them to concentrate on destroying Germany's synthetic oil plants and the country's transportation system. This policy met with the approval of the commander of the US Eighth Air Force, General Carl Spaatz, but was bitterly opposed by the commander-in-chief of the RAF's Bomber Command, Air Chief Marshal Sir Arthur Harris. It was, of course, more difficult to carry out 'pinpoint' bombing of targets with a force which operated mainly at night, especially when many of the targets were beyond the range of radar aids from stations in England. During October 1944, over two-thirds of the bombs the RAF dropped on Germany continued to be aimed at cities. This led to a further directive on 1 November 1944 in which the new policy was set out with greater clarity. Harris still continued with his policy and wrangled with the Chief of Air Staff, Air Chief Marshal Sir Charles Portal, until 18 January 1945 when he offered to resign. His resignation was not accepted and the policy was modified to permit him to carry it out only whenever conditions for bombing at night permitted.*

---

* Postwar evidence from the American and British Bombing Survey Units confirms that bombing of oil plants and the transportation system did seriously impair Germany's capacity to wage war. Estimates from West Germany after the war give the figures for civilians killed during the bombing campaign in the Greater German Reich (as it existed on 31 December 1942) as 635,000. By comparison, about 61,000 civilians were killed by air raids in Britain during the entire war. The number of dwellings destroyed in Germany is given at 3,370,000, about one-fifth of the total residential units in the country.

Troops of the US First Army entered the Hürtgen Forest, east of the German city of Aachen, on 13 September 1944 but found the conditions extremely difficult. There were almost no roads and the wooded terrain was intersected with deep valleys. German resistance was fierce and effective. American records show that their First Army suffered 12,707 casualties in this sector during the next 99 days. In this photograph, an American soldier is aiming a 'Bazooka' anti-tank thrower at a German pillbox while his comrade dives to the ground after loading a 6cm rocket. *The National Archives: CAB 106/1010*

On 17 September 1944, paratroopers of the US 101st Airborne Division dropped on assigned areas near Son, Sint Oedenrode and Veghel in the Netherlands, as part of operation 'Market Garden'. They were advancing towards Nijmegen when German tanks began to fire on them, hitting some ammunition trucks. This photograph shows US troops taking cover in a ditch. Typhoons of the RAF's Second Tactical Air Force soon arrived and knocked out the tanks. *US Official*

The German 'fortress' of Boulogne was attacked in daylight on 17 September 1944 by 762 aircraft of Bomber Command, in preparation for an assault by Allied ground forces. More than 3,000 tons of bombs rained down, in and around the city. This photograph shows marker flares, bombs falling, and a Lancaster below on the left. The German garrison surrendered five days later, but it was not until 12 October that Allied supply ships were able to enter the shattered dock area. *The National Archives: AIR 37/1231*

The effect of flooding after the operation by Bomber Command on 3 October 1944, showing a gap of about 100yd in the sea wall at Westkapelle in Walcheren Island, with water gushing through. The Dutch citizens in this area had been warned by leaflets dropped the day before of an impending bombing attack. *The National Archives: AIR 37/1231*

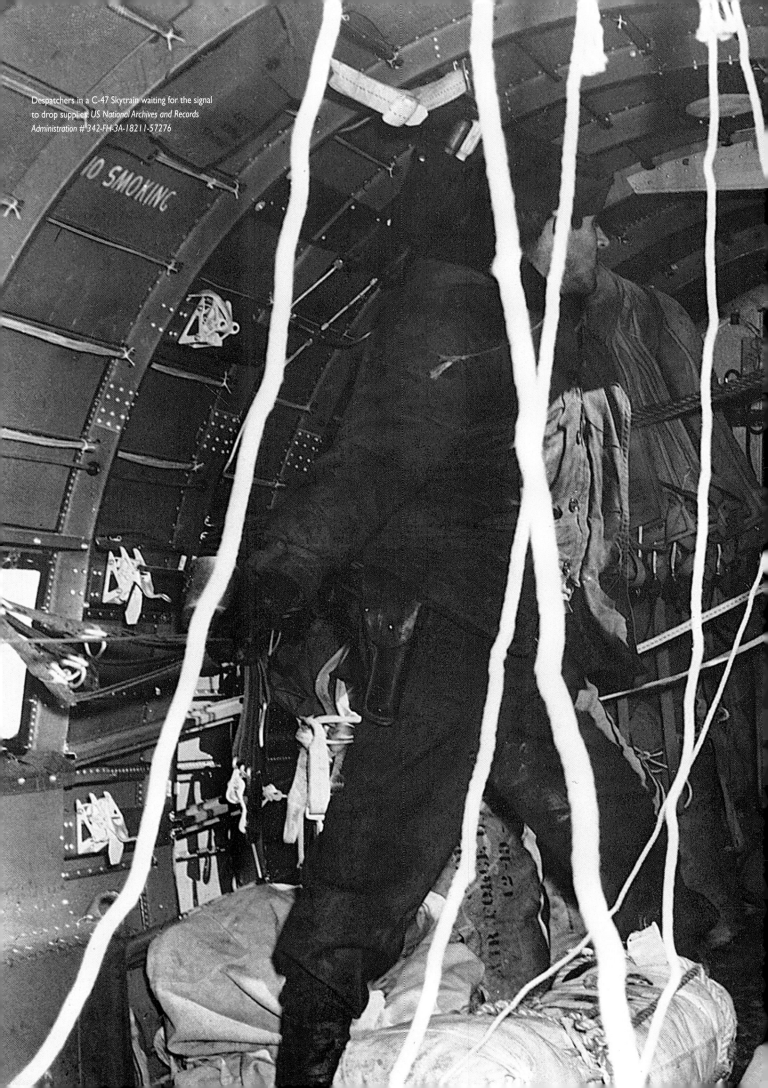

NO SMOKING

Despatchers in a C-47 Skytrain waiting for the signal to drop supplies. *US National Archives and Records Administration # 342-FH-3A-18211-57276*

The Northrop P61 Black Widow nightfighter first entered service in March 1944. It was equipped with air interception radar, powered by two Pratt & Whitney R-2800-65 engines of 2,000hp, carried a crew of three and was armed with four 20mm cannons and four .50 machine-guns. The 422nd and 425th Nightfighter Squadrons of the US Ninth Air Force were equipped with these machines from May 1944. *US National Archives and Records Administration # 18-WP-46-100521*

A-20 Havocs of the 416th Bombardment Group, US Ninth Air Force, began to arrive at Colommiers airfield in France on 27 September 1944. Despite the wreckage caused by Allied bombing, the airfield was soon back in operational condition. *US National Archives and Records Administration # 342-FH-3A-17341-A-61347*

A mosaic built up from three vertical photographs taken on 19 September 1944, showing Airspeed Horsa and General Aircraft Hamilcar gliders littering the landing ground at Renkum Heath, 3 miles south-west of Wolfheze near Arnhem. Units of the British 1st Airborne Division, commanded by Major-General Robert Urquart, had landed in that area two days before. *The National Archives: AIR*

French civilian workers on 27 September 1944, repairing a runway on an airfield for P-61 Black Widow nightfighters of the US Ninth Air Force. The first to arrive in France was the 422th Nightfighter Squadron, based at Maupertus near Cherbourg for a month from 25 July 1944. *US National Archives and Records Administration # 342-FH-3A-17283-C-61349*

This A-20 Havoc 'La France Libre', photographed in France with its three aircrew and two ground crew, was the first in the US Ninth Air Force to complete 100 operational missions against German military objectives. *US National Archives and Records Administration # 342-FH-3A-16953-A-54752*

A British infantryman watching a Sherman tank passing burnt-out houses in Asten, 4 miles south-south-west of the Dutch town of Deurne, in late September 1944. The forces had thrust north and east of Eindhoven, crossed the Bois le Duc canal, and were about 18 miles from the German border. *British Official*

A long line of German civilians leaving the town of Ubach-Palenburg, 10 miles north-west of Aachen, after it had been captured by the US 30th Infantry Division on 3 October 1944. Two battalions of the German 246th Infantry Division counter-attacked on the following day and a fierce battle raged with tanks of the US 2nd Division, continuing until 8 October. The town began to fall into ruins and the civilians were evacuated to an uncertain future. American jeeps can be seen driving in the opposite direction. *US Official*

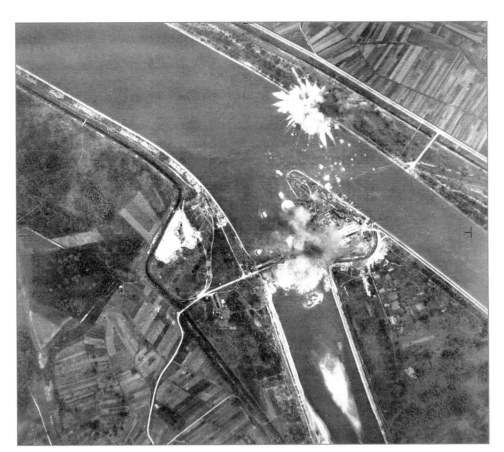

On 7 October 1944, No. 617 Squadron of Bomber Command despatched thirteen Lancasters on a special operation against the lock gates of the Kembs dam on the Rhine, near the Swiss border, with the objective of preventing the Germans from flooding the valley near Mulhouse and hindering the advance of American and French troops. The Lancasters were escorted by P-51 Mustangs of the USAAF. Seven Lancasters dropped 'Tallboy' bombs of 12,000lb from about 7,500ft, as shown in this photograph, while the others bombed from 1,000ft. The lock gates were put out of action, but two Lancasters in the low-level section were shot down by flak. *The National Archives: AIR 14/4677*

The German city of Aachen, near the Belgian border, was ruined by British and American air attacks before it was surrounded by units of the US First Army on 14 October 1944. The air attacks continued until the German commander Lieutenant-Colonel Wilck, signed an unconditional surrender seven days later. *The National Archives: CAB 106/1010*

This photograph shows the historical day of 1 October 1944 when the first British forces crossed the frontier into Germany. After capturing the town of Beek in the south-west Netherlands on 25 September, they fought their way past Sittard to the frontier. A British tank has passed the sentry box on the left and is heading towards the German town of Tüddern, with an American soldier lying prone in the firing position. The Sherwood Foresters worked in co-operation with American airborne troops in this operation. *British Official*

The RAF made an attempt to widen the gap in the sea wall at Westkapelle in the afternoon of 17 October 1944, when Bomber Command despatched forty-seven Lancasters and three Mosquitos, escorted by twenty-four Spitfires of Fighter Command. Although the bombing was accurate and more sea water gushed through the opening, the gap appeared to be little changed. *The National Archives: AIR 37/1231*

Girls of the Women's Auxiliary Territorial Service running through snow to their anti-aircraft posts, south-west of Antwerp, during the battle against V-1 flying bombs. The first British anti-aircraft unit was placed in position on 11 October 1944 and more units, including American, soon followed. They were all placed under the command of an American, Brigadier-General Clare H. Armstrong, and continued in action for several months. A range-finder can be seen in the centre of this photograph. *British Official*

The US Eighth Air Force bombed Minden in Nordrhein-Westfalen on several occasions. Its main target was the aqueduct of the Mittelland canal over the river Weser, which was used by barges and small ships carrying cargoes between the river Rhine in the Ruhr area and the river Elbe. The first attack took place on 26 October 1944, when 246 B-24 Liberators were despatched with an escort of 205 P-51 Mustangs and 36 P-47 Thunderbolts, all of which returned without loss. This photograph shows the collapsed aqueduct and bomb splashes in the river Wesser. *Author's Collection*

Bomber Command provided seventy-five Lancasters on 21 October 1944 for a daylight attack on a German coastal battery at Flushing in the Dutch island of Walcheren. Bombing was extremely accurate but one Lancaster was lost. This photograph was taken from a Lancaster of No. 115 Squadron based at Witchford in Cambridgeshire.
The National Archives: AIR 14/3677

Bombs falling accurately on the road–rail bridge at Zutphen in the Netherlands, 15 miles north-west of Arnhem, on 14 October 1944. The attack was made by thirty-five Mitchells and Bostons of the Second Tactical Air Force, but unfortunately the bombs dropped by six Mitchells were less accurate and destroyed 105 houses, killing seventy-three civilians. *The National Archives: AIR 34/845*

In a determined low-level attack on 31 October 1944, twenty-five Mosquitos of the Second Tactical Air Force, escorted by eight Mustangs, attacked two four-storey buildings in the University of Aarhus in Denmark. This was a Gestapo headquarters where thousands of records of the Danish resistance were held. Both buildings were destroyed. *The National Archives: AIR 37/1231*

The assault on the city of Flushing (Vlissengen) in the Dutch island of Walcheren on 1 November 1944, supported by fire from warships of the Royal Navy, with troops advancing along the waterfront. *British Official*

British Commandos landing on the Dutch island of Walcheren, near the mouth of the Scheldt, on 1 November 1944. They have disembarked from amphibious 'Buffalo' tanks. *British Official*

The landings on the Dutch islands of Walcheren and South-Beveland began on 1 November 1944, with 176 Buffalo tank landing craft manned by units of the Royal Marine Commandos, the 52nd Lowland Division and the 11th Royal Tank Regiment. This Buffalo was manoeuvring into position shortly before the assault took place. *British Official*

CHAPTER SEVEN

ATTACKS AND COUNTER- ATTACKS

In early November 1944, the Allied forces facing the Wehrmacht consisted of three Army Groups, with General Dwight D. Eisenhower as the Supreme Commander. In the northern sector, there was the British and Canadian 21st Army Group commanded by Field-Marshal Sir Bernard Montgomery. Within this, there was the British Second Army commanded by Lieutenant-General Sir Miles C. Dempsey and the First Canadian Army commanded by Lieutenant-General Henry D.G. Crerar, who had returned to active duty following his sick leave. In the central sector, there was the US 12th Army Group commanded by General Omar N. Bradley and consisting of four Armies; these were the US First Army commanded by General Courtney H. Hodges, the US Third Army commanded by General George S. Patton, the US Ninth Army commanded by Lieutenant William H. Simpson, and the US Fifteenth Army commanded by Lieutenant-General Leonard T. Gerow. In the southern sector, there was the US 7th Army Group commanded by General Jacob L. Devers, formed from the forces which had invaded the south of France. These consisted of the US Seventh Army commanded by Lieutenant-General Alexander M. Patch and the French First Army commanded by General Jean de Lattre de Tassigny. In addition to these three Army Groups, there was the First Allied Airborne Army commanded by Lieutenant-General Lewis H. Brereton and consisting of two British and four US divisions.

With the capture of Antwerp and the clearance of its approaches, General Eisenhower could begin to implement the next phase of the Allied operations. This was to be in three parts, although they would overlap. In the first phase, the US 12th Army Group in the central sector would commence operations on 10 November 1944 by advancing eastwards from the German city of Aachen, which it had captured on 21 October after a siege lasting five days. It would then cross the Rhine north of the Ardennes, in order to establish a bridgehead south of Cologne. At the same time, the British and Canadian 21st Army Group in the northern sector would attack the enemy holding the area west of the Maas (Meuse) and then advance to the Rhine from the Venlo area of the Netherlands. In the second phase the US 12th Army Group would strike into the Saar, timing

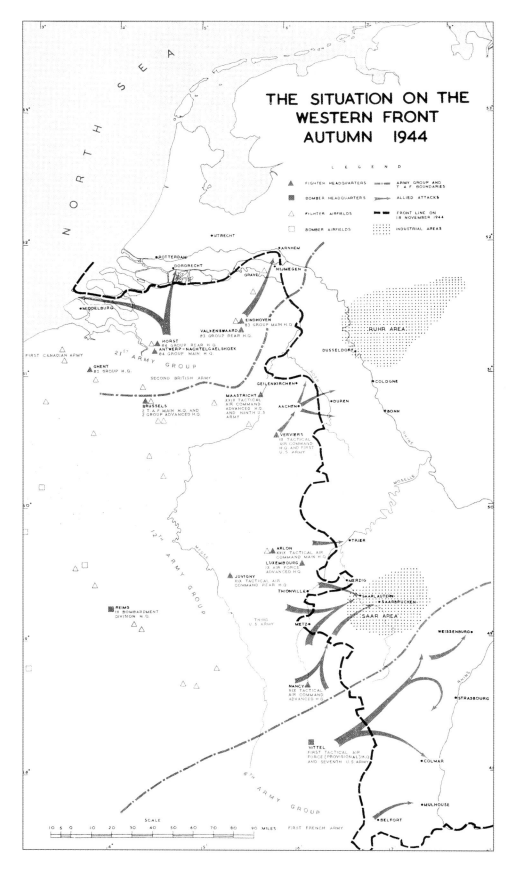

THE SITUATION ON THE
WESTERN FRONT
AUTUMN 1944

its operation so as to assist the operations of the British and Canadians. The third phase would concern a general advance of all three Groups into the German hinterland.

Opposing these formidable forces, Adolf Hitler was both the Supreme Commander of the German Armed Forces and the Commander-in-Chief of the German Army. On 10 November 1944, his Oberkommando West was commanded by Feldmarschall Gerd von Rundstedt, who in turn commanded three reorganised Army Groups. In the northern sector was Army Group H commanded by Generaloberst Kurt Student, consisting of the First Parachute Army and the Twenty-Fifth Army. In the central sector was Army Group B under Feldmarschall Walther Model, consisting of the Fifth Panzer Army, the Sixth SS Panzer Army, the Seventh Army and the Nineteenth Army. In the south was Army Group G under Generaloberst Johannes Blaskowitz and consisting of the First Army and the Nineteenth Army.

Meanwhile, the US First Army had suffered severely during October from a stubborn and skilful defence by the Germans in the Hürtgen forest, on the approaches to the German town of Düren on the river Roer. This thickly wooded country had proved very difficult to penetrate, while military supplies had not been replenished at the required rate. The Americans had driven out most of the enemy, but at the cost of very heavy casualties. In order to implement a directive from Eisenhower in early November, General Bradley regrouped his US 12th Army Group. The US Ninth Army was moved to the north of Aachen, to support the troops of the US First Army in an advance towards Düren and then the Rhine.

The weather was unsuitable for air support when the American troops were ready to start operations and there was a delay until 16 November, when the US Eighth Air Force delivered a massive raid with over 1,200 B-17 Fortresses and B-24 Liberators, escorted by 265 fighters, against communications in the rear of the enemy front lines. On the same day, RAF Bomber Command despatched over 900 Lancasters, Halifaxes and Mosquitos, heavily escorted by fighters, in daylight against similar targets. The German towns of Düren, Jülich and Heinsberg were almost completely destroyed, with civilian casualties known to have exceeded 3,000. Nevertheless, the American troops met determined resistance and it was not until 28 November that leading elements of the US Ninth Army managed to reach the river Roer, less than halfway towards their objective of the Rhine south of Cologne. At the same time, the US First Army had great difficulty in clearing the enemy from the north-eastern edge of the Hürtgen forest and once more suffered heavy casualties. Reinforcements arrived and renewed the attack, but they did not reach the river Roer until 15 December. By this time, the two US armies had taken over 25,000 casualties against stiffening German resistance and were still 25 miles from the Rhine.

In this period, RAF Bomber Command made daylight attacks against dams on the river Roer and its tributary the Urft, at the request of General Bradley. It was hoped that these could be breached in the same way that the RAF had breached the sea wall at Walcheren and flooded part of the German defences. Fifty-six Lancasters, escorted by fighters, made an attempt on 5 December against the Schwammenauel dam on the Roer but the target was covered with cloud. The next attempt was made on 8 December by 205 Lancasters and Mosquitos, escorted by fighters, but once again the bombing was affected by low cloud. A final raid was made on 11 December against the Urft dam by 238 Lancasters and Mosquitos, escorted as usual by fighters. Hits were scored on this occasion but the dam was not breached. These attacks were then discontinued since they were diverting effort from the strategic bombing campaign. Indeed, the adverse weather conditions and the difficult terrain prevented both the American and the British strategic and tactical air forces from giving effective support to the ground forces in this period.

In the northern sector, the British and Canadian 21st Army Group also began to advance. The First Canadian Army took over responsibilities on the Nijmegen front while on 14 November two corps of the British Second Army fought their way eastward towards the area of Venlo on the east bank of the river Maas. The British made good progress at first and on 23 November reached Blerick, on the west bank of the river opposite Venlo. Here the ground was so soft and heavily mined that tanks made slow progress. The troops were stalled for a while, but on 3 December they made a successful attack on the town with the aid of artillery and support from the RAF's Second Tactical Air Force. By then, the winter weather had arrived and the Maas was in full flood. To their south, the third corps attacked eastward towards Geilenkirchen where it linked up with the advancing troops of the US 12th Army Group. The German town fell on 17 November after a stiff fight. It was on the river Wurm, a tributary of the Roer, which in turn flowed into the Maas.

By then, the combined Allied advance had halted and it seemed that the troops in the northern and central sectors would have to sit out the winter and await more favourable weather. Although they had managed to fight their way over the Siegfried Line (known as the 'West Wall' by the Germans) in the area of Aachen, they had not reached the Rhine.

Only in the southern sector, in the approaches to the Saar, did results reach expectations and even exceed them. Here, General Patton's US Third Army began to advance on 13 November, with Lieutenant-General Patch's US Seventh Army (from the US 6th Army Group) on its right. Two days later, these crossed the German frontier and forced the enemy back on a broad front as far as the Siegfried Line. Moreover, General de Tassigny's First French Army, also from the US Sixth Army Group, advanced further south along the Swiss border to the north of Basle, leaving only a pocket of German troops in the area of Colmar. These operations were not without heavy loss, however, for the US Sixth Army alone suffered 28,000 casualties.

There was disappointment in SHAEF at the failure to achieve a bridgehead over the Rhine. Field-Marshal Montgomery saw this as justifying his objection to attacking on such a broad front. On 30 November, he wrote to General Eisenhower recommending that the US 12th Army Group and the British and Canadian 21st Army Group be placed under the single command of General Bradley, who in turn would serve under his operational command. Eisenhower did not agree with this proposal and in subsequent meetings the status quo was maintained. Winston Churchill was unusually gloomy in a telegram he sent to President Roosevelt on 6 December. He bemoaned the facts that the Rhine had not been breached, the Allied advance up the Italian peninsula had stalled, the bulk of the German forces in the Balkans had escaped back to their homeland from Russian advances, the British were making little progress in Burma, and the Chinese were no longer an effective fighting force in their own country.

Although Roosevelt did not share in this despondency, there was indeed a 'winter of discontent' among the Allies facing the Germans along the Siegfried Line. Hopes had been dashed after the heady days of the late summer when routed German forces were fleeing in disorder through France and Belgium, while taking enormous losses. The surviving enemy

An RAF reconnaissance photograph showing some of the havoc caused by the German military to Dutch homes when they breached the dykes in parts of the country. Hamlets and other buildings were left isolated in the Dutch island of Schouven-Duiveland, flooded to prevent possible seaborne landings by the British and Canadians. *British Official*

An example of the conditions under which the British and Canadians fought from 4 December 1944 in the Arnhem–Nijmegen area, after the Germans breached dykes to stem their advance. Parts of North and South Holland were flooded, as well as the area north of the Nijmegen–Kleve road. *British Official*

forces had rallied and regrouped, recovered their morale, and were fighting skilfully in defence of their Fatherland. There was no longer any doubt about their resolution, for they contested every metre of ground and counter-attacked whenever possible. Another difficulty was the temporary reduction in Allied tactical air support, for the squadrons on the airfields and advanced landing strips were frequently grounded in foul winter weather.

Allied Intelligence believed that the three German Army Groups on this front contained sixty-four divisions on paper but that many were considerably below strength. Their true fighting strength was considered to be equivalent to only about thirty-one divisions, compared with the Allied strength of sixty-five divisions. However, Allied Signals Intelligence (Sigint) reported on 10 December a significant increase in the movement of German train and motor transport in the sector facing Aachen. This was interpreted by SHAEF as evidence that the Ardennes was being used by the enemy as a training ground for new divisions, and to some extent this was true. The Allies appreciated that an attack through this sector by the Sixth SS Panzer Army was a possibility, but so far there was no sign of this happening. Then, on 14 December, decrypts of Luftwaffe signals gave evidence that this air arm was preparing to give support to ground forces for a large-scale offensive. Nevertheless, Field-Marshal Montgomery issued a directive on 16 December to his 21st Army Group stating that the enemy was fighting a defensive campaign and did not have the transport or fuel to mount mobile operations.

Montgomery's appreciation was perfectly logical, but Hitler's military mind dwelt on strategic fantasies rather than logic, despite his remarkable memory for precise details of his Wehrmacht and undoubted frenetic activity. As early as 22 October, he had summoned the Chiefs of Staff of both Feldmarschall von Rundstedt and Feldmarschall Model to attend a conference at his headquarters in East Prussia. They were told that newly formed divisions on the Ardennes front would become available in November but these were to be employed solely on attack from the Eifel district of Germany.

The Eifel is a district of dense pine forests, broken by ridges and the rivers Our, Sauer and Moselle. It faces westwards towards the wooded and hilly area of the Ardennes where the frontiers of Belgium, France and Germany meet, and slopes eastwards to the Rhine. In the centre is a ridge called the Schnee Eifel of over 2,250ft, which formed part of the Siegfried Line defences. The new divisions were intended to join in an attack by Army Group B from this area, with the objective of advancing through the Allied forces north of a line from Luxembourg to Brussels and then Antwerp. The Ardennes was the region through which the Germans had attacked in 1914 and 1940. On this occasion, the assault was intended to separate the British and Canadians from the Americans, deny the Allies their main lines of supply, and transform the campaign in the West.

On 2 December, Hitler sent his instructions to von Rundstedt. The Sixth SS Panzer Army was to attack in the north and the Fifth Panzer Army in the centre, while the Seventh Army covered their flank on the south. The three Armies were to advance simultaneously on a broad front. The operation was codenamed *Die Wacht am Rhein* (The Watch on the Rhine), to give the impression that it concerned the defence of the Rhine south of Cologne. The preliminary movements of the forces were made with the greatest possible secrecy.

Both von Rundstedt and Model agreed privately that it was impossible to achieve the required objectives but they had no option but to obey orders. It also became clear that Hitler himself was in direct command of day-to-day developments. He had planned to begin the assault in late November but a particularly bad period of flying weather was required, to limit the activities of the Allied Air Forces. This did not occur until 16 December when low cloud blanketed the area, with mist and fog obscuring ground movement. These weather conditions were forecast to continue for several days. There could be only very limited operations by Allied strike aircraft and almost no air reconnaissance or photography.

The Sixth SS Panzer Army consisted of LXVII Corps with two Infantry Divisions, I Corps with two Panzer Divisions and one Parachute Division, plus II SS Panzer Korps with two SS Panzer Divisions in reserve. The Fifth Panzer Army consisted of LXVI Corps with two Infantry Divisions; LVIII Panzer Korps with one Panzer Division and one Infantry Division; and XLVII Panzer Korps with one Panzer Division and one Infantry Division, plus the Panzer Lehr Division and the Führer Begleit (Bodyguard) Brigade in reserve. Lastly, the Seventh Army consisted of LXXXV Corps and LXXX Corps, each with two Infantry Divisions.

There was an additional and unusual special force on this occasion, devised by Hitler. This was 150th Armoured Brigade, formed from about 3,500 Commandos who spoke English with varying degrees of proficiency, some with a knowledge of British and American slang and idioms. They wore American uniforms and were equipped with captured American jeeps and scout cars, as well as some Panzers disguised as American tanks. They were commanded by Oberst Otto Skorzeny, an Austrian Nazi who was a favourite of Hitler and had already carried out some daring missions. Among these was an operation when he led a force of airborne Commandos who, on 12 September 1943, had rescued Benito Mussolini from imprisonment in the Abruzzi mountains and then delivered him safely to Germany, where he had formed an Italian puppet government. The orders of Skorzeny's 150th Armoured Brigade were to follow the advanced divisions of the Sixth SS Panzer Army, work their way eastwards, create confusion behind enemy lines, and then seize three bridges over the Maas.

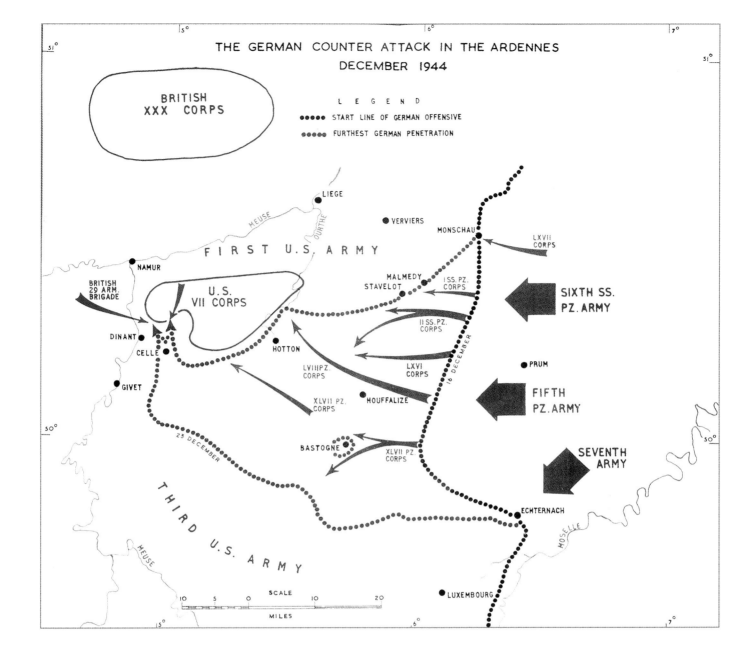

THE GERMAN COUNTER ATTACK IN THE ARDENNES
DECEMBER 1944

BRITISH
XXX CORPS

LEGEND
●●●●● START LINE OF GERMAN OFFENSIVE
●●●●● FURTHEST GERMAN PENETRATION

The German counter-attack in the Ardennes,
December 1944. *The National Archives: AIR 41/68*

The weather before dawn on 16 December was ideal for Hitler's purpose. The 'Battle of the Bulge', as it became generally known, began with a barrage of enemy artillery and mortar fire against the American lines, while V-1s streaked overhead towards Antwerp. The German attacks took place along the broad front, with the Sixth SS Panzer Army in the northern sector, the Fifth Panzer Army in the centre and the Seventh Army in the southern sector.

Infantry led the advance, closely followed by Panzers. The most significant achievement was made by the 3rd Parachute Division of the Sixth SS Panzer Army, which broke through the forward screen of the US First Army between its V and VIII Corps in the area of Losheim. A brigade commanded by SS-Obersturmbannführer Jochen Peiper, part of the 1st SS Panzer Division-Leibstandarte Adolf Hitler, advanced through this gap and reached the Belgian town of Stavelot, over 20 miles distant, by the following evening.

On the left of the Sixth SS Panzer Army, the Fifth Panzer Army attacked on a front of about 30 miles against VIII Corps of the US First Army. The Americans managed to hold their positions until the following day, when the 2nd Panzer Division broke through in the river Clerf area but was held by determined resistance. To the south, the Seventh Army attacked against lightly held positions of XII Corps, US Third Army, but met determined opposition. It managed to penetrate as far as the town of Wiltz but suffered very heavy casualties. The Americans even counter-attacked.

The skies were not completely free of aircraft during the first two days. The Luftwaffe put in an appearance over their ground forces, trying to provide support, but the airfields of the US Ninth Air Force were closed down by the weather on the first day. This cleared partially on the second day and the Ninth managed as many as 1,200 sorties, mainly attacking enemy movements behind the front line and seeking out enemy aircraft. Arrangements were made for the RAF's Second Tactical Air Force to provide additional support on following days in the northern area.

By coincidence, General Eisenhower was discussing plans with General Bradley at SHAEF headquarters in Versailles when news of the German attack first arrived. Although exact details were not then available, it was decided to reinforce VIII Corps of the US First Army with two divisions, the 7th Armoured from the US Ninth Army in the north and the 10th Armoured from the US Third Army in the south. These were not in the front line at the time but were able to set out immediately, arriving in the evening of 17 December. The disposition of enemy forces still remained unclear, partly because air reconnaissance was not effective, while reports from some advanced positions had not arrived and there was disruption created by Skorzeny's Armoured Brigade 150, which had infiltrated American positions. On this day, 17 December, Eisenhower also ordered two divisions of the Allied Airborne Army to reinforce the US First Army, from their reserve positions at Reims. On the following day, he ordered more reinforcements, an airborne division based in England and the 11th Armoured Division from Normandy. At the same time, he ordered General Patton to cancel his proposed operations against the Saar and move three more divisions to reinforce the hard-pressed VIII Corps of the US First Army, while the US 6th Army Group took over a section of his front. At the same time, Eisenhower ordered the British Sixth Airborne Army to leave England and join the 21st Army Group. If the German Army Groups succeeded in breaking through, there were no other reserves to stop them reaching Brussels.

A patrol of the US First Army searching the woods between Eupen and Bütgenbach in Belgium for German paratroopers dropped in the area on 17 December 1944, during the Battle of the Bulge. *The National Archives: CAB 106/1010*

Although this assault caught SHAEF by surprise, the American troops in the Ardennes front fought with skill and tenacity in trying to hold back the enemy. They managed to blow bridges and form block roads in front of the advancing Germans, despite the confusion that accompanied the failure of communications. The 106th Infantry Division on the western ridges of the Eifel, composed of new recruits without battle experience, was soon surrounded yet fought stubbornly until ordered to withdraw to the Belgian town of St-Vith. The men tried to break through the enemy lines but on 19 December were forced to surrender. Over 7,000 were taken prisoner.

Meanwhile, General Bradley tried to coordinate his defences and re-establish broken communications. By 20 November, the Sixth SS Panzer Army had failed to capture the Belgian town of Malmédy in the northern sector, while its 1st SS Panzer Division had been driven back from Stavelot by the newly arrived US 82nd Airborne Division. To the south, the Fifth Panzer Army made more progress, surrounding the Belgian town of Bastogne with three divisions. This was an important road junction held by the US 7th Armoured Division from the US Ninth Army, with elements of VIII Corps from the US First Army and from the US 101st Airborne Division. The defence of this town became a famous episode in the story of the 'Battle of the Bulge'.

On 19 December, General Eisenhower decided on a change in command. General Bradley's forces were so badly split by the German attack that he decided to place those in the northern sector, consisting of the major part of the US First and Ninth Armies, under the operational command of Field-Marshal Montgomery. Part of the US Ninth Air Force was passed to the command of Air Marshal Sir Arthur Coningham of the RAF's Second Tactical Air Force. These British commanders were able to maintain contact with the American forces in the combat area.

General Bradley retained command of his forces in the more southerly sectors. He was not happy with this temporary arrangement but could see the logic from a geographical standpoint, since the forces he lost were so close to those of the British. He was unable to visit his Army commanders in this area but could maintain contact with General Patton in the south.

The weather deteriorated even further during 19–22 December, with low cloud persisting over all the tactical airfields. Air operations by the Allies and the Luftwaffe became severely limited. The conditions favoured the German ground forces to some extent, but constant rain turned many roads through the Ardennes into muddy tracks which hampered the movement of Panzers and other vehicles. This bad weather began to clear on 23 December, giving way to cold, clear and frosty conditions. These were ideal for the Allied tactical air forces, since enemy forces suddenly became conspicuous. Both the US Ninth Air Force and the RAF's Second Tactical Air Force came out in droves. The main attacks were made by the US Ninth on that day. Its fighter-bombers flew 696 sorties, destroying numerous ground targets and enemy aircraft. At the same time, 624 light and medium bombers attacked railway and road bridges, marshalling yards and other enemy centres. The bombers hit their targets but lost 36 aircraft from enemy fire while 190 others were damaged, some seriously. Enemy fighters were particularly active on this day.

The strategic bombers also re-entered the fray. On the night of 22/3 December, RAF Bomber Command despatched 274 Lancasters, Halifaxes and Mosquitos on raids against railway yards at Koblenz and Bingen in Germany, causing enough damage to hamper the supply routes to the Ardennes front. These were followed by a daylight attack on 23 December when 153 Lancasters escorted by fighters bombed the German town of Trier near Luxembourg. This was a communications centre and

A machine-gunner of the US First Army in a defensive position on 20 December 1944 during the Battle of the Bulge, in the area of Bullange in Belgium, facing smoke rising from an American artillery barrage. Bullange was the site of a large American fuel dump, where German tanks had replenished their advance three days before. *The National Archives: CAB 106/1010*

it was heavily hit. On the same day, the US Eighth Air Force despatched 423 Fortresses and Liberators, escorted by 636 fighters, to bomb marshalling yards and communications centres behind the German lines. There was even better weather on 24 December, when 338 Lancasters, Halifaxes and Mosquitos were sent against airfields behind the German lines, while the Eighth sent 1,884 Fortresses and Liberators, escorted by 804 fighters, against similar targets. Attacks by tactical fighter-bombers and other bombers also continued.

The results of these Allied air operations were devastating for the Germans. Their troops had been unable to capture any major stocks of fuel which were so necessary for further advances. There is a vivid example of the difficulties they experienced. The Fifth Panzer Army had entered St-Vith on 21 December, a town which the US 7th Armoured Division had defended for five days before retreating under orders from Montgomery, who wished to straighten out a salient. But then the Panzers ran out of fuel. The brigade under Obersturmbannführer Peiper, which had been in the forefront of the advance, was forced to abandon its tanks and other vehicles. All the crews, numbering 600 men, had no option but to make their way back on foot through the woods to the Siegfried Line.

The tide of war began to swing decisively against the Germans. On Christmas Day, a combined force of Americans and British attacked the Sixth SS Panzer Army's 2nd Panzer Division in the area of the Belgian town of Foy-Notre-Dame. Within the next three days, this German division was almost completely wiped out. It lost all its tanks, guns and vehicles, while 1,200 men were taken prisoner. On 26 December, the long siege of Bastogne by the Fifth SS Panzer Army came to an end when the 4th Armoured Division of General Patton's Third Army fought its way through to the hard-pressed defenders. The enemy had been foiled, not only by the courage of these defenders but with the aid of supplies dropped from the air or brought in by gliders. The relieving troops had fought their way through 120 miles from the area of the Saar.

With the German advances stalled, General Eisenhower was anxious to regain the ground lost in the last fortnight, but Montgomery's 21st Army Group was committed with other measures until 3 January. General Bradley began a counter-attack on 30 December with the forces of the US 12th Army Group which remained under his command. Some very fierce fighting developed around the area of Bastogne, particularly when General Patton's Third Army came up against three additional divisions which had been brought up to the area. The winter weather had set in and the going was difficult, but the Americans made steady progress.

In this period, the Luftwaffe was making final preparations for its last major assault on the Western Front. Hitler had recognised that the RAF's Second Tactical Air Force and the US Ninth Air Force had been largely responsible for bringing the attack of the Panzers to a halt. German soldiers hated and feared tactical fighter-bombers and the rockets they fired. These screamed towards them, armed with 60lb high-explosive warheads capable of destroying any Panzer or other armoured vehicle. An operation codenamed 'Bodenplatte' was planned to destroy as many as possible of these Allied aircraft on the ground. Many of these were grouped in a small number of serviceable airfields in Belgium and the Netherlands, with up to six RAF or USAAF squadrons on a single station. Their heavy anti-aircraft guns and camouflage netting had been withdrawn, under the impression that the Luftwaffe in this region was a spent force.

The Germans were well aware that these airfields were congested and could make excellent targets. They codenamed the operation 'Hermann' and made preparations with the greatest possible secrecy. A miscellany of single-engined aircraft were gathered from other German airfields, including training units. These even included some of the small communications Fieseler Fi.158C Storch, which were then armed with light bombs. In total, between 750 and 800 aircraft were accumulated. Some experienced pilots were drawn from bases all over Germany and occupied territories in the east of Europe, but many of the others were unskilled or even trainees.

Allied decrypts of enemy signals on 14, 15 and 22 December revealed that the Luftwaffe was practising with aircraft guiding others on low-level flights, but there was no warning of the proposed operation. When the attacks were delivered, they came unexpectedly in the early morning of 1 January. The formations were guided towards their targets by coloured smoke shells fired from the ground and by searchlights pointing directions. Junkers Ju88s led sections of the variegated armada of single-engined aircraft but these twin-engined bombers turned away before Allied territory was reached. All flew at extreme low level to keep under the Allied radar screen, while maintaining strict radio silence.

For security reasons, the pilots had not been briefed until the last moment and some aircraft were late on take-off. A few collided en route in the congestion, but the others caused considerable damage. The leading aircraft, Messerschmitt Bf109s and Focke-Wulf Fw190s, came out of the low sun and delivered their attacks along the runways and dispersal areas. They were followed by aircraft flown by less experienced pilots. In all, 144 RAF aircraft were destroyed and 84 damaged, as well as patrol bowsers and other vehicles. About 40 RAF servicemen were killed and 145 injured. The Americans suffered less severely, losing about 40 aircraft.

But the Luftwaffe losses did not justify this achievement. Many RAF and USAAF aircraft were able to take off and air combats ensued. German records disclose that about 220 of their aircraft failed to return. Most of these crashed

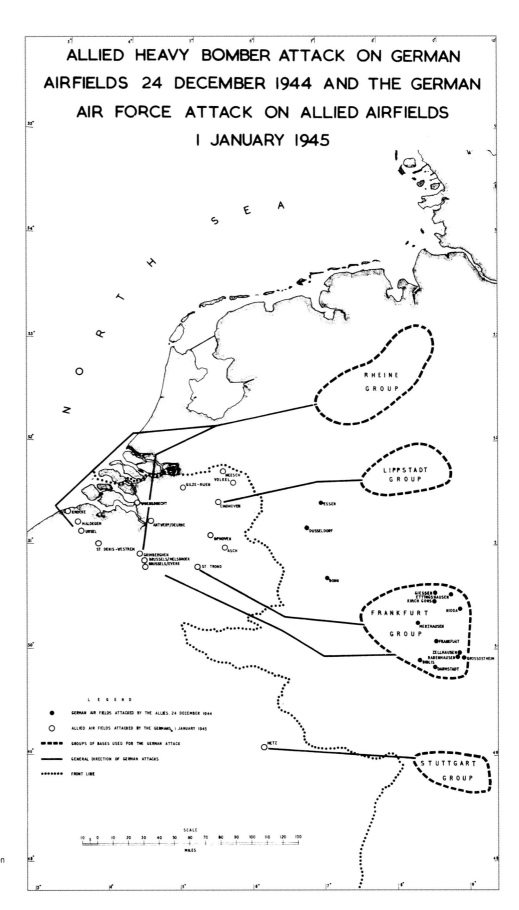

The Allied bomber attacks on German airfields,
24 December 1944, and German Air Force attacks on
Allied airfields, 1 January 1945. *The National Archives:*
AIR 41/68

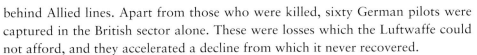

behind Allied lines. Apart from those who were killed, sixty German pilots were captured in the British sector alone. These were losses which the Luftwaffe could not afford, and they accelerated a decline from which it never recovered.

Field-Marshal Montgomery duly began his counter-offensive in the northern sector on 3 January, employing divisions from the British Second Army and the US First Army, as well as the British 6th Airborne Division from the First Allied Airborne Army. The divisions struck towards the south-east and there was hard fighting over the next few days, with some areas changing hands several times. It was not until 13 January that contact was made with VIII Corps of the US Third Army, attacking from the south. On 15 January, the US VII Corps from this force entered the Belgian town of Houffalize, which was in complete ruins after attacks by RAF Bomber Command on 30/1 December and 5/6 January while it was in German hands. With the meeting of the US First and Third Armies, command of the First was returned to General Bradley, although Field-Marshal Montgomery retained his command of the US Ninth Army for the time being.

By the end of the month, all the territory lost during the Battle of the Bulge had been regained. The human cost to the Germans was estimated to have been about 85,000 men, including about 50,000 taken prisoner. The losses on the Allied side are known more accurately. The US Armies suffered about 8,500 killed, over 46,000 wounded and almost 21,000 missing but probably taken prisoner. The British lost 200 killed, over 950 wounded and almost 250 wounded. The Allied Air Forces lost almost 650 aircraft during these protracted attacks and counter-attacks.

Of course, the Ardennes was not the only front where fighting took place. Before the German offensive began on 16 December, von Rundstedt had ordered his Army Group H to exert pressure on the northern flank of the British and Canadian 21st Army Group in the area of Nijmegen. More troops had been moved to the front line. A garrison of the 6th Parachute Division was stationed in the Dutch town of Kapelsche Veer on the Maas, and Montgomery wanted it forced back. Attacks began on 30 December by the 1st Polish Armoured Division and fierce fighting resulted, with the Poles reinforced on 13 January by the 47th Royal Marine Commandos. The Germans still held on until 26 January when a Canadian Infantry Brigade and an Armoured Division attacked over the frozen ground. After five more days of combat in the bitter weather, the position was at last gained.

Nearer Nijmegen, the Germans made a further attempt on 13 January to blow the bridges with seventeen *Biber* midget submarines, but all these were wiped out by gunfire or failed to reach their targets. On 18 January, the German 6th Parachute Division launched an attack at Zetten, 10 miles south-west of Arnhem, but they suffered heavy casualties and were driven back when the British 59th Division counter-attacked.

There was also a German salient on the east of this northern front, south-west of the river Roer between the Dutch town of Roermond and the German town of Geilenkirchen, which Montgomery was determined to eliminate. It was in front of the Siegfried Line but had been strengthened by the Germans, who used slave labour to dig three lines of trenches with weapon pits and reserve positions. The salient was roughly in the form of a triangle, with the British and Americans on two sides, to the west and the south. They faced positions occupied by two divisions of Volksgrenadier defenders, well supported by artillery. The attack against them was codenamed operation 'Blackcock' and was to be carried out by XII Corps of the British Second Army. This was composed of an armoured division, two infantry divisions, two armoured

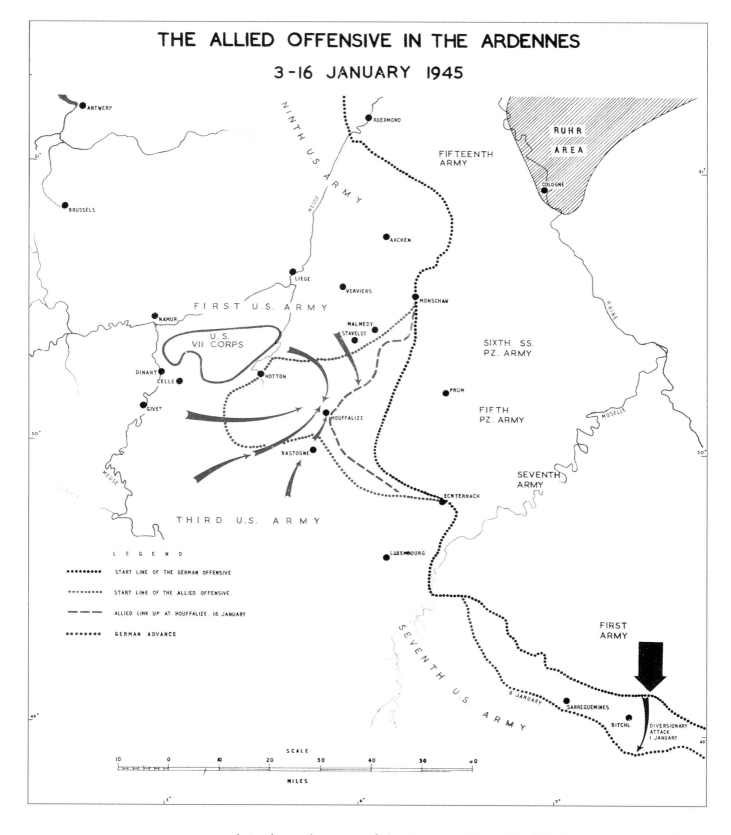

THE ALLIED OFFENSIVE IN THE ARDENNES
3-16 JANUARY 1945

brigades and groups of the Royal Artillery. The US Ninth Army was able to provide its XIII Corps to assist on the southern flank, while the RAF's Second Tactical Air Force was in strong support together with some squadrons of the US Ninth Air Force.

The attack began in the early morning of 16 January, towards the Dutch town of Susteren in the centre of the line, against heavy shelling and small-arms fire. This town was captured during the following day and a counter-attack repelled, but it became obvious that every village and hamlet would be hotly contested by the enemy, who knew the ground well. The approaches were thickly mined all along the front, fog hampered some of the assaults by the RAF's Second Tactical Air Force, and an unexpected thaw resulted in mud which bogged down the advance of some of the British armour and heavy equipment. The Typhoons came in with rockets whenever possible and medium bombers of the US Ninth Air Force made attacks in daylight.

The Germans brought up reinforcements, including self-propelled guns and a few Tiger tanks. The conflict took place in bitter weather, which alternated between snow and rain. Once the first line of enemy defences was breached, the British faced a second line. Some of the heaviest fighting took place around the Dutch hamlet of St Joost, near the town of Echt. The conditions were similar to those of the First World War, but with even deadlier weaponry. Two Victoria Crosses were awarded posthumously to British soldiers during this intense fighting.

To the relief of the attackers, the weather cleared on 22 January and the RAF's Second Tactical Air Force were able to fly over 700 sorties during daylight. These good weather conditions lasted for two more days, during which the Allied air forces hammered the German frontal positions and supply lines. To the dismay of the defenders, the Luftwaffe was unable to put in more than token appearances. At last there were signs that the enemy was beginning to give way, with the British forcing their way through the second defence line. Advanced elements of the British XII Corps were able to link up with the US XIII Corps advancing north from the area of Geilenkirchen.

By 26 January most of the survivors of the German divisions had withdrawn to the Siegfried Line and the British were busy mopping up pockets of the remainder. The German salient ceased to exist, although it had taken longer to clear than anticipated. British casualties had risen to over 1,500 killed and wounded, while over 100 tanks were destroyed. Some of the latter were mine-clearing or flame-throwing vehicles, put out of action by mines or anti-tank weapons. Over 2,000 Germans were captured by the end of the month.

Meanwhile, there was another German salient in the far south of the Allied front, the so-called 'Colmar pocket' in the Alsace district of France. This was south of Strasbourg and close to the Swiss border, with the Vosges mountain range on the west. The German forces backed on to the Rhine in the east, behind which was the southern end of the Siegfried Line and then the Black Forest. These forces were contained by the French First Army, commanded by General de Tassigny, part of the US Sixth Army Group.

The Allied front to the north of this salient, facing the Siegfried Line in the Saar Palatinate, had been weakened when part of Patton's Third Army had been directed on 19 December to attack the southern flank of the German forces invading the Ardennes. The gaps in the lines after they left were filled by extending the front held by the US Seventh Army commanded by Lieutenant-General Patch, also part of the US Sixth Army Group. It was acknowledged that Patch might have to retreat if the German pressure became too strong. This could have involved evacuating Strasbourg, a contingency which General Charles de Gaulle vehemently opposed. In deference to his objections, General Eisenhower ordered the reorganisation of the US Seventh Army to strengthen the forces around this major French city.

The Germans were fully aware of the American troop movements and duly attacked this weakened front at midnight on 31 December, employing seven divisions from the Saar in the north. Five more joined in, including two Panzer divisions, from across the Rhine in the east. The US Seventh Army was forced back in a fighting retreat but managed to hold the Germans in the region of the river Moder. The Germans made little further progress and by 25 January decided they had had enough and withdrew all their forces.

During these operations, the seven German divisions within the Colmar pocket made strong attempts from 7 January to enlarge their area by attacking northwards in the direction of Strasbourg, but their advances were resisted strongly by the French First Army. Eight divisions of the latter launched counter-attacks from 20 January, and eventually were joined by four American divisions, thus attacking the Colmar pocket from both the north and the south. There was some extremely bitter fighting until the German resistance began to crumble and their divisions evacuated the pocket, narrowly avoiding becoming trapped in a pincer movement. By 9 February, the surviving Germans were back behind the Rhine, having blown all the bridges to prevent the French and Americans from further pursuit. These fierce engagements had cost the French over 10,500 casualties and the Americans over 4,500, but they had caused huge casualties to the enemy and taken over 15,000 prisoners.

The Rhine bridges. The National Archives: AIR 41/68

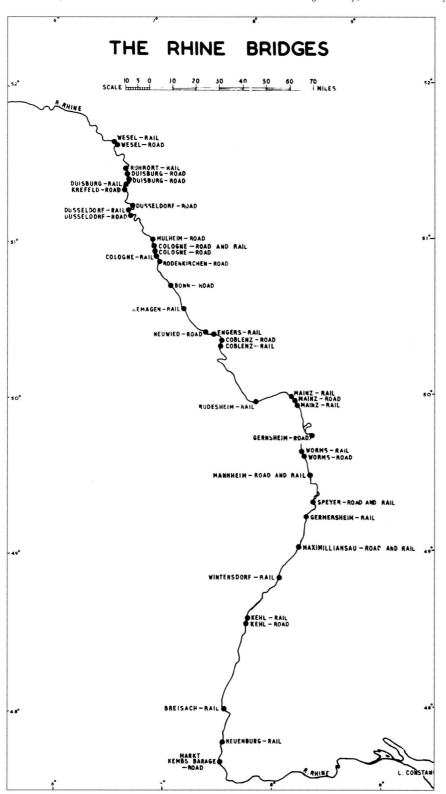

British infantry march into the German village of Bauchem, a few kilometres from Geilenkirchen, on 19 November 1944. A Bren Mark I machine-gun can be seen on the carrier in the foreground. *British Official*

The few snipers left in Bauchem who survived the shelling are rounded up and sent into captivity, after the British entered the German village. A Bren carrier is on the left. *British Official*

On 18 November 1944, British and American units began their attacks on the German town of Geilenkirchen, near the Dutch border. The town was defended by concrete strongholds, forming part of the Siegfried Line, but it was captured in the late afternoon of 19 November. This photograph shows one of the British tanks, with American soldiers, entering the devastated town.
British Official

The first Allied convoy to reach Antwerp, the third largest port in Europe, docked on 28 November 1944. It was preceded by minesweepers and accompanied by destroyers of the Royal Navy. In all, nineteen Liberty ships arrived. The *Fort Cataraqui* was the first to arrive, at Dock 22, in the presence of the Allied Naval Commander-in-Chief, Admiral Sir Bertram Ramsay, the Deputy Burgomaster of Antwerp, Emiel Van Puc, high military officers and crowds of onlookers. British troops immediately began off-loading supplies of oil, cement and ordnance into waiting trucks destined for the front line. *British Official*

The rocket-firing Sherman tank, officially the 'Rocket Launcher T-34 Calliope', was a fearsome weapon used on the Western Front. Sixty 4.5in rockets were mounted on the turret of the tank and could be fired singly or in salvoes. The rockets in this photograph were fired against enemy rearguards, to support American engineers building bridges. *US Official*

Some of the 95,000 German prisoners, dishevelled and weary, taken prisoner by the Americans after the fierce battle for the Hürtgen area of Germany, which lasted for a month from 16 November 1944. Both the US First Army and the US Ninth Army were involved, losing 127,000 soldiers killed, wounded or captured. German losses were even higher. *US Official*

The British forces began a heavy artillery
bombardment of the German bridgehead in the Dutch
town of Blerick, on the west bank of the Maas near
Venlo, in the early morning of 3 December 1944. Then
they breached a wide anti-tank ditch in five places and
occupied the town in the afternoon. In this
photograph, soldiers of the 6th Royal Scots Fusiliers
are tackling German snipers in the houses. Then they
helped civilians to evacuate the town while it was
being shelled by German artillery. *British Official*

The 105mm howitzer was the main artillery weapon employed by the Americans during the Battle of the Bulge. The 101st Airborne Division had a battalion of these highly efficient guns. In this photograph, men of the 101st Field Artillery Battalion are manoeuvring their guns into position and preparing to dig in, to repel the German attack. *US Official*

In the late afternoon of 26 December 1944, elements of three US Divisions (the 101st Airborne with the 9th and 10th Armoured), which had been trapped in the Belgian town of Bastogne during the Battle of the Bulge, were relieved by the 4th Armoured Division, US Third Army, under Lieutenant-General George Smith Jnr. This photograph shows soldiers of the relieving force, which had broken through from the south, inspecting some of the wrecked American vehicles littering the Place du Carré in the centre of Bastogne. *US Official*

On Christmas Day 1944, the advance elements of the German 2nd Panzer Division stood on high ground near Dinant in Belgium, ready for a thrust towards the river Maas. While waiting for reinforcements, the US 2nd Armoured Division blocked their supply route and the Panzers in the woods near Celles were cut off. By 27 December the German spearhead was mostly destroyed and the opportunity of crossing the Maas had gone. This 88mm Flak 41 gun was put out of action by the retreating Germans. *US Official*

American soldiers in the snow during the counter-attack in the Battle of the Bulge, which began with the German assault of 16 December 1944. The man on the left is covering his ears from the violent crashes as self-propelled 155mm guns known as 'Long Toms' are fired at the enemy. *US Official*

Christmas Eve 1944 at a dispersal point for Hawker Tempest fighters of the RAF's Second Tactical Air Force was celebrated when a choir from the ground crew toured the airfield and sang carols to the guards. They were conducted by the station padre, Squadron Leader K.J. Morgan. Illumination from a hurricane lamp suspended from a fishing rod gave an unusually grim setting instead of a traditional Christmas scene. *British Official*

The British Second Army dug in near the German border, where snow fell in the last two days of 1944, resulting in a temporary period of trench warfare. These soldiers were photographed on 31 December 1944 while bringing up mattresses for the men in the trenches. *British Official*

This photograph seemingly taken on the Russian Front in fact shows a British patrol on reconnaissance in Germany, near the Dutch border. It was taken by an Army photographer in January 1945 who accompanied the patrol. The men on this front and in the Ardennes were issued with white camouflage cloaks and trousers. Their guns, rifles and radios were also wrapped in white cloth. *British Official*

A patrol of the US First Army marched 20 miles in freezing weather over snow-covered hills and on 16 January 1945 made contact with these troops of the US Third Army crossing a bridge near Houffalize in Belgium. *The National Archives: CAB 106/1010*

Men of the 387th Fighter Group of the US Ninth Air Force, equipped with P-38 Lightnings, devised a sleigh train towed by a jeep for transport over the snow from the briefing hut to the dispersal areas. This Group was based at Juvincourt in France from 28 October 1944 to 1 February 1945. It was then re-equipped with P-47 Thunderbolts. *US National Archives and Records Administration # 342-FH-3A-10748-B-50738*

British troops experienced fierce fighting at St Joost, a little hamlet 2 miles from Etch in the south-east of the Netherlands, when this picture was taken on 21 January 1945, but two platoons of infantry were able to take the position with the help of Crocodile tank flame-throwers. *British Official*

A camouflaged patrol of the 7th Armored Division, US First Army, on the outskirts of St-Vith in Belgium on 23 January 1945. By this time the Americans were poised to re-take the devastated town from the German garrison. *The National Archives: CAB 106/1010*

A remarkably clear photograph taken by the RAF at night in January 1945, with the aid of a huge flash bomb. It revealed a camouflaged shelter on the right as well as the vehicles and trees against the snow. This oblique photograph was taken at low level with the camera facing south, showing enemy field guns being towed *eastward* from the Dutch city of Venlo to the German frontier. *British Official*

American soldiers of Combat Command B, 7th Armored Division, US First Army, led by Brigadier-General Bruce Clarke, captured St-Vith in the Ardennes salient on 23 January 1945, in spite of repeated counter-attacks by the Germans. This photograph shows American reinforcements moving up to the town on the next day. *US Official*

Churchill tanks of the British Second Army moving over the snow-covered German countryside in January 1945, in order to cut the road between Heinsberg and Geilenkirchen. *British Official*

An oil mill at Heldon, on the Rhine near the German town of Emmerich, was bombed by 56 Mitchells of No. 2 Group, Second Tactical Air Force, on 2 February 1945. This photograph shows a salvo of bombs falling across the centre of the mill. Reconnaissance photographs taken the following day showed the power station in the centre of the target area completely gutted and most of the other buildings damaged by direct hits or blast. *The National Archives: AIR 37/46*

Opposite page: A boy soldier of the Wehrmacht, age 15, breaks down and weeps after capture, probably after having undergone terrible experiences. *US Official*

An infantryman of the 9th Division, US First Army, photographed on 6 February 1945 while firing his Browning automatic rifle at retreating German forces in the area north-east of Morsbach in Germany, overlooking the river Urft. *The National Archives: CAB 106/1010*

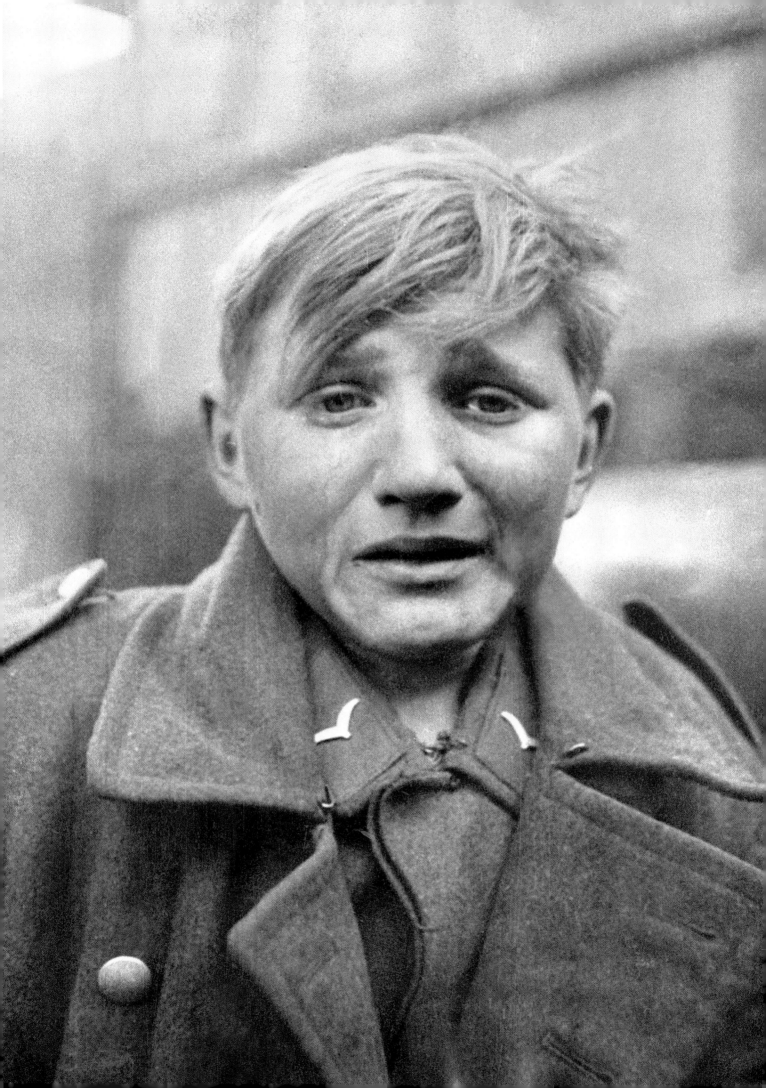

Infantrymen of the US Seventh Army plodding through snow, mud and mist en route to the French city of Colmar, near the west bank of the Rhine, where the Germans held a strong bridgehead. French and American units attacked this German pocket on 20 January 1945. The action was completed in early February, when the pocket fell to the Allies. *US Official*

On 3 February 1945, the US Eighth Air Force despatched 1,003 B-17 Flying Fortresses to the Tempelhof area of Berlin, escorted by 613 P-51 Mustangs. This photograph was taken over the target, partly obscured by fires and smoke. Losses were 23 Fortresses and 7 Mustangs. *Author's Collection*

Troops of the 51st Highland Division marching towards the Belgian town of La Roche-en-Ardenne, which had been occupied successively by the Germans and the Americans. It was attacked by the US Ninth Air Force on 26 December, 27 December and 1 January, causing the deaths of 114 civilians. Shock waves from the surrounding hillsides intensified the damage considerably. The town was finally liberated on 11 January 1945. *British Official*

CHAPTER EIGHT

VICTORY IN THE WEST

Although this stage of the assault from the west had not fulfilled the hopes of the American President and the British Prime Minister, they were sufficiently confident about its ultimate outcome to coordinate their next moves with those of the Russians on the Eastern Front. They also began to prepare plans for the future of Germany when the Wehrmacht was finally vanquished. A conference was arranged for 4 February 1945 with the Soviet leader, Marshal Josef Stalin, at Yalta in the Crimea. Both Churchill and Roosevelt would attend, together with the Combined Chiefs of Staff of all three Powers. As a preliminary, Churchill and Roosevelt would meet a few days earlier at Malta under the codename of 'Argonaut'. They had already received some encouraging news from the Deputy Supreme Commander, Air Chief Marshal Sir Arthur Tedder, who had headed a mission which arrived in Moscow on 15 January. Marshal Stalin had informed this mission that he planned a huge attack on Germany with over 150 divisions as soon as the weather was favourable. When he learnt of the American and British plans, Stalin said that he would launch the attack irrespective of the weather and that his forces would continue until they reached the river Oder.

Roosevelt and Churchill duly met in Malta and discussed such matters as the war against U-boats, operations in Italy and the situation in Greece. They left on 2 February with their Combined Chiefs of Staff and arrived safely in Yalta. The first discussion with Stalin and his Chiefs of Staff, on 4 February, was mainly concerned with an exchange of information on military operations. Then the three leaders arrived at a political agreement which would have far-reaching effects for the remainder of the century and beyond. This concerned the unconditional surrender of Germany and its partition into three zones, each under the military control of one of the three Powers, Russia, the United States and Britain. France would be invited to take over part of one of these zones. Berlin would be within the Soviet zone but partitioned among all four Powers. These terms would not be made known to the world generally until Germany had been finally defeated. It was intended that all German forces would be disarmed and that the country would never again be able to disturb the peace of the world.

Meanwhile, plans had been made by the Americans and the British to destroy all the remaining German forces west of the Rhine, with the Allied attack advancing through the Siegfried Line. The first was codenamed operation

'Veritable', which would take place in the north of the sector, with the Canadian First Army and the British Second Army playing the major part. In the southern sector, the US Ninth Army would begin operation 'Grenade', still under the command of Field-Marshal Montgomery. These attacks were scheduled to begin in the second week of February and would be strongly supported by Allied strategic and tactical air forces. It was believed that the three Allied armies faced about twelve enemy divisions, with perhaps eleven more which could be brought into the battle area. After success against these had been gained, General Eisenhower would resume his objective of establishing bridgeheads over the Rhine in the north and the south. The next phase would be to capture the great industrial centre of the Ruhr and then an advance into the German heartland.

Meanwhile, the two major strategic air forces, RAF Bomber Command and the US Eighth Air Force, continued to hammer the enemy. Still based in England, they were intended to follow the official policy of destroying the enemy's synthetic oil production and his transport system, whenever they were not called

Mitchell and Boston medium bombers of No. 2 Group, Second Tactical Air Force, were also despatched on 22 February 1945 to attack the enemy's transport system, escorted by fighters. An accurate concentration of bombs fell on the railway junction and canal bridge outside the Dutch town of Coevorden, close to the border with Germany.
The National Archives: AIR 37/46

upon to support the ground forces. This policy was enthusiastically endorsed by General Carl Spaatz, who commanded the Eighth Air Force. His heavy bombers went into Germany on daylight raids whenever possible, escorted by swarms of long-distance fighters, and inflicted heavy damage. But the Commander-in-Chief of the RAF's Bomber Command, Air Chief Marshal Sir Arthur Harris, was never convinced that this was the right policy. On 8 January 1945 the RAF's Chief of Air Staff, Air Chief Marshal Sir Charles Portal, sent him a dossier of Enigma decrypts demonstrating that attacks on oil were having a serious effect on Germany's capacity to wage war. Harris was unmoved by the evidence, although the records show that his heavy bombers did make frequent attacks on these designated targets, while continuing to obliterate German cities. There was a minor diversion in January when these two strategic air forces were engaged on attacks against targets involved in the production of the new Me163 Komet jet aircraft, which had been operating for about six months in small numbers, and U-boats equipped with the new 'Schnorkel' breathing tube. In the event neither of these inventions had a serious effect on the course of the war.

The two tactical air forces, the RAF's Second Tactical Air Force commanded by Air Marshal Sir Arthur Coningham and the US Ninth Air Force commanded by Major-General Hoyt S. Vandenberg, were based mainly in France and Belgium. Their medium bombers could reach into western Germany while their fighter-bombers devastated enemy defences in the front lines. Aircraft of the Luftwaffe were drastically reduced in numbers but the flak units remained numerous and extremely effective. Losses of Allied aircraft occurred mainly from ground fire rather than from aerial combat.

Clearance of the enemy from the areas west of the Rhine proved long and difficult, despite the defeats and losses the Germans had already suffered. The formidable barrier of the Siegfried Line stood in the way of the Allies and the Wehrmacht was still resolute in the defence of its homeland. The area was occupied by the tough First Parachute Army commanded by General Alfred Schlemm, a resourceful officer with much experience of fighting rearguard actions in Russia and Italy.

Operation Veritable, which took place in a south-easterly direction from Nijmegen in the north, opened in the early morning of 8 February 1945 with an enormous barrage from 1,050 guns of various calibres. This exceeded any concentration of firepower previously achieved by the British in the war. The front was about 6 miles wide, in a low-lying area between the rivers Waal (Rhine) and the Meuse (Maas), with flooding to the north. The initial barrage was followed by the laying of a smokescreen intended to persuade the enemy that troops were about to advance. When the enemy guns opened up in retaliation, fighter-bombers of the RAF's Second Tactical Air Force swept overhead and the British artillery fire was resumed, this time directed against enemy positions disclosed by their fire. This second barrage was lifted at 10.30 hours and infantry brigade groups from British and Canadian divisions began their advance, accompanied by gun-firing tanks from armoured brigades.

The initial stretch of battleground was flat and mostly open, crossing the German border towards the forested areas known as the Reichswald in the northern sector. The troops made good progress on the first day, with the German defences apparently stunned by the enormous bombardment. There had been an unexpected thaw and the advancing troops were more delayed by boggy ground than enemy fire. But inevitably there were pockets of stiff resistance. The Siegfried Line was breached and the infantry passed through gaps cleared of

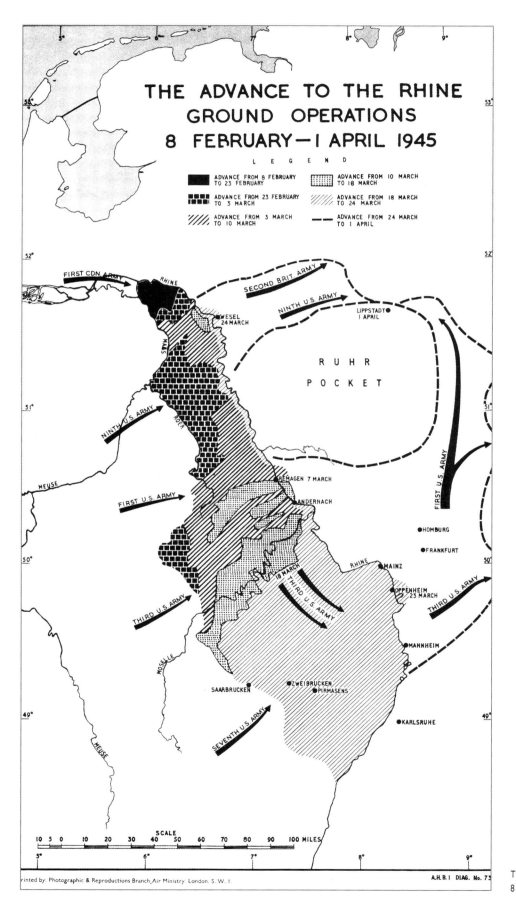

The advance to the Rhine, ground operations,
8 February–1 April 1945. *The National Archives: AIR 41/68*

mines by flail tanks, closely supported by Typhoon fighter-bombers despite cloudy weather. Assault boats were employed in the flooded area in the northern area south of the Rhine, while further afield air attacks were made on railways and roads leading to the battle area. Over 1,200 Germans were taken prisoner on this first day and it seemed probable that the German town of Kleve, south of the Rhine and about 10 miles from the start-line, would soon fall.

The weather on the following day was unfavourable, with constant rain saturating the ground, causing flooding and restricting movement of heavy vehicles. Close air support was almost impossible. Some further progress was made and there was heavy fighting on the outskirts of Kleve. This rain persisted on 10 February, preventing any air support and bogging down much of the movement along the muddy roads. On the other hand, the enemy was able to bring up reinforcements. Operation Grenade, which the US Ninth Army was due to start further south on this day, was postponed when the river Roer burst its banks and flooded the region. These waters were released when the Germans blew the dams in the reservoirs further south, resulting in a long-term flood. It was estimated that operation Grenade could not be launched until 23 February.

The troops in operation Veritable were reinforced by two British and two American divisions, but the campaign degenerated into a bitter slogging match with heavy casualties on both sides. The town of Kleve was entered on 11 February after fighting at close quarters, leaving almost every building in ruins. The Canadian divisions then struck south-east towards the German town of Kalkar, near the left bank of the Rhine. The British divisions began to fight their way southwards through the Reichswald towards the German town of Goch. This was an important road and rail junction, heavily defended with very strong fortifications. If these two towns were captured an advance could be made through more open country towards the German town of Wesel on the far bank of the Rhine, served by two bridges over the river.

The weather eventually cleared during the night of 13/14 February and the Allies made a colossal air effort. The RAF's Bomber Command despatched 796 Lancasters and 9 Mosquitos to Dresden in two waves at night, following a request from the Russians for attacks against targets in front of their advancing troops. This was followed during daylight by the US Eighth Air Force, which despatched 461 Fortresses, escorted by 316 Mustangs, to the same target. Deaths from the resulting firestorm were believed to have exceeded 50,000, mostly civilians. On the same day, the Eighth sent 832 heavies and 511 escorts against marshalling yards in Chemnitz and Magdeburg, also with the objective of assisting the Russian forces. It made a more modest attack with 84 heavies and 30 escorts on Wesel, one of the objectives for the British and Canadians in operation Veritable.

The ground forces involved in Veritable were gratified when the RAF's Second Tactical Air Force flew over 1,800 sorties on 14 February, many of them of the 'cab-rank' variety in close support of the advanced troops. The US Ninth Air Force flew an even greater number, mainly against enemy airfields, rail targets, depots and communication centres behind the front line. But the weather closed in once again and this air effort could not be repeated for several days. Nevertheless, British troops entered Goch and on 19 February the German garrison surrendered. Fighting on the outskirts continued for two more days, until the whole area was clear of the enemy.

The front of operation Veritable had been widened from its initial 6 miles to about 20 miles, as the rivers Meuse and Rhine diverged towards the south-east.

Everywhere there was a very hard going, through mud, mines and anti-tank ditches within a belt of prepared defences, and casualties mounted on both sides. A major push, codenamed 'Blockbuster', began on 22 February with an advance by the British divisions.

This coincided with a massive attack by the Allied strategic and tactical air forces against the enemy's transport, codenamed 'Clarion'. It was the brainchild of General Spaatz, endorsed by other air commanders. During the preceding night, the RAF's Bomber Command despatched 372 aircraft against Duisburg and 349 against Worms, both resulting in huge damage. But the most valuable for the Allied ground forces resulted from an attack by 177 aircraft against the vital Mittelland canal at Gravenhorst. The structure of the canal was shattered and one of the most important links in the German transport system rendered unusable. During the day, the US Eighth Air Force despatched 1,428 heavies escorted by 862 fighters against rail and road communications behind the German front lines. The RAF's Second Tactical Air Force made 1,735 sorties during the day, strafing locomotives, trucks and barges. Bombers of the US Ninth Air Force made 503 sorties while fighter-bombers made 1,082 more against transportation targets immediately behind the German front lines. Photo-reconnaissance revealed enormous damage to the German lines of communication leading to the battlegrounds.

Operation Grenade began in the early morning of the following day, since the floods along the river Roer had subsided enough for the US Ninth Army to begin

A British infantryman taking cover on 11 February 1945 in the ruins of a building in the German town of Kleve, an important rail and road junction behind the Siegfried Line where a strong enemy concentration is being attacked. Further down the street, a tank machine-gunner is firing at German snipers. *British Official*

A British soldier trying the pick off isolated snipers in the factory area before Goch was finally cleared in the evening of 21 February 1945. The fighting was extremely bitter, but the British used tanks and flame-throwers. *British Official*

its advance towards the Rhine. This was opened with another enormous artillery barrage by over 1,000 guns from that army, together with others from the British Second Army on the northern flank and the US First Army on the southern flank. Two corps of the Ninth entered assault boats and began crossing the Roer, hampered by strong currents as much as by enemy fire. Bridgeheads were established by nightfall on the far bank and pontoon bridges were soon built by the engineers. American casualties numbered about 1,000 on this first day, but the defending German infantry and Volksgrenadier divisions suffered badly and yielded numerous prisoners.

At the same time, troops of the US First Army managed to cross the Roer in the region of Düren. Both US armies were provided with close tactical support by the US Ninth Air Force, contributing greatly to the initial success. During the next day, the Americans managed to build up their strength across the river and took more prisoners. The Luftwaffe made attempts to bomb the pontoon bridges at night, with limited success while losing several aircraft from anti-aircraft fire. By the evening of 26 February, almost the whole of the US Ninth Army had succeeded in crossing the river and was beginning its main thrust in the direction of Düsseldorf on the far bank of the Rhine.

Operation Blockbuster in the north continued on this day with a barrage of 600 guns on the front leading to Kalkar. Two Canadian infantry divisions then moved forward, accompanied by their armoured division, while two British divisions attacked from the area of Goch on their right flank, with their front extending as far as the Moselle. The German parachute divisions stood their ground everywhere and intense fighting took place, with heavy losses on all sides. The Canadians found conditions extremely difficult while attempting to advance through dense forest, bogs, mines, enemy artillery fire and roadblocks. Their progress was again hampered by heavy rain which also prevented close air support. The RAF's Second Tactical Air Force was unable to fly sorties of any magnitude for the fortnight before 28 February, when the weather cleared and 1,117 were flown.

Nevertheless the Canadians gradually made ground, as did the British divisions. By early March, the British managed to link up with the US Ninth Army in the area of Kevelaer and a more general advance was made. General

An attack in clear daylight on 16 February 1945 when 100 Lancasters and a single Mosquito bombed Wesel on the Rhine, smothering the town and its railway stat on with bomb attacks. The photograph was taken from a Lancaster of No. 149 Squadron from Methwold in Norfolk. The Lancaster below looks far too close for comfort but no aircraft were lost in this operation. The National Archives: AIR 14/3701

Schlemm had hoped to hold a bridgehead along the left bank of the Rhine so that coal from the Ruhr could be carried as far as Wesel before turning up the Lippe canal to the Dortmund-Ems canal towards northern Germany. But this objective was not achieved, although his forces fought bitterly for every yard lost. The German bridgehead shrank until the last of the forces retreated over the bridges at Wesel and then blew both of these.

Meanwhile, the US Ninth Army made excellent progress. The weather conditions were less unfavourable in its area than in the north, and the US Ninth Air Force was able to fly sorties on most days, on close support missions as well as on more distant bombing raids. By 1 March, the troops had captured the large German city of München-Gladbach, about 10 miles from the Rhine east of Düsseldorf, despite reinforcement from the Panzer Lehr Division by the Germans. It was hoped that they would be able to capture intact at least one of the eight Rhine bridges in their sector, but these were being blown by the enemy forces when they retreated to the far bank. By 5 March the last of these was destroyed.

Casualties in these operations had been very heavy. The British and Canadians suffered 15,500 killed, wounded or taken prisoner and the Americans 7,300. But it was estimated that in operation Veritable the Germans had lost 22,000 killed or wounded, while another 22,000 were taken prisoner. On operation Grenade, German killed or wounded amounted to 16,000 while 29,000 prisoners were taken.

These two fronts were not the only active ones during this period. To the south of the US Ninth Army was the US First Army, which also had had to wait until the floods on the river Roer had subsided. However, on the right flank of this army, General Patton's US Third Army had pushed eastwards through the densely forested district of the Eifel towards Prüm, a communications centre, as well as Bitburg to its south. This advance was difficult over ground made boggy from heavy rains and thaws, and the formidable barrier of the Siegfried Line had to be breached. But the troops forced their way through with strong assistance from the US Ninth Air Force and by 22 February had captured both towns.

The following day was the opening of operation Grenade by the US Ninth Army. The US First Army could also advance on its right flank over the Roer towards Düsseldorf, increasing pressure on all the German forces in the region. Thus both the First and the Third Armies joined in a general assault, striking eastwards towards the Rhine, under the cover of their Ninth Air Force. Enemy resistance crumbled and both armies made rapid headway, despite some pockets of resistance. By 1 March, the Rhine was within range of American guns. On its left bank, Cologne was entered by troops of the First on 5 March and street fighting began. Two days later, the railway bridge at Remagen, to the south of Bonn, was seized before the Germans were able to blow it. The US First Army achieved the distinction of establishing the first Allied bridgehead over the Rhine.

On 10 March, the veteran Feldmarschall Gerd von Rundstedt was finally retired on Hitler's orders and his place as Commander-in-Chief West was taken over by Feldmarschall Albert Kesselring, who had achieved much success in the fighting retreat of the German forces in the Italian peninsula.

The US Seventh Army captured Koblenz, on the confluence of the Moselle with the Rhine, and then advanced further. By 22 March it cleared the left bank of the latter river as far south as Oppenheim. Nearby, it achieved a second bridgehead over the Rhine for the Americans and then moved even further south to Mannheim. This town had been captured by the US Seventh Army, which had crossed minefields to breach the Siegfried Line near Saarbrücken and then advance eastwards. During this period, the Third and Seventh Armies had sustained more than 12,000 casualties but they had captured 107,000 prisoners and inflicted an unknown number of casualties on the retreating Germans.

By this time the Allies had cleared all the German forces west of the Rhine and were ready to begin their major assault into the heartland of their enemy. But the bridges seized or built over the Rhine were all in the American sectors, in the centre and the south of the Allied line. There was an obvious need for a crossing further north. This had been anticipated by Field-Marshal Montgomery and extensive plans had been prepared for the three armies of his 21st Army Group – one British, one Canadian and one American. His directive had been issued as early as 9 March and involved establishing bridgeheads in the region of Wesel on the far bank, by means of a massive ground and airborne operation codenamed

'Varsity'. The river itself was in full spate but pontoon bridges could be built further north at Emmerich. The operation would isolate the Ruhr, deprive Germany of a huge industrial capacity and precede a drive into the north of the country. The area was known to be defended by five German divisions and there was likely to be a tough fight ahead.

Operation Varsity was preceded by a stream of attacks on the Ruhr by the RAF's Bomber Command, the US Eighth Air Force and the two tactical air forces. These were intended to disrupt communications and obliterate airfields or barracks, but inevitably caused much destruction of other property and civilian casualties.

The ground operation began with a crossing of the Rhine on the night of 23/4 March by four battalions and duplex drive tanks of XXX Corps in 150 Buffalo amphibious landing craft, covered by a barrage of about 3,500 guns of various calibres. The troops landed successfully on the far bank near Rees, about 12 miles north-west of Wesel, and met little initial opposition but later were fiercely opposed by German parachute troops.

An hour later, Commandos of XII Corps crossed and formed another bridgehead about 2 miles north-west of Wesel. As they landed, 195 Lancasters

Support to operations Varsity and Plunder, 24 March 1945. *The National Archives: AIR 41/68*

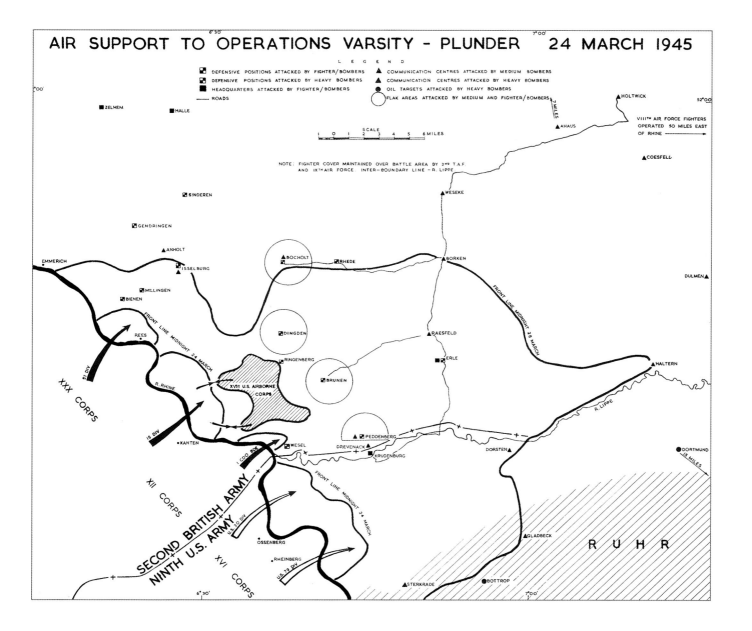

and 23 Mosquitos of RAF Bomber Command dropped 1,100 tons of bombs on this town. Already damaged by previous attacks, Wesel was reduced to rubble. The number of civilian casualties from its original population of 23,000 could not be counted before the British Commandos began to enter the outskirts. With only 3 per cent of its buildings left standing in the centre, this unfortunate town was considered to have been the most intensively bombed in Germany, in relation to its size. About 6 miles south of Wesel, another crossing was made by troops of the British XII Corps while even further upstream XVI Corps of the US Ninth Army made yet another landing.

The Second Tactical Air Force despatched 39 Mosquitos of its No. 2 Group on 22 February 1945 to attack the transport system behind enemy lines in north-west Germany. One of the targets was this railway station at Soltau, about 40 miles south of Hamburg. Freight cars, passengers and railway tracks were heavily damaged. Eight Mosquitos failed to return from these dangerous low-level operations. *The National Archives: AIR 37/46*

With the break of dawn, the airborne assault began. Medium bombers of the two tactical air forces attacked the enemy's supply lines, while a huge operation was carried out by the US Eighth Air Force. This despatched about 1,750 heavy bombers during the day, escorted by almost 1,500 fighters, mainly against enemy airfields in the vicinity.

In the midst of these air attacks, the Allied First Airborne Army arrived. This had been rebuilt into a colossal armada by Lieutenant-General Brereton after the disaster of Arnhem. Over 19,000 men were involved, from the British 6th Airborne Division from airfields in East Anglia and the US 17th Airborne Division from airfields near Paris. The first to arrive were 541 Dakotas carrying paratroops, followed by 1,050 aircraft towing 1,350 gliders, some in double tow. All were strongly escorted by British and American fighters. Aircraft of the Luftwaffe were unable to interfere with this armada but the flak units were presented with a huge target. These shot down 53 aircraft and damaged a further 440. The landings took place behind enemy lines to the north of Wesel and the airborne troops were involved in fierce fighting, but by the end of the day had linked up with advancing ground troops.

By midnight, the attackers and their reinforcements had achieved all their objectives and their engineers were busy building bridges over the Rhine. The British, Canadians and Americans consolidated their gains until, on 27 March, the bridgehead was 35 miles wide and 20 miles deep. Casualties up to this date amounted to almost 4,000 British and Canadian ground forces and about 1,500 American. In addition, the airborne forces had suffered 1,400 casualties. But over 16,000 prisoners had been taken and Allies were already beginning to break out from the bridgehead.

It must have been obvious to all but the most blinkered of the German senior commanders that the war was lost. Nevertheless they were still under the thrall of Adolf Hitler who, although a shambling physical wreck, held the power of life or death over his subjects. The Germans continued to fight, perhaps with broken morale in some divisions. These were estimated to number 65 on the Western Front, with some in no more than cadre form, while those of the Allies numbered 94 and were fully equipped. Moreover, the Allies could muster 10,000 strategic and tactical aircraft, with numerous forward airfields restored or built, while the Luftwaffe possessed only about 1,000 in the west and was short of experienced pilots and fuel. Transport behind the Allied lines was working well, with the railways rebuilt and other supplies arriving by road, canal and pipeline. It was time for the final push.

The German forces were seriously weakened when the US First Army broke out of its bridgehead at Remagen, which by 25 March was about 30 miles wide and 9 miles deep. By 1 April, it had wheeled north around the east of the Ruhr and then met the advanced units of the US Ninth Army, under Montgomery, which had also broken out of its bridgehead. Thus the Ruhr was completely enclosed by American forces. Within this area were twenty-one German divisions and over 300,000 men.

Montgomery was intent on a dash with his 21st Army Group for the Elbe and then Berlin, which hitherto had been regarded as the 'main prize', but his hopes were dashed when Eisenhower ordered the US Ninth Army to revert to the command of General Omar Bradley's 12th Army Group, partly in order to help contain the German forces in the Ruhr. This transfer took place on 4 April. Eisenhower knew that the Russians were only about 40 miles from Berlin and were certain to get there first. His plan was to direct the US Army Groups across central Germany and to link up with the advancing Russians in the area of Leipzig, the most important industrial area after the Ruhr.

The 21st Army Group was thus reduced to the British Second Army and the First Canadian Army. But, meanwhile, the US Ninth Army had left one corps in the Ruhr area but its other two corps had sped across central Germany. By 8 April these reached Hildesheim, beyond the river Leine, over 100 miles distant. On their left flank, two corps of the British Second Army reached an area north of Hannover on the same river and Verden on the river Aller. At the same time, a Canadian division advanced on the far left flank to reach Meppen on the river Ems. These troops had not met any coherent fronts although they had had to fight their

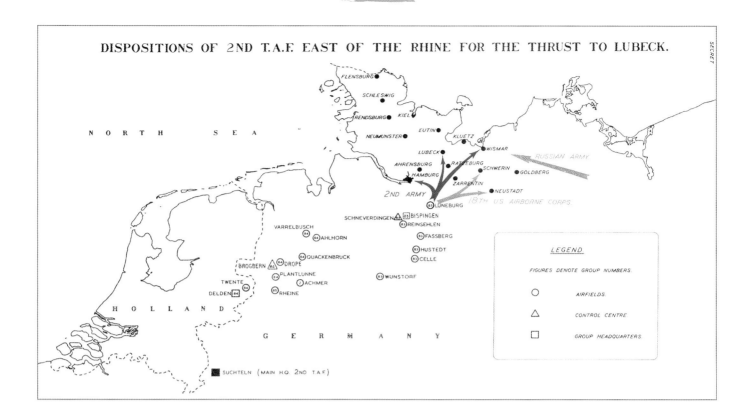

DISPOSITIONS OF 2ND T.A.F. EAST OF THE RHINE FOR THE THRUST TO LUBECK.

way past the enemy in improvised positions. The weather had been good and they were supported at all stages by tactical fighters and fighter-bombers.

Further to the south, the US 12th and 6th Army Groups made equivalent advances across Germany, closely supported by the US Ninth Air Force. From the former, the US Third Army had consolidated its bridgehead over the Rhine at Oppenheim and struck north-east and then east to reach Gotha on 8 April. From the latter, the US Seventh Army had crossed the Rhine at Worms on 26 March, created another bridgehead, and then headed south-east from Heidelberg. On its right flank, the First French Army crossed the Rhine at Speyer on 31 March and then struck south as far as the Black Forest.

These advances necessitated a change in the German high command, for Feldmarschall Kesselring had lost touch with those forces cut off in the north. On 7 April he retained his position of Commander-in-Chief West, consisting of Army Group G and five armies, but Feldmarschall Ernest Busch became Commander-in-Chief North-West. The latter was formed from Army Group H and consisted of three armies, defending a huge territory stretching from the Netherlands to Bremen and then to Magdeburg on the river Elbe.

But these rearrangements availed little, for the Allied forces proved unstoppable. On 15 April the 11th Armoured Division of the British Second Army reached the village of Belsen, 10 miles north-west of Celle and near the village of Bergen. Here they discovered the horror of the sadistic cruelties perpetrated by Nazis on their victims in concentration camps. If any British soldiers had any doubts about the justice of their cause, these were dispelled by the sight of thousands of dead bodies and other inmates barely alive. Photographs bore witness to the world of the vicious and inhuman regime created by Adolf Hitler and his henchmen.

By 19 April advanced elements of the British XXX Corps had fought their way to the approaches of Bremen, XII Corps was within a few miles of Hamburg, and

Dispositions of 2nd TAF east of the Rhine for the thrust to Lubeck. *The National Archives: AIR 41/68*

XIII Corps had reached the Elbe at Lauenburg. On their left, the First Canadian Corps had cut through to the north of the Netherlands and was attacking the German forces bottled up in that country. All these achievements took place under the umbrella of the RAF's Second Tactical Air Force. Strategic raids on German cities by RAF Bomber Command ceased on 16 April but attacks in support of ground and naval operations took place until the end of the war. Eisenhower decided that further advances by the British Second Army needed additional support and allocated the American XVIII Airborne Corps to right under its command.

Meanwhile, on 12 April, the world learnt that President Franklin D. Roosevelt had died suddenly and that his position had been taken over by the Vice-President, Harry Truman. The final victory that these men had sought was only a few weeks away. Before that day, four corps of their US First and Ninth Armies had surrounded most of the German Army Group B's Fifth Panzer and Fifteenth Armies in the Ruhr, as well as contingents of Army Group H's First Parachute Army. All attempts of the German forces to break out were thwarted and the Americans steadily overcame enemy resistance, which in some strongpoints was fanatical. It was all over on 21 April when the last pockets of Germans surrendered. Huge quantities of equipment and over 320,000 prisoners fell into

American hands. Their commander, Feldmarschall Walther Model, killed himself. This Allied victory was greater than that of Stalingrad.

At the same time, the US 12th Army Group continued its remorseless advances, supported at all times by the US Ninth Air Force. In the north of its sector, spearheads of two corps of the US Ninth Army met little resistance and reached the Elbe at Magdeburg on 11 April. They crossed the Elbe on the next day, despite enemy artillery fire and attacks from German aircraft. On the right flank, the US First Army encountered stiffer opposition from German divisions in the Harz mountains, but these were encircled and bypassed. Two bridges over the river Mulde, south of Leipzig, were seized intact on 15 April. On 25 April, a First Army patrol made contact with a vanguard of the Red Army at Torgau on the Elbe. The US Third Army experienced less opposition and sped south-east. By 11 April the troops had encountered more Nazi atrocities when they reached and freed the concentration camps at Nordhausen and then Buchenwald. Six days later, they reached the north-west border of Czechoslovakia and then swept across Bavaria to capture Munich and reach the Austrian border by the time hostilities ceased. Near Munich, they freed some 30,000 prisoners from the notorious concentration camp at Dachau.

In the southern area, the US 6th Army Group made similar progress. Its US Seventh Army advanced on the right flank of the US Third Army to reach Nuremberg on 18 April. It then progressed with extraordinary speed as far as Innsbruck, near the Brenner Pass, by the end of the war. At the same time the First French Army broke through the Black Forest to reach Lake Constance on the Swiss border.

Hitler remained in Berlin during the dramatic period when his remaining forces were disintegrating, living in his bunker underneath the German Chancellery. There was no cause for celebration on 20 April, his 56th birthday. The vicious Nazi regime was doomed, with its capital surrounded by the Russians. On 29 April Hitler appointed Grossadmiral Karl Dönitz as his successor, married his mistress Eva Braun and ordered that both their bodies be burnt after they committed suicide. He shot himself on the following day.

The British 21st Army Group made further advances in these final days. No. VII Corps crossed the Elbe and swept up to capture Lübeck and Kiel. On its right, the US XVIII Airborne Corps reached Wismar on the Baltic. On its left, XII Corps advanced from Hamburg to the Kiel canal. Further to the left, XXX Corps set off from Bremen and reached Cuxhaven. On the extreme left, the Canadian II Corps reached Wilhelmshaven.

Two of the final operations carried out by the RAF should be mentioned, one humanitarian and the other a dreadful accident. Operation 'Manna' by Bomber Command took place between 29 April and 7 May. A large pocket in the west of the Netherlands was still under the control of the Germans and the Dutch people were starving to death. A truce was arranged with the local German commander, so that Lancasters and Mosquitos could make about 3,000 sorties during which they dropped over 6,500 tons of food.

The other RAF operation was made by Typhoons of the Second Tactical Air Force and concerned victims of the concentration camp at Neuengamme, near Hamburg. When the Allies approached, the inmates were marched out by their guards and either murdered or dispersed to other localities. About 10,000 arrived at the port of Lübeck and were battened down in the holds of a liner and two freighters, in disgusting and inhuman conditions. At the time, the RAF was attacking U-boats and other vessels making for Norway, in the belief that the

Nazis would attempt to make a last-ditch stand in that country. Unaware of the existence of the victims, four squadrons of Typhoons attacked the ships with rockets on 3 April. Almost 7,000 prisoners who managed to swim to the shore were shot by the SS.

Grossadmiral Dönitz agreed to surrender unconditionally to the Allies. His delegation arrived at Field-Marshal Montgomery's tactical headquarters on Lüneburg Heath on the morning of 3 May and the final Instrument of Surrender was signed on the following day, to take effect from 08.00 hours on 5 May. Victory in Europe was celebrated on 8 May.

The Allied casualty figures in this campaign from 6 June 1944 to 7 May 1945 make grim reading. American, British, Canadian, French and other nationalities in the armies suffered 164,954 killed or died of wounds. There were 538,763 others who were wounded but survived. Those missing or captured numbered 78,657. The Royal Navy and the US Navy suffered 5,332 killed or died of wounds, plus 4,976 wounded. The Royal Air Force, the US Army Air Force and the French Air Force suffered 30,845 killed or died of wounds, 7,340 wounded and 23,439 missing or captured. This was a price which the Western countries had to pay for their part in the liberation of Europe.

Weary and demoralised German prisoners photographed on 25 February 1945 near Gogh, while British and Canadian forces were making steady progress between the Maas and the Rhine. British Official

British troops entered the German town of Kervenheim, 3 miles south of Uedem, on 1 March 1945. The Germans were forced to pull out after severe street fighting, as shown in this photograph of British troops dashing towards a building while houses are ablaze from shell and mortar fire. *British Official*

A Bren gun carrier of the British Army in the German town of Goch, part of the Siegfried Line about 6 miles south of Kleve, before it was completely cleared on 21 February 1945. The town had been subjected to an accurate attack by Bomber Command on the night of 7/8 February in preparation for the assault, destroying most of the buildings and causing 150 deaths among the forced labourers brought in to dig the local defences. *British Official*

Elements of the US 12th Army Group entered Cologne on 6 March 1945, accompanied by an RAF official photographer. This photograph shows an American tank on the right, hit by a shell, with a man being blown out of the turret. He was the only man in the crew to survive, although he lost a leg. Cologne Cathedral is in the background. *British Official*

An RAF reconnaissance photograph taken on the night of 2/3 March 1945, showing German transport, nose to tail, streaming west to east across the Duisburg–Homberg road bridge over the Rhine.
British Official

American infantrymen moving through Cologne, covered by one of their number in the doorway of a battered building. Most of the damage to the city was the result of heavy attacks by the RAF's Bomber Command and the US Eighth Air Force. *British Official*

Opposite page: Troops of the US Third Army storming into Coblenz on 6 March 1945, with a dead comrade lying against debris and his helmet in the road. Only a few defenders remained when the German city fell to the Allies. *US Official*

An American tank rumbling through a wreckage-lined street on the outskirts of Cologne. *British Official*

The Ludendorff railway bridge over the river Rhine,
south of Cologne, was captured in a damaged
condition by American units on 7 March 1945, in spite
of Hitler's orders that all Rhine bridges were to be
destroyed. The Germans made great efforts to
destroy it, using V-weapons, air bombardment and
frogmen. Ten days later, the damaged bridge began to
tremble and then crashed into the Rhine, as shown
here. *The National Archives: AIR 37/1231*

The centre of Coblenz captured by the US Third Army
after stiff resistance from German defenders. The city
had been ruined by numerous heavy raids by the
RAF's Bomber Command. *US Official*

Near misses of 22,000lb 'Grand Slam' and 12,000lb 'Tallboy' bombs dropped on 14 March 1945 by Lancasters of No. 617 Squadron on the railway viaduct at Bielefeld in Germany created an earthquake effect which caused part of it to collapse. The photograph was taken by a Lockheed F-5 of the US Eighth Air Force. *Author's Collection*

During the weeks before the Allied troops crossed the Rhine, No. 2 Group of the Second Tactical Air Force attacked many railway centres and enemy troop areas behind the proposed bridgehead sites. On 13 March 1945, an attack by 48 Mitchells and 12 Bostons was made on the railway centre at Langerich, 12 miles west-south-west of Osnabrück, using GH radar in cloudy conditions. Photographs taken the following day showed a large crater at 'A' and a smaller one at 'B', which had blocked the tracks and sidings. A scorch mark at 'C' showed the result of a large fuel fire. Very severe damage had been done to a nearby cement works. *The National Archives: AIR 37/46*

On 21 March 1945, 29 Mitchells of No. 2 Group, Second Tactical Air Force, dropped 51 tons of bombs on the Bocholt railway centre in Germany, about 12 miles north of Wesel, as part of the preparation for the assault across the Rhine. Bombs burst on the tracks and nearby factories. Reconnaissance photographs taken six hours later showed considerable damage, with fires still burring in the factories. *The National Archives: AIR 37/46*

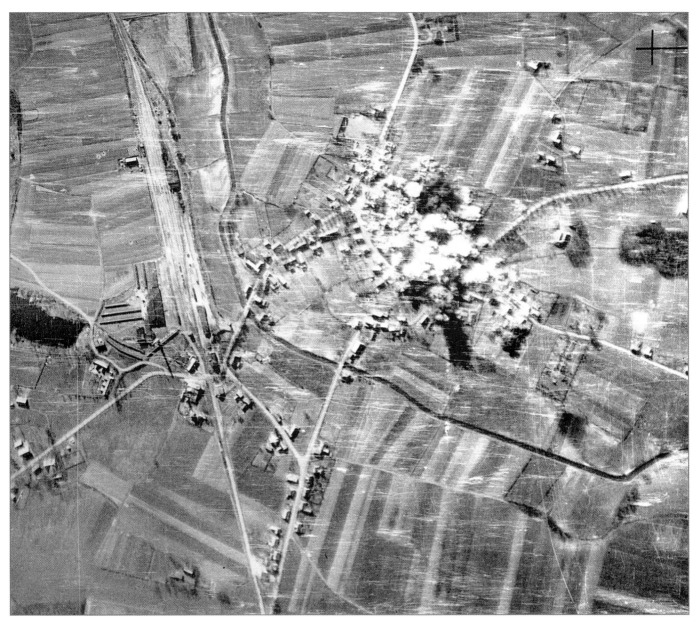

As zero hour approached for the great airborne assault, the main weight of the Second Tactical Air Force's attacks was brought closer to the Rhine. On 22 March 1945, 136 medium bombers concentrated on the billeting areas of German reserves along the battle front. This photograph is typical of such attacks. It shows the German village of Alstätte, about 6 miles south of the Dutch city of Enschede near the German border, almost blanketed by bomb bursts. *The National Archives: AIR 37/46*

Troops of the US Seventh Army in March 1945, advancing through the German village of Scheibenhardt on the Siegfried Line, after having crossed the river Lauter. They advanced through the Bien forest, where the enemy counter-attacked with tank support. After repulsing this attack they captured the town of Landau, north-west of Karlsruhe, on 23 March. US Official

The German town of Bocholt, full of troops and supplies in front of the British armies near the Dutch border, was bombed in daylight on 22 March 1945 by 100 Lancasters in Bomber Command. It was left in flames, with columns of smoke rising high in the sky. No bombers were lost. *British Official*

In the early evening of 23 March 1945, the British 1st Commando Brigade made a surprise crossing of the Rhine in their assault craft, following a terrific artillery pounding of German positions on the east side of the river. Then they halted while Lancasters and Mosquitos of Bomber Command made an attack on their main objective, the town of Wesel. The men in this photograph are from the 1st Battalion of the Cheshire Regiment, who landed from Buffalo amphibious tanks on the following day to support the Commandos. *British Official*

This photograph was taken at dawn on 24 March 1945, when British forces crossed the Rhine in assault craft. On the next day they linked up with their Airborne Army and the US Ninth Army. A bridgehead about 30 miles long and 7 miles deep was established on the right bank of the Rhine by the British and Canadians. *The National Archives: DEFE 2/502*

The largest air armada of the war followed the capture of Wesel. On 24 March 1945, 541 C-47 Dakotas dropped parachutists on key points east of the Rhine, while a total of 1,050 Halifax and Stirling tugs towed 1,350 gliders (some on double tow) carrying airborne troops. Over 21,000 men were carried, in an armada which stretched over 500 miles. They were supported by almost 900 fighters of the US Ninth Air Force and the RAF's Second Tactical Air Force. These Stirlings were photographed over the Rhine. *British Official*

British troops of the 6th Airborne Division were carried in a train of 440 Horsa gliders and landed in wooded country north-west of Wesel. These are advancing over a fie d while a body lies in the foreground alongside a crashed Horsa glider. British Official

The 1st Commando Brigade entered the town of Wesel in the early morning of 24 March 1945, while the remaining German defenders were still dazed from the tremendous artillery and air bombardments. Over 350 German prisoners were taken. These men of the Wehrmacht were sitting in one of the many bomb craters amid the ruined houses, awaiting transport to a POW centre. *British Official*

The British 51st Highland Division and the Canadian 3rd Division crossed the Rhine near Rees and Emmerich between 23 and 24 March 1945. The German soldiers in this photograph have discarded their weapons and are carrying white flags as they walk towards a British infantryman. *British Official*

British airborne troops dug in on the banks of the river Issel, about 2 miles east of their dropping zone, photographed on 25 March 1945. *British Official*

Winston Churchill visited the Rhine on 25 March 1945 when General Eisenhower was absent. He took the opportunity to cross the river in an American LCVP (Landing Craft Vehicle Personnel) before stepping ashore on the east bank. He was photographed chatting to the American helmsman while Field-Marshal Sir Bernard Montgomery talked to the commander of the US 1st Army Group, General W.H. Simpson. *US Official*

On 26 March 1945, 48 Mitchells of No. 2 Group, Second Tactical Air Force, attacked the marshalling yards at Potraus-Bochen, north-east of Lüneburg, dropping 67 tons of bombs. This was the most successful of the last five attacks made by the Group in the war. The photograph shows the railway centre completely obscured by smoke from bombs dropped by the first box of aircraft, with smoke from the second box falling on the track. *The National Archives: AIR 37/46*

On the left flank of the British Second Army, the Guard's Armoured Division and the 3rd Infantry Division captured the German town of Lingen, about 13 miles north-east of Nordhorn, on 7 April 1945. This photograph shows infantry clearing the town of snipers. Afterwards they advanced 10 miles to the east against determined resistance from the German 7th Paratroop Division. Their objective was to cross the river Ems and cut the Dortmund-Ems canal. *British Official*

By 31 March 1945, armoured forces of the British Second Army had fanned out over the Westphalian Plain and were 70 miles beyond the Rhine. They had encountered spasmodic opposition and taken 17,000 prisoners during this advance. This photograph shows soldiers of the 7th Armoured Division clearing a village near Stadholm, about 6 miles from the Dutch border. *British Official*

On 15 April 1945, elements of the British Second Army relieved the huge Nazi concentration camp at Belsen in north-west Germany. They found about 60,000 emaciated and starving civilians – men, women and children. Hundreds lay dead while many others were dying from typhus and dysentery. This skeletal survivor was trying to delouse his clothes. *British Official*

On 19 April 1945, troops of the 15th Scottish Division cleared the town of Uelzen, about 6 miles south-south-east of Lüneburg, after several days of stiff fighting. This Bren gunner is taking cover behind a memorial while some houses are ablaze in the background. A white cloth of surrender hangs from the house on the left. *British Official*

On 17 April 1945, seven Mosquitos of No. 2 Group, Second Tactical Air Force, bombed the headquarters of the Gestapo at Odense on the Danish island of Fünen, between the Little and Great belts. This photograph shows smoke from bombs bursting precisely on the main target building. Luckily there were no civilian casualties and the Gestapo's hold on Denmark was broken at last. *The National Archives: AIR 37/46*

On 18 April 1945, the Second Tactical Air Force despatched sixty Mitchells to attack enemy barracks at Oldenburg, west of Bremen. They dropped 105 tons of high explosive. This photograph was taken towards the end of the attack, showing smoke rising from the barracks and more bombs bursting in the target area. *The National Archives: AIR 37/46*

One of the most famous photographs of the Second World War was taken on 25 April 1945 when infantrymen of the 69th Division, 6th Army Corps, US First Army, shook hands with Russian soldiers of the 58th Guards Division on the broken bridge over the Elbe at Torgau, 31 miles north-east of Leipzig. *US Official*

German prisoners walk down the central island of an autobahn near Giesen, about 12 miles south-south-east of Hanover, in April 1945. The vehicles driving in the opposite direction are part of the 6th Armored Division, US Third Army. *US Official*

British forces clearing the centre of the devastated
city of Bremen, which was captured by the 30th Army
Corps on 26 April 1945. *British Official*

Dunkirk was invested by the First Canadian Army
from late September 1944 but the German garrison of
about 10,000 men, under Admiral Frisius of the
Kriegsmarine, did not surrender until the end of the
war. They destroyed the docks and harbour
installations, sank blockships to render the port
useless and flooded large areas inland to make
approach difficult. Dunkirk was invested by Canadian,
British, French and Czechoslovakian forces but no
major attempt was made to assault the port. Admiral
Frisius signed the instrument of surrender on 9 May
1945, in the presence of the Czechoslovakian Major-
General A. Liska. This photograph was taken after the
German evacuation. *The National Archives: AIR 37/1231*

British prisoners housed in this factory at Brunswick in Lower Saxony put this large sign on the roof in the hope that it would prevent attack from the RAF. However, such signs were unlikely to be effective against 'area bombing' at night from high level. *The National Archives: AIR 34/742*

The best-known POW camp in the Second World War was Oflag IVC at Colditz Castle, a cluster of fortress-like buildings near the river Mulde about 25 miles east-south-east of Leipzig. The first to be incarcerated were Polish officers, later followed by Dutch, Belgian, French and British officers. Although supposed to be a place of maximum security, a total of 130 officers managed to escape, although only 30 reached safety. Colditz was liberated by American troops on 15 April 1945. *The National Archives: AIR 40/230*

The Henschel Hs 117, known as the 'Schmetterling' (Butterfly), was a ground-to-air missile powered by a BMW 109-558 rocket motor. It was also fitted with two auxiliary Schmidding 109-553 motors for take-off, one above the fuselage and one beneath it. The weapon flew at subsonic speeds and was controlled from the ground by a joystick, with the purpose of bringing down enemy aircraft at medium and low altitudes. The first was tested in May 1944 near Peenemünde. Four months later twenty-two tests had been made, some from a Heinkel He111E-1. Although mass production was planned, this missile never went into service. The example here is on a modified mounting for a 37mm flak gun. *The National Archives: AIR 40/2532*

The Rheinmetall-Borsig RhZ-61/9, also known as the 'Rheinbote' (Rhine Messenger), was a long-range surface-to-surface missile. The first version carried 88lb of high explosive and had a range of about 100 miles, but the final version had a range of 136 miles. The weapon was launched from a 'Meilerwagen', a modified mobile V-2 transporter. After launching, three of its stages fell away, leaving the final stage with the warhead to continue its trajectory at a speed of Mach 5.55. Many of these missiles were launched against Antwerp after this important port had been captured by the Allies. *The National Archives: AIR 40/2532*

RAF officers examining the remains of some Junkers Ju88-1s on a captured Luftwaffe airfield. The Germans collected the wreckage of their own and Allied aircraft from crash sites all over Europe and assembled them in dumps where unskilled workers stripped the airframes. Any reusable equipment such as engines, instruments and radios was stored in warehouses at a 'Beutepark'. The aluminium alloy was melted down and sent by rail to aircraft factories. The Allies were presented with a colossal amount of scrap at airfields and stores. *The National Archives: AIR 37/1441*

A captured V-2 rocket at a railway station, en route to England for examination. *The National Archives: AIR 37/1441*

During the later stages of the war, the Germans were forced to use railway tunnels to protect war materials from Allied bombing attacks. *The National Archives: AIR 37/1441*

RAF officers and airmen standing cheerfully in front of a concealed bomb dump in Germany. *The National Archives: AIR 37/1441*

In the forest of Hahnenberg near Leese, west-north-west of Hannover, British troops discovered a well-camouflaged chemical factory, probably built in connection with V-2 rockets. Many rockets were also found, most of them already destroyed but a few remaining intact. *British Official*

This trainload of V-2 rockets was captured by American soldiers at Bromskirchen, west-south-west of Kassel, in the closing weeks of the war in Europe. They were intact but had not been assembled, being found under camouflage foliage in freight cars. Note the wording *Vorsichtig Rangieren* (shunt carefully) on the right of the nearest freight car. *Author's Collection*

At 02.41 hours on 7 May 1945, the German plenipotentiaries surrendered unconditionally to the Allies at Rheims in France. From far left clockwise around table: General Frederick E. Morgan (UK, mainly obscured); Major-General Francois Sevez (France); Admiral Sir Harold M. Burrough (UK); General Walter Bedell Smith (USA); Major-General I. Susloparov (Russia); General Carl A. Spaatz (USA); Air Marshal Sir James M. Robb (UK); Major-General Harold R. Bull (USA); Senior Lieutenant-Colonel I. Zenkovich (interpreter USSR); Major Wilhelm Oxenius (Germany); Colonel-General Alfred Jodl (Germany); General-Admiral Hans Georg von Friedeburg (standing, Germany). *British Official*

At 18.25 hours on 4 May 1945, in an Army tent at the headquarters of the British 21st Army Group, Lüneburg Heath, German plenipotentiaries put their signatures to the surrender of their land, sea and air forces in northern Germany. Left to right around the table: Major Friedal; Konteradmiral Magner; General-Admiral Hans Georg von Freideburg; Field-Marshal Sir Bernard Montgomery; General der infanterie Kinsel; Colonel Pollek. *British Official*

The remains of the synthetic oil plant in the Ruhr, which had been a primary target for both the RAF's Bomber Command and the US Eighth Air Force, photographed at the end of the war. The remains of the compressor house are in the foreground, the reaction cylinders (in which the coal paste was made) are on the left, and the tanks for the lubricating oil plant are in the background. *Author's Collection*

This was the first official RAF picture of Berlin since its fall, issued in May 1945. It was taken from a low-flying Mosquito by the RAF's Film Production Unit and showed the devastation in the heart of the German capital, with many people in the streets. *British Official*

The German plenipotentiaries at the unconditional surrender at Rheims in France at 02.41 hours on 7 May 1945. Left to right: Major Wilhelm Oxenius (Aide to General Jodl); Colonel-General Alfred Jodl (Nazi Chief of Staff); General-Admiral Hans Georg von Friedeburg (Commander-in-Chief of German Fleet). The surrender was formally ratified by the Russians in Berlin shortly before midnight on 8 May. *US Official*

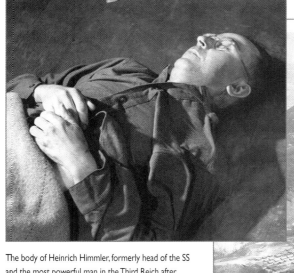

The body of Heinrich Himmler, formerly head of the SS and the most powerful man in the Third Reich after Adolf Hitler, was photographed on 23 May 1945, after he had bitten open a small glass capsule and swallowed cyanide of potassium. He had disguised himself by shaving off his moustache, putting a black patch over his right eye and taking the uniform of a discharged Feldwebel (Sergeant) of the Secret Field Police under the name of Heinrich Hitzinger. He and his companions were arrested on 22 May by troops of the British 2nd Army at Bremervörde, east of Bremerhaven. On the following day they were transferred to Westerimke, then Barnstedt and then Lüneburg, where he committed suicide in the course of a body search. He was buried in an unmarked grave in Lüneburg Heath. *British Official*

Hitler's tea house, near his mountain retreat at Berchtesgaden on the Oversalzberg in the Bavarian Alps, was photographed by the US Eighth Air Force at the end of the war in Europe. Known as the 'Eagle's Nest' by the Americans, it was built on top of the Kehlstein mountain and could be reached by an elevator in a shaft 120m deep which led to a tunnel 120m long. In fact, Hitler visited it on only five occasions. His house nearby, the Berghof, was heavily damaged by Bomber Command in the morning of 25 April 1945 when 359 Lancasters and 16 Mosquitos were despatched to the target. The houses of Goering and Bormann were also hit and the barracks housing the SS were completely wiped out. *Author's Collection*

Paris after the liberation, viewed down the Champs Elysées to the Arc de Triomphe. *The National Archives: AIR 37/1231*

The headquarters staff of No. 2 Group, Second Tactical Air Force, marked 8 May 1945 (V-E Day) by parading at 08.30 hours on the open square of the parade ground in Brussels. The photograph was taken when the men and women had been called to attention for an address by the Air Officer Commanding, Air Vice-Marshal Sir Basil Embrey. *The National Archives: AIR 37/46*

GIVE THANKS BY SAVING

A general view of the celebrations in Trafalgar Square, London, during V-E Day, 8 May 1945. *British Official*

The Prime Minister, Winston Churchill, giving his famous victory sign on the eve of V-E Day from the balcony of the Ministry of Health, to the thunderous cheers from a jubilant crowd of about 60,000 people in Whitehall and Parliament Square in London. He acknowledged the ovation with the words 'God bless you all'. Eleven weeks later, he and his Conservative Party lost the General Election. *British Official*

Opposite page: St Paul's Cathedral in London, floodlit for the first time in nearly six years, standing bright against the sky on the night of V-E Day, 8 May 1945. *British Official*

Happy V-E Day revellers in Fleet Street, London. They may have forgotten that there was still a major war to be won against Japan, estimated by the many who knew nothing about the atomic bomb to last for two more years. *British Official*

SELECT
BIBLIOGRAPHY

Titles published in London, unless stated otherwise.

Bradley, Omar N. *A Soldier's Story*. Eyre & Spottiswoode, 1951
British Bombing Survey Unit. *The Strategic Air War Against Germany 1939–1945*. Frank Cass, 1998
Bryant, Arthur. *Triumph in the West*. Collins, 1959
Cooke, Ronald C. & Nesbitt, Roy Conyers. *Target: Hitler's Oil*. William Kimber, 1985
Craven, W.F. & Cate, J.E. *The Army Air Forces in WW2, Vol III*. University of Chicago Press, 1951
Donald, David. *American Warplanes of World War II*. Aerospace Publishing, 1995
Eisenhower, Dwight D. *Crusade in Europe*. Heinemann, 1949
Ellis, L.F. *Victory in the West, Volume I*. HMSO, 1962. *Volume II*, HMSO, 1968
Elstob, Peter. *Hitler's Last Offensive*. New York: Ballantine Books, 1973
Freeman, Roger. *The Mighty Eighth War Diary*. Arms & Armour, 1990
Galland, A. *The First and the Last*. Methuen, 1955
Halley, James J. *The Squadrons of the Royal Air Force & Commonwealth 1918–1988*. Tonbridge: Air Britain, 1988
Hamlin, John F. *Support and Strike!* Peterborough: GMS Enterprises, 1991
Harris, Arthur T. *Despatch on War Operations*. Frank Cass, 1995
Henshall, Philip. *Hitler's V-Weapon Sites*. Stroud: Sutton Publishing, 2002
Hinsley, F.H. et al. *British Intelligence in the Second World War, Volume 3 Part 2*. HMSO, 1988
Hogg, IV. *German Secret Weapons of World War 2*. Arms & Armour, 1970
Jones, R.V. *Most Secret War*. Sevenoaks: Hodder & Stoughton, 1978
Masterman, J.C. *The Double-Cross System 1939–1945*. Pimlico, 1975
McKee, Alexander. *Caen: Anvil of Victory*. Pan Books, 1972
Middlebrook, Martin and Everitt, Chris. *The Bomber Command War Diaries*. Penguin Books, 1985
Montgomery, Bernard L. *Normandy to the Baltic*. Hutchinson, 1947
Overy, Richard. *Why the Allies Won*. W.W. Norton, 1995
Patton, George S. *War as I Knew it*. W.H. Allen, 1947
Roskill, S.W. *The War at Sea, Vol. 3 Part II*. HMSO, 1961
Rust, Kenn C. *The 9th Air Force in World War II*. Fallbrook: Aero Publishers, 1970
Saunders, Hilary St G. *Royal Air Force 1939–45, Volume 3*. HMSO, 1975
Taylor, John W.R. *Combat Aircraft of the World*. Ebury Press, 1969
Thetford, Owen. *Aircraft of the Royal Air Force since 1918*. Putnam, 1988
Trevor-Roper, H.R. *The Last Days of Hitler*. Macmillan, 1947
Weeks, John. *Assault from the Sky*. David & Charles, 1978
Wilmot, Chester. *The Struggle for Europe*. Collins, 1952

INDEX